100 THINGS
CLEMSON FANS
SHOULD KNOW & DO
BEFORE THEY DIE

100 THINGS
CLEMSON FANS
SHOULD KNOW & DO
BEFORE THEY DIE

Lou Sahadi

TRIUMPH
BOOKS

Library of Congress Cataloging-in-Publication Data

Sahadi, Lou.
  100 things Clemson fans should know & do before they die / Lou Sahadi ; foreword by Dabo Swinney.
     pages cm
  Includes bibliographical references.
  ISBN 978-1-60078-997-7 (paperback)
  1. Clemson University—Football—Miscellanea. 2. Clemson Tigers (Football team)—Miscellanea. I. Title. II. Title: One hundred things Clemson fans should know & do before they die.
  GV958.C56S23 2014
  796.332'6309757—dc23
                                    2014018183

This book is available in quantity at special discounts for your group or organization. For further information, contact:
  Triumph Books LLC
  814 North Franklin Street
  Chicago, Illinois 60610
  (312) 337-0747
  www.triumphbooks.com

Printed in U.S.A.
ISBN: 978-1-60078-997-7
Design by Patricia Frey
All images courtesy of the Clemson University Sports Information Department unless otherwise indicated

For Sam Blackman, who has bled orange every day since growing up in Central, South Carolina, and is by far the best researcher any author would want, which is a tribute to his mentor, Tim Bourret.

Contents

Foreword

I have been at Clemson as an assistant coach and head coach since 2003, but my ties to Tiger football feel a lot longer.

There has been a tie between the Clemson and Alabama football programs since 1931 when former Alabama player Frank Howard became an assistant coach under first-year head coach Jess Neely. Howard was in his first year out of school after playing on Alabama's Rose Bowl team of 1930, but he landed the job thanks to high praise from then Alabama head coach Wallace Wade.

Howard was a top assistant under Neely for nine seasons. In his final season as head coach, Clemson defeated Frank Leahy and Boston College in the Cotton Bowl. After that season, Neely decided to take the head coaching job at Rice, and Howard became Clemson's head coach. He kept the job for 30 years, leading Clemson to eight conference championships, still more than anyone else.

When I was a youngster growing up in Pelham, Alabama, my parents and I met Frank Howard at a dinner. Little did I know that many years later I would become the head coach of the program he built. It was not just the victories and championships Coach Howard accomplished; he set a standard in many other areas of the program. He had players who went on to success in the NFL, but he had many more who were success stories in many areas outside athletics.

Of course there are many other ties between Clemson and Alabama. Charley Pell and Danny Ford were both products of Bear Bryant's system. Pell coached Clemson to its most significant turnaround season in 1977, leading the Tigers to their first bowl game and final top 20 ranking in 17 seasons. I have gotten to know Danny Ford during my career, and we all took great joy in his induction into the Clemson Ring of Honor in 2013. Leading Clemson to the 1981 national championship is the most significant accomplishment in Clemson athletics history.

Lou Sahadi's documentation of the unique ties between Clemson and Alabama over the years is just one of the many stories in *100 Things Clemson Fans Should Know & Do Before They Die*. The book recounts our great history from the days of John Heisman to our back-to-back top 10 seasons of 2012 and 2013. Lou has a close relationship with Clemson, and you can feel it in this book. After the national championship season of 1981, he authored the book, *1896 to Glory*, a book I still recommend to all Clemson fans. That year he spent many months documenting Clemson history through his research and through his interviews with Clemson greats, including Coach Howard.

As you will see, this book covers it all, whether it be the exciting plays and games, the special color and pageantry of a Clemson football weekend, or the personalities that have made Clemson a special place.

I was recently honored with a long-term contract to remain at Clemson. I look forward to the opportunity to add to the glory that is Clemson football.

"ALL IN."

—Dabo Swinney

Preface

There are many reasons you fall in love with Clemson.

Clemson is all about family. Everyone pulls together and bonds together as one. It is also a great place to raise a family. I know that Deborah and I have had a great time raising our children and grandchildren in this area.

We also fell in love with Clemson because of its unique atmosphere. It's a small town, but it has big opportunities. The Tigers play big-time sports, but yet it has a college-town atmosphere. Young people come to Clemson from small towns and large cities and they graduate and become very successful in varied occupations. It's fun to see how this place changes people for the better.

It's hard to describe what Clemson has meant to the Fords. But I know that I love calling Clemson and the surrounding area my home, and I would not want to be anywhere else.

Winning the national championship in 1981 has meant a lot to me and to Clemson. I am so thankful that I was a part of this and I will never forget it.

I have been very blessed in my years at Clemson as a coach and now as a farmer.

Clemson means the world to me, and I am thankful that I'm a Tiger and will always be a Tiger.

—Danny Ford

Acknowledgments

Amy Blalock, a priceless assistant; Kathryn Everett; Denise Largo; Allison Dalton; Susan Moran; Karen O'Brien, a punctilious editor; Noah Amstadter and Tom Galvin, who shared my vision; Mitch Rogatz, who supported it; and everyone at Triumph Books for their efforts.

Introduction

Clemson Football History

Football has always been important at Clemson. The school opened its doors in 1889, and just seven years later it had a football team. Four years after that, in 1900, it hired John Heisman as its head coach, and the man they named the trophy after led Clemson to an undefeated season and a conference championship. Georgia, South Carolina, and Alabama were among the conquests in Heisman's first season.

A second future Hall of Fame coach led Clemson to a landmark season in 1939 when Jess Neely developed Banks McFadden into one of the top all-around football players in the nation. The Tigers completed a 9–1 season with a No. 11 ranking with a 6–3 victory over Frank Leahy's Boston College team.

Frank Howard followed Neely and led Clemson to six conference titles, two undefeated seasons, and the 15th-best record in college football in the 1950s. His legendary personality promoted the Clemson team, the university, and the game of football in the state of South Carolina for 30 years.

As impactful as the sport was at this agricultural and military school during its first 80 years, the last 36 have brought the program to new heights. It has been my good fortune to work in the Clemson athletic department for all 36 and witness some of the great moments and great players in the history of the sport.

My first year was 1978, and it was a remarkable year that saw the Tigers finish with an 11–1 record. Thanks to the efficient play of quarterback Steve Fuller and receiver Jerry Butler, Clemson finished the year tied for sixth in the final UPI poll with Notre Dame, my alma mater, for whom I had worked as a student the previous year.

Tying Notre Dame in a final poll, just a year removed from an Irish national championship, brought national acclaim to Clemson. A victory over Ohio State in the 1978 Gator Bowl in what proved to be Woody Hayes' final game as head coach of the Buckeyes also improved Clemson's national profile.

Clemson was coached by 30-year-old Danny Ford, another coach who is destined to join Heisman, Neely, and Howard in the Hall of Fame someday.

Ford's grand accomplishment and the most noteworthy of Clemson seasons took place in 1981 when the Tigers won the national championship. The final of three wins over top 10 teams that year took place in the Orange Bowl, a 22–15 conquest of Nebraska and future Hall of Fame head coach Tom Osborne.

A pair of 9–1–1 seasons followed, and by the end of the decade Clemson had the third-best winning percentage in college football for that 10-year interval. Barry Switzer of Oklahoma, Joe Paterno of Penn State, Bobby Bowden of Florida State, and Vince Dooley of Georgia were all Hall of Famers who lost to Ford's Tigers.

Now Clemson has returned to glory days with a 32–8 record over the three most recent years under head coach Dabo Swinney. The program won an ACC Championship in 2011 with a resounding victory over Virginia Tech and future Hall of Fame coach Frank Beamer.

The 2012 and 2013 seasons saw the Tigers register 11–2 seasons that have been culminated by victories over top 10 programs LSU and Ohio State.

The manner in which the Tigers have gained victory over the last five years has been exciting thanks to the highlights of All-Americans C.J. Spiller, Dwayne Allen, Sammy Watkins, and Tajh Boyd.

With Swinney's enthusiasm, the enhancement of all facilities, including the legendary "Death Valley," and the enduring traditions such as rubbing Howard's rock and running down the Hill, Clemson is a program that has a firm foundation and will continue to bring great joy to its fans for many years to come.

In these pages, Clemson fans will re-live some of these memorable years of Clemson football. Enjoy.

—Tim Bourret

Author Credits

The Long Pass (World Books; Bantam Paperback)

Miracle in Miami (Henry Regnery Books)

Pro Football's Gamebreakers (Contemporary Books)

Broncos! (Stein & Day)

Super Sundays I-XII (Contemporary Books)

Steelers: Team of the Decade (New York Times Books)

Super Steelers (New York Times Books)

Super Sunday's XV (Contemporary Books)

L.A. Dodgers (William Morrow)

The 49ers (William Morrow)

The Clemson Tigers: From 1896 to Glory (William Morrow)

The Redskins (William Morrow)

Johnny Unitas: America's Quarterback (Triumph Books)

One Sunday in December (Lyons Press)

Affirmed...The Last Triple Crown (St. Martins Press)

Autobiographies

Len Dawson: Pressure Quarterback (Cowles Books) by Len
   Dawson with Lou Sahadi

The Winning Edge (EP Dutton; Popular Library Paperback) by
   Don Shula with Lou Sahadi

They're Playing My Game (William Morrow; St. Martins
   Paperback) by Hank Stram with Lou Sahadi

Say Hey! (Simon & Schuster; Pocketbook Paperback) by Willie Mays with Lou Sahadi

Winning My Way (Tiger Press) by Jim Donnan with Lou Sahadi

They're Playing My Game (Revised—Triumph Books) by Hank Stram with Lou Sahadi

Television Credits

Remembering Marshall (ESPN; November 2001)

Precis

When Triumph Books approached me to write this book, I was ecstatic. I had been the only author to write a tome on Clemson's 1981 championship season. Writing that book was quite an invigorating challenge because I had never written anything about college sports. I asked my literary agent, "Who would want to read a book about Clemson football?" She informed me that Clemson had a huge, passionate fan following, among the best in the nation.

I found that out the day I arrived in Clemson to begin my research. Every way I looked I was mesmerized by waves of orange. In the week that I was there, I discovered a history of Clemson football that I had never imagined. It was deep and emotional.

For me, this book is a homecoming and yes, one can come home again, so much so that Tim Bourret and Sam Blackman are still there. When I informed them about my offer to write this book, they resoundingly said that I should accept. They, along with Bob Bradley, led me on a wonderful journey into what Clemson football was all about in 1982, beginning one evening at 93 Fish Camp, where Bradley introduced me to catfish for the first time.

In December 2013, I returned to Clemson to see how much had changed since I was there in 1982. I looked for some of the places that I had experienced—Bob Higby's Esso Club, Mr. Knickerbocker, Ibrahim's Tiger Shop, Pixie & Bill's, Calico Corners, and the Holiday Inn where Coach Frank Howard hosted his daily morning coffee klatch with four or five of his cronies. I was a perfect foil for Howard, who addressed me as "the Yankee from New York." We had a warm, jovial camaraderie.

"I don't have a drop of likker to offer you, but I can offer you a good chew of tobacco," he drawled in his best country twang the first time I met him.

That was then. My December Clemson observance was so much different. It appeared as if the town had doubled in size. There were more banks, hotels, restaurants, traffic lights, and yes, students. The campus was overgrown, so much that I had a difficult time finding the Jervey Athletic Center. And through the years, Clemson football also grew to the extent that it is looked upon across the country as a football power.

Over the years, I relished the relationship I nurtured, not only with Bourret and Blackman, but with others like Danny Ford, Allison Dalton, Frank Howard, and B.C. Inabinet, one of Clemson's biggest boosters.

My kinship with Inabinet was special, a bonding one. He wanted me to live in Myrtle Beach and offered to provide a house. When I told him I couldn't because my literary agent was in New York, he told me, "So what, Mickey Spillane lives in Myrtle Beach, why can't you?"

I couldn't give him an answer. Unfortunately, B.C. died at a young age before I saw him again. I received the news of his death after I attended a Mass on a Sunday morning. I was shocked. I sat down in my backyard and cried. That's the effect B.C. had on me and what makes the Clemson populace so special.

Several years later, his widow, Kitty, and daughter, Dixie, visited me on a trip to New York. They hired a limo to come to my home in Palisades, New York, some 20 miles from the city. That said a lot. With tears in our eyes, we reminisced about B.C. I didn't know when I would go back to Clemson again.

But it happened unexpectedly a year later. My daughter, Elizabeth, couldn't find a college to attend during a late week in May. Yet, I did. I called Clemson and got an acceptance over the phone. She left home and never returned. Elizabeth did her part at Clemson one year by being one of the basketball team's statisticians under Tim Bourret's supervision.

A year after graduating, Elizabeth married, not in her hometown, but her new one, Clemson. She settled in Easley, is a third grade teacher at Chastian Road Elementary in Liberty, and raised four beautiful children—Hannah, Bennett, Sam, and Emma.

I hope Clemson fans will enjoy what I have lived and am now reliving. Go Tigers!

—Lou Sahadi

1981 National Championship

The 1980 campaign, when Clemson stumbled into mediocrity with a 6–5 record, haunted Coach Danny Ford all winter. He had believed his squad was capable of being in a bowl game that year, but three close losses to Georgia, North Carolina State, and North Carolina by a combined total of 13 points had made it only an average season.

Yet, after preseason practice was over, Ford had a good feeling about the 1981 campaign with 53 returning lettermen waiting. He didn't know how good. The Tigers went unbeaten and won the national championship for the first time in their history. Nobody could ask for more.

Game 1: Wofford

The season-opening game against Wofford was truly an accommodation by the small South Carolina school. Villanova was originally scheduled to play Clemson; but when the Philadelphia school abruptly dropped its football program, it left Clemson with an Opening Day void. Quickly, Clemson athletic director Bill McLellan reached for the phone and called Wofford's athletic director George "Buddy" Sasser, who also happened to be the Terriers' football coach, and he agreed to the game.

Under a hot sun, Wofford received the opening kickoff of the 1981 season. Donald Igwebuike buried the kick in the end zone, and the Terriers put the ball in play on the 20-yard line. They surprised the sold-out crowed by keeping the ball for more than 8:00 and reaching the Clemson 7-yard line before being stopped. Don Hairston gave the Terriers a 3–0 lead with a 24-yard field goal.

Perry Tuttle immediately made his presence felt. He returned Hairston's kickoff 38 yards to position a Clemson field goal. Igwebuike displayed a powerful leg when he tied the game with a 52-yard field goal.

It wasn't until six minutes had gone by in the second period that Clemson got the lead. It came suddenly and dramatically. Homer Jordan and Tuttle combined on a picture-book 80-yard touchdown pass that had Tigers fans roaring. Bob Pauling's conversion gave Clemson a 10–3 edge. The next time they got the ball the Tigers scored again. Jordan completed an eight-play, 76-yard drive by running the last 14 yards around left end on a keeper. Pauling's kick made it 17–3 minutes before the first half ended.

Clemson received the second half kickoff and marched 73 yards for a touchdown. Jordan hit wide receiver Frank Magwood with an 11-yard throw. Pauling's kick stretched Clemson's lead to 24–3. Just before the third quarter ended, Clemson scored again. Jordan scored his second touchdown by going over from three yards out. Pauling added the extra point to give the Tigers a 31–3 lead.

On its first series in the final period, Clemson scored its fifth touchdown. Chuck McSwain sped around left end for five yards to complete a 56-yard drive. Igwebuike converted; and the Tigers led 38–3. Wofford finally scored again when it recovered a fumble on the Clemson 39-yard line. Ten plays later, Barry Thompson hit tight end Dirk Derrick with a 15-yard scoring pass. Hairston's conversion made it 38–10. Clemson closed out the scoring a minute from the end when Jeff McCall broke over right tackle for 10 yards for a touchdown. Pauling booted the extra point that made the final score 45–10.

CLEMSON	3	14	14	14	45
WOODFORD	3	0	0	7	10

Game 2: Tulane

There were two areas of concern that confronted Ford as he began his preparations for Tulane.

For one thing, Clemson had never played a game indoors before. That wasn't all. It was playing its first night game in five years, which didn't seem too important except for the fact that it allowed the players a lot of free time before the game in the city's famed French Quarter—a nearby distraction.

"Playing in the Superdome, the Astroturf, a night game, that's all new to us," Ford said.

Clemson received the opening kickoff but couldn't do much. The offense managed to reach Tulane's 37-yard line but Igwebuike's 55-yard field-goal attempt was short. Tulane took over at that point and drove to Clemson's 28-yard line before stalling. However, Vince Manalla booted a 46-yard field goal that provided Tulane with a 3–0 lead.

Misfortune struck Clemson following the kickoff. After failing to produce a first down, Dale Hatcher was sent in to punt from the 26-yard line. However, the ball was snapped over his head and rolled into the end zone. Hatcher managed to cover the ball for a safety that gave Tulane a 5–0 lead.

It wasn't until midway through the second period that Clemson finally scored. Defensive end Joe Glenn made it possible. He recovered a Tulane fumble on the 25-yard line to set up tailback Cliff Austin's four-yard touchdown run. Pauling converted to give the Tigers a 7–5 edge, which they kept when the half ended.

Clemson had an opportunity to score first in the third period but lost it. It recovered a Tulane fumble on the 33-yard line following the kickoff. Clemson got to the Tulane 16, which was close enough for Pauling to attempt a 33-yard field goal. Unfortunately, the snap was bad, and Pauling never got the kick off. When the quarter ended, the score remained 7–5 and neither team could produce a serious scoring threat, although Clemson was driving at the end.

On the very first play of the fourth quarter, Pauling was on the field again. This time his 31-yard field-goal attempt was good, and Clemson led 10–5. It was apparent at this point that the tenacious Tigers defense would have to control the game. They met the challenge by intercepting a Tulane pass two plays after the kickoff. Minutes later, Pauling returned to the lineup. He looked at a 37-yard field goal try and came through to give the Tigers a 13–5 lead with just more than 12:00 remaining in the game. Nobody realized at the time that the game would end that way. Clemson's defense was the deciding factor, limiting Tulane to just five first downs and 177 total yards. Ford was relieved when it was over.

| CLEMSON | 0 | 7 | 0 | 6 | 13 |
| TULANE | 5 | 0 | 0 | 0 | 5 |

Game 3: Georgia

It may have appeared insignificant at the time, but by winning its first two games Clemson achieved something it hadn't been able to do since 1970. More significant was the fact that the Tigers had to face Georgia in Death Valley. The Bulldogs were the No. 1 college team in 1980 and owned the nation's longest winning streak that stood at 15 games.

The game was expected to be close. It began that way with a scoreless first quarter. Georgia did manage to threaten toward the end of the period. They had a first down on the Clemson 17-yard line; after gaining four yards, Walker fumbled and safety Jeff Suttle recovered.

Even when the second period began, Jordan had trouble moving the offense. However, with about 9:00 left, he was given a great opportunity when safety Tim Childers intercepted Buck

Belue's pass on the Georgia 18. After moving to a first down on the 8-yard line, Jordan threw a touchdown pass to Tuttle that got the crowd of 62,000-plus to its feet. Pauling converted to give Clemson a 7–0 lead.

Near the end of the half, Clemson struck again. Walker again fumbled and middle guard William Perry recovered on the Georgia 35-yard line. Three plays later, with only 11 seconds showing on the clock, Igwebuike booted a 39-yard field goal to provide Clemson with a 10–0 halftime advantage that made Tigers followers happy.

However, Georgia managed to come back with the second half kickoff. The Bulldogs marched 56 yards, basically on two plays—a 21-yard run by Herschel Walker and a 14-yard pass completion from Belue to Lindsay Scott, before being stopped. A 40-yard field goal by Kevin Butler managed to trim Clemson's lead to 10–3.

Early in the final period, Igwebuike gave Tigers fans more to cheer about. With 14:01 left in the game, he was accurate with a 29-yard field goal that extended Clemson's margin to 13–3. From then on, it was up to the defense, and they responded with swarming intensity to intercept Belue five times before the game ended while keeping Walker out of the end zone. Tigers fans celebrated well into the night.

"It was the biggest win I've ever had in football," beamed a happy Jordan. "It's going to be a lot easier going back to Athens. I can go home and talk a little bit."

CLEMSON	0	10	0	3	13
GEORGIA	0	0	3	0	3

Game 4: Kentucky

The convincing victory over Georgia awakened the nation's pollsters. After the third week of the young season, Clemson cracked the top 20 and was ranked 18th by United Press. The Clemson triumph was so impressive to the United Press that Ford was also voted the Coach of the Week by its panel of experts.

While the United Press poll, the one voted on by a panel of coaches, picked the Tigers 18th, the Associated Press in its poll of writers ranked Clemson a notch below, at 19th. Clemson was beginning to generate some national recognition.

Unbeaten Clemson lured a sellout crowd of 57,453 fans to Commonwealth Stadium. Neither team could get a first down the first time it had the ball. On their second series, the Wildcats drove 47 yards in 11 plays, at which point Tom Griggs booted a 40-yard field goal that sent Kentucky into a 3–0 lead. When the quarter ended, the troubled Clemson offense had not produced a first down.

Clemson's offensive woes continued in the second quarter. Yet, the Tigers appeared ready to score when Jeff Bryant recovered a fumble on the Kentucky 16-yard line. They moved for a first down on the 6-yard line where they failed on four successive runs by Cliff Austin. They never seriously threatened the rest of the period except for a 49-yard field-goal attempt by Igwebuike that fell short six seconds from the conclusion of the first half.

Clemson looked like a different team when it took the second-half kickoff and drove 83 yards in 13 plays with Kevin Mack slipping off tackle for a six-yard touchdown run. Pauling added the extra point that gave the Tigers a 7–3 lead.

Some 2:00 later, defensive end Andy Headen positioned Clemson's second touchdown by recovering a fumble on Kentucky's 21-yard line. After only six plays, Jordan raced into the end zone from three yards out. Pauling's kick gave Clemson a 14–3 edge when the third period ended.

Midway through the final period, the Tigers secured their victory. They put together an 87-yard drive in 12 plays that consumed more than six precious minutes. McSwain carried for 41 of the yards, scoring a touchdown from two yards out. Pauling's kick provided Clemson with its final margin of victory at 21–3.

CLEMSON	0	0	14	7	21
KENTUCKY	3	0	0	0	3

Game 5: Virginia

Clemson was now entering the second phase of its schedule. The Tigers' first four wins had been secured against non-conference opponents. Their trip to any bowl would begin in earnest during the fifth week with the campaign against Virginia, the first of Clemson's six consecutive ACC games. The Tigers were ready to start their hunt for an ACC title in Death Valley.

A threat of rain hovered over Death Valley on Homecoming Day. Once again the Tigers started slowly. It wasn't until there were 22 seconds left in the first period that they got on the scoreboard. Igwebuike kicked a 22-yard field goal to give Clemson a 3–0 lead.

As time was winding down in the second quarter, Clemson scored its first touchdown. And did so quickly. Jordan connected with Tuttle for a 20-yard completion. On the very next play, Tuttle picked up 22 more yards on an end around. Austin then brought the crowd to its feet when he broke loose around right end on an exciting 43-yard touchdown gallop. Pauling's kick sent the Tigers into their dressing room with a 10–0 halftime lead.

Taking the second-half kickoff, Clemson kept right on going and scored its second touchdown. Except for one 16-yard pass, the Tigers kept the ball on the ground, driving 77 yards in 11 plays. McCall got the final five yards for the touchdown. Pauling's conversion attempt was good as Clemson stretched its lead to 17–0.

The next time the Tigers got the ball, they scored again. This time they traveled 67 yards in 13 plays. Jordan mixed his plays well, completing all three passes he threw. Austin slammed over left tackle from a yard out. When Pauling made good on his conversion, the Tigers extended their margin to 24–0.

They added to it early in the final period. The first time they got the ball, they scored once more. After they reached the Virginia 16-yard line, they were held in check. However, Igwebuike was accurate with a 32-yard field-goal attempt that sent Clemson into an insurmountable 27–0 bulge with only 10:00 reaming in the game. Much to the delight of the Homecoming crowd, the game ended that way. The defense basked in glory. It was the first time since 1979 that Clemson had shut out an opponent.

CLEMSON	3	7	14	3	27
VIRGINIA	0	0	0	0	0

Game 6: Duke

By now, some of the postseason bowl game executives were taking an interest in Clemson. Mickey Holmes, the executive director of the Sugar Bowl, warmed to the thought of the Tigers celebrating New Year's Eve in New Orleans.

When the game began, the Tigers took charge. The first time they got their hands on the football, they scored. Jordan led them on a 64-yard drive in seven plays with seldom-used Brendon Crite going over from the 4-yard line. Pauling's conversion gave the Tigers a quick 7–0 lead.

When the second period opened, Clemson was working on an 80-yard drive that had begun late in the first quarter. The offense got down to the Duke 3-yard line before stalling. Pauling made an appearance again, booting a 20-yard field goal that sent the Tigers into a 10–0 lead. The very next time Clemson took over on offense, it scored again. The team went 49 yards in eight plays with Cliff Austin breaking loose on a 15-yard touchdown run. Pauling's conversion made it 17–0.

Austin wasn't finished yet. On the next series, he brought the crowd to its feet by shaking free up the middle for 77 yards before he was tripped up on the Duke 4-yard line. Three plays later Jordan put the finishing touches on the 98-yard drive by sneaking over from the 1. Pauling converted, and the Tigers were on their way to a romp 24–0. Seconds before the half ended, Duke managed a field goal that still left it far behind at 24–3.

Clemson wasn't about to let up. The special teams took the second-half kickoff and went 59 yards for another touchdown. Austin punched it across from two yards, and when Pauling tacked on the extra point, Clemson's lead ballooned to 31–3.

Duke managed to score a touchdown, being the first team to do so in 18 quarters of play against Clemson's defense. Quarterback Ben Bennett accomplished it with a 21-yard touchdown pass to split end Cedric Jones. However, Clemson answered back. Completing a 65-yard drive, Jordan hit Tuttle with a 29-yard touchdown throw. Pauling's kick restored Clemson's margin 38–10. It was the last scoring of the day. Clemson had its revenge.

| CLEMSON | 7 | 17 | 14 | 0 | 38 |
| DUKE | 0 | 3 | 7 | 0 | 10 |

Game 7: North Carolina State

The one ingredient confronting Ford as his undefeated Tigers roared to their sixth straight triumph was finding a method to keep his squad from getting complacent the rest of the season. After soundly drubbing Duke, Clemson moved up in the national polls. It was ranked fourth by the Associated Press and fifth by the United Press.

It was a chilly 48 degrees when the teams lined up for the opening kickoff. Austin rushed for 15 yards on two carries but fumbled the ball away the third time he ran. State recovered on its own 41-yard line and moved for a touchdown from there. Larmount Lawson scored it with a 13-yard burst. Todd Auten converted to give the Wolfpack a 7–0 lead with half the period gone.

Clemson took the kickoff and got as far as the Wolfpack 23-yard line before being stopped. Igwebuike then booted a 39-yard field goal that narrowed State's margin to 7–3 when the first quarter ended.

Both team's defenses controlled the action during the second quarter. It appeared as if the half would come to a conclusion without any more scoring. Yet, with just more than 3:00 remaining, Jordan quickly led the Tigers to a touchdown. He ran for 22 yards and passed for 22 more to account for 44 of the 65 yards the drive covered. Austin got the touchdown from a yard out, and Pauling added the conversion that gave the Tigers a 10–7 halftime lead.

However, the defense took over again, which resulted in a scoreless third quarter. It wasn't until midway through the final period that Clemson ensured its seventh straight victory. The clinching touchdown came on a 52-yard drive. Jeff McCall broke loose on a 15-yard run off tackle to score standing up in the end zone. Pauling again kicked the extra point to provide Clemson with a hard-fought 17–7 victory.

CLEMSON	3	7	0	7	17
NC STATE	7	0	0	0	7

Game 8: Wake Forest

There were some whispers around the Clemson campus. The Tigers had won their first seven games, and ever so quietly people thought that maybe Clemson would keep going in its last four games and finish the season undefeated. The Tigers were getting stronger in the polls, too. They climbed to the third spot in the Associated Press poll. Never had a Clemson team been ranked so high.

The Deacons received the opening kickoff, and quarterback Gary Schofield began throwing the ball all over Death Valley. The first five times he touched the ball, he threw. When he tried for a sixth straight time, he fumbled and tackle Dan Benish recovered at midfield. With Cliff Austin leading the way, Clemson scored a touchdown in seven plays, all on the ground. Austin gained 43 of the yards, taking over the ball from the 4-yard line. Pauling converted and Clemson jumped in front 7–0.

The Tigers scored again the next time they got the ball. Again, they went 50 yards with Austin going in from the 3-yard line. Pauling's kick made it 14–0. Near the end of the quarter, Wake Forest got on the scoreboard when Schofield hit Kenny Duckett with a 17-yard touchdown pass.

In the second quarter the Tigers erupted for five touchdowns. It was the biggest offensive display in Clemson history and sealed the Deacons' doom. First, Chuck McSwain scored on a one-yard run. Then Kevin Mack scored on a 10-yard run. Jordan got into the scoring act with a seven-yard keeper around left end. Jeff McCall made his presence felt by breaking away on a 24-yard touchdown gallop. McSwain again got into the scoring column with a 16-yard run that mushroomed Clemson's lead to 49–7. Before the first half ended, Wake Forest managed to score a touchdown that seemed meaningless. Clemson had an insurmountable 49–14 lead.

It was now a question of how many points Clemson would score. On the first play of the second half, Jordan connected with Tuttle on a beautiful 75-yard touchdown pass to up Clemson's margin 55–14. After a Wake Forest field goal, Clemson scored once more when reserve quarterback Mike Gasque hit Tuttle with a 15-yard touchdown pass to give Clemson a 62–17 lead. Moments later the Tigers scored again when McSwain stepped around right end for a touchdown. When the quarter was over, Clemson led 69–17.

There was no stopping the Tigers. They scored 5:00 into the fourth period when Duke Holloman scored a touchdown from three yards away. Five minutes later, Craig Crawford broke loose on a 72-yard touchdown jaunt that further added to Clemson's lead 82–17. The Deacons got one more touchdown before the carnage was over, which made the final score 82–24! Unbelievable.

CLEMSON	14	35	20	13	82
WAKE FOREST	7	7	3	7	24

Game 9: North Carolina

What was paramount in the Clemson–North Carolina meeting was the fact that the eventual winner would emerge as the ACC champion and automatically be awarded a major bowl bid. So attractive was the game that representatives of eight bowl events were attending with hope of eventually landing the winner of the contest, which was looked upon as the biggest game in the state of North Carolina since anyone could remember.

Because the Tigers were the only undefeated team in the nation with eight victories, they had inched their way to No. 2 in the Associated Press poll behind Pittsburgh and No. 3 in the United Press tabulation. Since North Carolina was ranked eighth in the AP and ninth in the UPI, it marked the first time ever that two schools from the same conference faced each other after being ranked nationally.

A standing-room-only record crowd of 53,611 overflowed Kenan Stadium on a sunny, cool day to witness the struggle for ACC supremacy. Clemson couldn't do anything after receiving the opening kickoff, and neither could North Carolina the first time it had the ball. The defenses of both teams were waging a fierce struggle in the trenches. The closest any team came to scoring was when Igwebuike was wide with a 50-yard field-goal attempt, and the period ended scoreless.

In the early minutes of the second quarter, the Tar Heels broke through. Working on a 64-yard drive, quarterback Rod Elkins, limping slightly from his sprained ankle, got North Carolina to the Clemson 5-yard line before being stopped. Nevertheless, it allowed Brooks Barwick to kick a 22-yard field goal that gave the Tar Heels the lead 3–0.

Clemson answered back. The Tigers took the ensuing kickoff and brought it downfield on a finely executed 81-yard drive in 14 plays. Jeff McCall got the touchdown on a seven-yard burst off right tackle, and Pauling converted to push the Tigers in front 7–3.

It appeared as if the score would remain that way. However, with only 19 seconds left in the half, Dale Hatcher's punt was blocked, and the ball was recovered in the Clemson end zone to narrow the halftime margin to 7–5.

Halfway through the third period, the Tigers got just a bit more breathing room. Igwebuike gave it to them when he booted a 39-yard field goal that sent Clemson into a 10–5 lead. However, just before the third quarter ended, Barwick kicked a 26-yard field goal that cut Clemson's edge to 10–8. The tenacious battle ended that way when both teams failed to come close to scoring in the final period. Clemson had its important win and a bowl bid in its pocket.

CLEMSON	0	7	3	0	10
UNC	0	5	3	0	8

Game 10: Maryland

Danny Ford claims he isn't superstitious. However, in the approaching days before the Maryland game, he certainly acted as if he was. He sat in his cluttered office sucking on a lemon, something he had done with regularity through this unbeaten season, which had lasted nine weeks.

The biggest crowd of the season, 63,199, sat in the orange seats in Death Valley on a cool, sunny day, expecting to see the

Tigers win their first ACC championship since 1978 and only their second since 1967. After a series of misfortunes in which they lost the ball on an interception and a fumble, the Tigers finally scored just before the first period came to an end. Passing as expected, Jordan completed all four passes he threw in a six-play, 61-yard drive for a touchdown. The payoff was a 14-yard strike to Tuttle. Pauling converted and Clemson led 7–0.

The Jordan-Tuttle combination struck again midway through the second quarter. This time Clemson went 88 yards for a touchdown. On second down, Jordan found Tuttle in the end zone from the 5-yard line. Pauling added the conversion to send Clemson into a 14–0 lead. The next time the Tigers got the ball, Jordan again went to the air. It only took him three plays to get Clemson another touchdown. First, he hit Tuttle for 30 yards, then Frank Magwood for 13, and finally, Jerry Gaillard for a 12-yard touchdown. Pauling kicked his third extra point to send Clemson into a 21–0 halftime bulge.

Clemson moved closer to the ACC title after a scoreless third period. There was only a brief moment of concern early in the fourth quarter when Jordan fumbled on the Tigers' 7-yard line and Maryland quickly scored on the next play. However, the tenacious Clemson defense preserved Clemson's 21–7 triumph. The fans knew what the victory meant, tossing oranges onto the field in anticipation for the trip to the Orange Bowl. Jordan had his biggest game of the year, completing 20-of-29 passes for 270 yards, while Tuttle caught 10 passes to break Jerry Butler's career reception record—and he still had one more game to add to his 142 total.

| CLEMSON | 7 | 14 | 0 | 0 | 21 |
| MARYLAND | 0 | 0 | 0 | 7 | 7 |

Game 11: South Carolina

It was inconceivable to suspect that Ford would conjure any incentives for his players before the South Carolina game. The game itself said it all. Nobody in the state of South Carolina needed to be reminded of its importance. Their backyard rivalry had been nurtured with each passing year since they first began playing one another back in 1896.

Clemson took the opening kickoff but was stopped after three plays. Their opponents didn't wait long to score, which left the sold-out crowd of 56,971 stomping with excitement at the thought of an upset. The Gamecocks went 51 yards in eight plays with Johnnie Wright scoring a touchdown from a yard out. Mark Fleetwood's conversion gave South Carolina a quick 7–0 lead.

Again, Clemson's offense was ineffective. However, the defense came through. Attempting to punt, Chris Norman's kick was blocked by McSwain, and Johnny Rembert recovered the ball in the end zone for a Clemson touchdown. However, Pauling shocked Tigers fans by missing his first conversion attempt of the season after 31 straight to leave Clemson short 7–6.

Yet, in the early minutes of the second period, Pauling atoned. He booted a 24-yard field goal to push Clemson in front 9–7. After Jordan suffered an interception, Clemson scored again on its second series. Hollis Hall positioned it with an interception on the South Carolina 28-yard line. Six plays later, Jordan squirmed around left end for an 11-yard touchdown. Clemson then decided on a two-point conversion attempt which failed. Nevertheless, the Tigers led 15–7 at halftime.

South Carolina took the second-half kickoff and drove 67 yards for a touchdown, with Gordon Beckham hitting Horace Smith in the end zone with a 10-yard pass. Beckham's two-point conversion try was foiled when he was sacked by Jeff Suttle, which preserved the Tigers' 15–13 lead. Clemson answered right back after the kickoff. Jordan led the Tigers on an 86-yard march, with McSwain getting the final yard and the touchdown. Pauling's conversion stretched Clemson's lead to 22–13 when the period ended four minutes later.

On its first series in the fourth quarter, Clemson sealed its victory. This time the Tigers went 80-yards for a touchdown with Chuck McSwain breaking loose up the middle on a 23-yard run. Pauling kicked an extra point, which gave the Tigers a 29–13 triumph and an unbeaten season. The "Tiger Rag" was heard all night—and all the way from Columbia to Clemson.

CLEMSON	6	9	7	7	29
USC	7	0	6	0	13

2 1982 Orange Bowl

January 1, 1982
Miami, Florida
Clemson 22, Nebraska 15

Even though Clemson was the only undefeated team in the nation and Nebraska had two losses, the Cornhuskers were a four-point favorite entering the clash that would be nationally televised, the only time all season someone in California could see the Tigers play. The Cornhuskers had great tradition and they still do, but they won two National Championships in 1970 and 1971 and had the third-best record in college football during the 1970s.

In fact, they had won the 1971 national title in an Orange Bowl win over Alabama and assistant coach Danny Ford, so Ford was trying to erase his own demons in the Orange Bowl 10 years later.

The media did not give the ACC much respect, calling it a "basketball conference." In fact, Ford's parting comment to the media after this game was, "Well, it's on to basketball season."

While looking back, it seems odd that Nebraska was favored in this game.... They did come in riding an eight-game winning streak, averaging 330 yards per game on the ground. They had just won at Oklahoma by a score of 37–14, only the second time in the last nine years they had defeated the Cornhuskers. And they had a backfield that included Mike Rozier, the winner of the 1983 Heisman Trophy, and Roger Craig, who would go on to a successful NFL career with the San Francisco 49ers. They had played a tough schedule, with non-conference games against Iowa, Florida State, Penn State, and Auburn.

The Clemson players were excited enough prior to the game, but NBC held the start of the game 17 minutes due to the length of the Rose Bowl game between Penn State and Southern California. The game finally kicked off at 8:17 PM, and it did not take long for things to go Clemson's way.

On Nebraska's first drive and third play from scrimmage, Cornhusker quarterback Mark Mauer fumbled and William Devane recovered at the Nebraska 33. Mauer had been the second-string quarterback for Nebraska much of the season but was the starter in this game due to an injury to Turner Gill.

"We had been forcing turnovers all year, and that play told us that this game would be no different," Jeff Davis said. "It gave us confidence."

Clemson could not score a touchdown after the fumble, but Donald Igwebuike came on to boot his first of three field goals, this one a 41-yarder that would have been good from 60 yards.

The Cornhuskers came right back and drove 69 yards for a score in just eight plays on the ensuing drive. They used a trick play to score, as Rozier threw a 25-yard halfback pass to Anthony Steels for six points. Clemson added a field goal and trailed 7–6 after the first quarter, the eighth time in 12 games Clemson went to the second quarter without holding the lead in 1981.

The second quarter was the most dominant for the Tigers in 1981, outscoring the opposition 133–15 for the season, and this game was no different. A fumble by Nebraska's Phil Bates that was recovered by Davis, his record fourth recovered fumble of the season, gave Clemson the ball at the Nebraska 27. A series of runs brought the ball to the 2-yard line, where Cliff Austin scored on a sweep.

Clemson held a 12–7 lead at halftime. While Clemson did not score on its first possession of the second half, it did record a touchdown on its second possession. The Tigers drove 75 yards in 12 plays on their best drive of the night. Homer Jordan connected with Perry Tuttle on the 13-yard scoring pass in the left corner of the end zone.

For Tuttle, it was his eighth touchdown catch of the season, establishing a school record. His post-touchdown celebration was captured on the cover of *Sports Illustrated* the only time a current Tiger athlete has made the cover of the publication. That gave Clemson a 19–7 lead.

Clemson forced a three-and-out on the next Nebraska possession, and freshman Billy Davis returned the punt 47 yards to the Nebraska 22. It would be the longest punt return of his career. Igwebuike booted a 36-yard field goal to give Clemson a 22–7 lead. The Tigers had scored 19 consecutive points.

On the first play after the kickoff, Mauer attempted a pass in the left flat. Johnny Rembert, a backup linebacker who would go on to a 10-year NFL career, jumped into the passing lane and had the ball in his hands for an easy touchdown. But he could not hang on. Had he done so, this game might have turned into a rout.

Nebraska was a championship team and certainly was not down, even with a 15-point deficit. Mauer took the Cornhuskers 69 yards in eight plays, and Nebraska scored on a Roger Craig 26-yard run. It was the longest run all year against the Tigers. Nebraska lined up to go for two points but was penalized for delay of game. Much to everyone's surprise, they still went for two, and Craig scored from the 8-yard line on a pitchout to the left. Momentum appeared to have shifted with more than 9:00 left.

The Clemson defense shut down the Big Red on their final extended drive, then the offense held on to the ball for nearly five-and-a-half minutes to run down the clock to six seconds. Andy Headen deflected Mauer's desperation pass to preserve the win and the championship for Clemson.

Jeff Davis led the Tigers defense with 14 tackles in his final game. He also recovered a fumble, giving him a school-record eight for his career. Bill Smith added a career-high 10 tackles from his defensive end position.

Clemson then went three-and-out, so Nebraska took over the ball with 5:24 left, and Jordan and the Tigers offense worked their ball-control magic. Nebraska could not stop Clemson's offensive line. The Tigers converted two important third downs, including a 23-yard run by Jordan on third-and-4 from the Tiger 37.

Jordan was physically dehydrated after this drive, and one has to wonder if he wouldn't have been able to come back to another possession. He was virtually carried off the field after the game and was given IV's. Even though he was voted Offensive MVP, you will not find any quotes from him after the game because it was far past the media's deadline before he came out of the locker room.

Clemson ran the clock down to six seconds before giving up the ball. The Cornhuskers had one last chance from their own 46, but Andy Headen knocked away their final long pass, and

Clemson became the first ACC team to win the national title since 1953.

CLEMSON	6	6	10	0	22
NEBRASKA	7	0	0	8	15
CU Igwebuike 41 FG, 1st, 11:39					
NEB Steels 25 pass from Rozier (Seibel kick), 1st, 6:43					
CU Igwebuike 37 FG, 1st, 1:03					
CU Austin 2 run (pass failed), 2nd, 3:56					
CU Tuttle 13 pass from Jordan (Pauling kick), 3rd, 6:12					
CU Igwebuike 36 FG, 3rd, 2:36					
NEB Craig 26 run (Craig run), 4th, 9:15					
Attendance: 72,748					

3 IPTAY—Lifeblood of Clemson Athletics

When Josh Cody retired in 1930 after four highly successful years as head coach, Clemson's football fortunes crashed along with the stock market. Cody had compiled a 29–11–1 record before he left and Jess Neely took over for the 1931 season. Although Neely later went on to become a successful coach at Rice University, his seasons at Clemson were referred to as the "Seven Lean Years." It took him five years to produce a winning season. His record was 27–33–7. There was some consternation among some influential alumni after Neely's first season in which Clemson finished 1–6–2.

After the 1931 Citadel game in Florence, in which Clemson was beaten 6–0, Captain Frank Jervey, Neely, assistant coach Joe Davis, and Captain Peter Heffner were sitting in a car outside the stadium talking quietly. Jervey was working in Washington as a liaison between the military and the school; and Heffner, who was a member of the military staff at Clemson, had a strong interest in athletics and assisted with the coaching in his spare moments.

"What we ought to do," he said, "is get the alumni to give Jess some backing by helping him finance the football team."

"How much do you think we should ask from each person?" Jervey asked Neely.

"How about $50 each?" Neely answered. "That way we can form a '50 Club.' If I could get $10,000 a year to build the football program, I could give Clemson fans a winning team."

During the drive back to Clemson, the four men continued their conversation and decided that Jervey would begin writing letters to the more influential Clemson alumni when he returned to Washington. (One of his first letters was to Rupert H. "Rube" Fike, M.D., a cancer specialist in Atlanta who had fallen in love with the Tigers in 1900 when he watched the Clemson-Wofford game through a knothole in a fence. He later graduated in the class of 1908.) After a year of correspondence, a dozen alumni gathered on October 20, 1932, in the Jefferson Hotel in Columbia, immediately following the game against South Carolina. From the outset, Fike believed the $50 figure was a bit too high for people to pay during the Depression years. Nevertheless, he agreed to start the 50 Club; but he still believed after returning to his practice in Atlanta that if a smaller amount was requested, it would attract a bigger list of people. The idea excited him. He decided to ask for $10 instead of $50. In Atlanta, he presented his idea to two other Clemson graduates, J.E.M. Mitchell, class of 1912, and Milton Berry, class of 1913.

Though it took another year, progress was made toward implementing Fike's plan to solicit $10 from Clemson alumni under the slogan, "I Pay Ten A Year."

According to Fike, a constitution was formulated and IPTAY was to be a secret organization.

It stated that the purpose of the Clemson Order of IPTAY "shall be to provide annual financial support to the athletic department at Clemson and to assist in every other way possible to regain for Clemson the high athletic standing which rightfully belongs to her."

Neely's initiation in the order took place at Clemson as scheduled on September 22, 1934, in the office of J.H. "Uncle Jake" Woodward. In addition to Fike, Berry, and Mitchell, who came from Atlanta, others present were Leonard R. Booker and J.C. Littlejohn. The seven were the vanguard of IPTAY. When the season was over, they began a statewide campaign to solicit memberships to the organization. By the end of 1935, they had succeeded in signing up 185 members.

Wealthy IPTAY members were informed that the "T" didn't necessarily have to represent $10 but could be for $20, $200, or $2,000. Some like Earl Glasscock, a farmer in Harmony, South Carolina, couldn't even afford $10. Instead, he traded $10 worth of sweet milk for his membership card. In the early years of the organization, other legal tender included such items as sweet potatoes and turnip greens. Neely had to acknowledge everything that came in through IPTAY. Not only did the $10 fee entitle the donor to a membership card, it also included such benefits as a subscription to the school's weekly newspaper; a weekly letter from the head coach; a windshield sticker that was dated every year; and finally, first rights on the purchase of tickets. Even a local bookmaker jointed IPTAY, but only because he picked up some tips from the coach's weekly letter.

Fired up by a new wave of spirit from the countryside, Clemson finished its 1935 season with a 6–3 record. After two break-even years, the 1938 team produced a 7–1–1 mark. In Neely's last season, in 1939, Clemson was 9–1 and defeated Boston College in the 1940 Cotton Bowl 6–3.

"When we came to Clemson in 1931," Neely said, "there wasn't 20 cents in the treasury; and when I left, there was over $20,000."

Indeed, IPTAY was beginning to grow. Just prior to World War II, its membership had risen to 1,620.

Today, there are more than 15,200 card-carrying IPTAY members who donated $20.5 million in 2013. The doctrine of IPTAY is spread throughout all of South Carolina's counties and even in the larger cities in Georgia and North Carolina. It is the largest fund-raising organization of any college in the country, and it presents a model for other colleges to follow.

Joe Turner had a simple explanation for the organization's success.

"We utilize massive marketing campaigns, TV shows, billboards, bumper stickers. We're like McDonalds."

He also pointed out that the "T" in IPTAY has ballooned to $30. "Some," Turner adds, "give more than $2,000."

The organization has, from its followers, raised millions over the years, 90 percent of whom live in South Carolina, Georgia, and North Carolina, almost defying the imagination in regard to fund raising. Member privileges include parking permits and priorities to purchase tickets. Larger donors have an extra incentive, an opportunity to buy tickets to the ACC basketball tournament or any bowl games the football team plays in.

Although the football program requires the largest budget, a total of 410 athletic scholarships in all sports are allocated through the monies raised through IPTAY. Once an IPTAY scholarship has been awarded to an athlete, it can never be withdrawn. However, there are two requirements that an athlete must maintain—one is good scholastic standing and the other is his obligation to conduct himself like a gentleman at all times, which in reality is demanded of all Clemson students.

B.C. Inabinet, chairman of the board of Defender Industries, was a former football star in the early 1950s who benefitted from an IPTAY scholarship. Inabinet himself was acknowledged as one of the top contributors to IPTAY. So valued was Inabinet's support that Clemson president Bill Atchley bestowed the honorary title of Ambassador of Clemson on the jovial Inabinet early in the spring of 1982.

Not only that, but the former lineman was the only non-player to receive a diamond Orange Bowl ring after Clemson defeated Nebraska in the 1982 bowl game. He is unabashed when expressing his love for Clemson.

"I never, never miss a game," Inabinet said. "Something like Clemson gets into your blood. In the early years, it was just like the spirit at West Point and The Citadel. Clemson spirit is one of the real identifiable things in this country. The people go way back. It's real family, and that's the most beautiful thing about it. There isn't anything like it. Why, I could get a Yankee to love Clemson."

Since he contributed $35,000 at the beginning, Inabinet was named a lifetime member of IPTAY.

Inabinet was a much sought-after prospect when he graduated from Dreher High School in Columbia. He could have gone to any one of 50 colleges who tried to recruit him. One would have imagined that he would have enrolled at South Carolina, which was located in his own hometown.

"Senator Strom Thurmond recruited me to Clemson, and the people in South Carolina wanted me to stay in the state," Inabinet said. "Columbia was my home, but I loved Clemson. It was no hard decision."

There is also no mistaking George Alley's love for Clemson, either. Like Inabinet, he, too, is from Columbia; and Alley's law offices are rampant with tiger designs on rugs, ashtrays, and desks. On the wall close to his desk is a photograph of Clemson wide receiver Jerry Butler's game-winning catch that defeated South Carolina in

1977. It is autographed. Alley is also a lifetime donor of IPTAY. He left Clemson in 1948 and earned his law degree from the University of Virginia several years later. He's never forgotten Clemson.

"I just love Clemson," Alley said simply. "I wish I had lots of money; I mean lots and lots of money. I'd give it all to Clemson. I go up there every chance I get. My wife graduated from Clemson. My son's wife did; her dad did, too. My daughter graduated from Clemson; her son did also. My daughter's husband graduated from Clemson, as did his father. My three grandchildren joined IPTAY as gold card [$500] members the day they were born."

"Anything that benefits Clemson, I want to get it before the public," Alley said. "I always wanted to go there. I've felt that way since I was a small boy. I remember seeing the cadets coming down to Columbia for football games. I just love that place."

Walter Riggs—Father of Clemson Athletics

Historians acknowledge Walter Riggs as the father of Clemson athletics. And, rightfully so. Not because he possessed football experience where he came from but because he was only one of two persons at Clemson to have ever seen a football game. The other when the sport debuted in 1896 was Frank Tompkins, who was in the Clemson backfield on Clemson's first football team that year.

An engineering professor, he was the only candidate to coach the embryonic Tigers, and he was well qualified to do so. At Auburn, he was manager and left end on the football team as well as a catcher and captain of the baseball team.

"When leaving Auburn, I had sworn off from athletics," Riggs confessed. "But when the fall of 1896 came around and the

Clemson boys wanted to get up a football team, the call of the wild was too strong and again, I found myself in a football suit and the single-handed coach of the first Clemson football team."

What Riggs saw his first year at Clemson was a campus covered with underbrush and underdeveloped land that had no groomed paths and very poor roads. There was but a single barracks, only three buildings, and a small one-room post office with a stretch of land in front where football had its beginning. It was far different what Riggs had experienced at Auburn.

The practice field was small, 50' x 200'. Equipment for the players was non-existent and was provided for with donations from the faculty and students. The uniforms consisted of very little padding except at the knees and elbows. Tightly fitted and laced leather or canvas served as body protection. A few of the players were fortunate to have nose and shin guards. It was only natural for the players to grow long hair for protection since there were no helmets anywhere.

Clemson's first game was against Furman University in Greenville on October 31. It was the first time the Clemson players ever saw a full-sized gridiron. Furman, who had been playing football for several years, was a prohibitive favorite to cage the Tigers. To the shock of everyone, Clemson beat Furman 14–6. Charlie Gentry was credited in scoring Clemson's first touchdown ever.

The win left a huge impression on center George Swygert.

"With Professor Riggs as our coach, we were ready," Swygert remembered. "We had a few trick plays. One was when a play ended near the sideline, our lightest end would hide the ball under his sweater. As the teams moved to the center of the field for the next play, he faked being injured and he then would make a bee-line for the goal."

Clemson's upset victory over Furman that day was a monumental milestone for the school. At the time, Furman was considered a strong team and had enjoyed success playing the game since 1889.

Riggs was very devoted to Clemson. The college was low in funds and wasn't able to hire a coach. They looked to Riggs and once again he contributed and guided the Tigers to a career record of 6–3. He became president of Clemson in 1911, and the field where it all began was named Riggs Field in his honor.

"In looking back over a service of several years, I regarded the introduction of intercollegiate football into Clemson College as one of the most valuable steps in development in the institution," he wrote. "Long before its graduates could spread its fame as an institution of learning, its football teams had made the name of Clemson College known and respected throughout the nation.

"In a well-rounded college life, play is just as indispensable to healthy growth as is work. Athletics should not interfere with studies, nor should studies exclude athletics. Each should have a proper and legitimate place in the thought and life of the students."

5 John Heisman

The arrival of John Heisman in 1900 ushered in the Golden Age of Clemson football. A budding genius, Heisman developed the Tigers into a football power in the South during his four years at Clemson.

It was Walter Riggs who was responsible for luring Heisman into coming to Clemson.

Heisman was a northerner, born of German parents in Cleveland, Ohio, and he grew up in Pennsylvania. His real given name was Johann Wilhelm, but he changed that to John William when he attended Brown and later the University of Pennsylvania before the turn of the twentieth century. A new game called

John Heisman. (Photo courtesy of the Clemson University Sports Information Department)

football was beginning to become popular on the campuses of colleges in the east and north. It interested Heisman immensely. After playing at both Brown and Pennsylvania, Heisman was so obsessed with the game that he started coaching at Oberlin College in 1892. In his first season there, Heisman produced an undefeated team. He coached at Akron University (then known as Buchtel College) in 1893 and the following year returned to Oberlin. However, in 1895 he was lured south to Auburn.

It was the same year that Heisman became infatuated with the possibilities of a forward pass, which was an illegal play during the formative years of the game. He saw it used for the first time while scouting a game between North Carolina and Georgia. While getting ready to punt, the North Carolina kicker was surrounded by Georgia linemen and couldn't get his kick off. Instead he inadvertently threw the ball toward a teammate who caught it and ran 70 yards for the game's only touchdown.

The Georgia players screamed in protest but to no avail. The referee admitted that he hadn't seen the ball thrown and allowed the touchdown. In the years ahead, Heisman championed for the legalization of the forward pass by the Football Rules Committee. In the meantime, he improvised by making use of a lateral. It was the second innovation that Heisman had developed. Years before, he had instituted the center snap a year before Amos Alonzo Stagg of the University of Chicago introduced it. Heisman produced strong teams at Auburn in the five years he was there.

In its very first game under Heisman, Clemson routed Davidson 64–0. The Tigers didn't stop there and went on to defeat Wofford 21–0, South Carolina 51–0, Georgia 39–5, Virginia Tech 12–5, and Alabama 35–0. In winning all six of its games, Clemson recorded its first undefeated season, thoroughly outscoring its opponents 222–10.

Heisman was a perfectionist. One of his ingenious characteristics was in originating plays. Only rarely did he ever use the same play twice. He didn't have any patience with players who were not bright and couldn't quickly learn his signal system or intricate tactics. For that reason, he barely substituted during games, making use of only three or four reserves at most. Heisman demanded that his players remain in excellent physical shape to play the expected 70 minutes of football required back them.

The following year, in 1901, Clemson finished with a 3–1–1 record. After opening with a 6–6 tie against Tennessee, Clemson stampeded Guilford 122–0 in the opener, which remains today as the most points ever scored by a Tigers football team. The Tigers went on to tie Tennessee 6–6, beat Georgia 29–5, lose to Virginia Tech 17–11, and close out the season with a 22–10 victory over North Carolina. The next year Clemson was 6–1, with its only loss occurring in the middle of the season, 12–6 to South Carolina. In between Clemson defeated North Carolina State 11–5, Georgia Tech 44–5, Furman 28–0, Georgia 36–0, Auburn 16–0, and Tennessee 11–0.

The 1902 team was considered the best that Heisman produced. The ploy he used that season before the Georgia Tech game was perhaps the cleverest ruse in the school's history. A day before the game, Heisman dispatched a group of cadets into Atlanta, masquerading as the Clemson football team. He gave them instructions to live it up around town and make certain that they were visible to Georgia Tech officials. They carried out their mission unfailingly. Not only were they seen, but they were entertained by the partisan local citizens. Since the supposed Clemson football players partied until the late hours, Tech was confident of an easy win the next day.

However, on game day, Heisman arrived with his team. They had spent the night in Lula, Georgia, a small railroad stop north of Atlanta. Clemson easily disposed of the stunned Tech eleven by a score of 44–5.

In 1903, the Tigers went 4–1–1, defeating Georgia 29–0, Georgia Tech 73–0, North Carolina State 24–0, and Davidson 24–0. They lost to North Carolina 11–6 and were tied by Cumberland in Heisman's final game as coach 11–11.

Once again Georgia Tech was victimized by Heisman's cunning. Vet Sitton, Clemson's left end who had played so brilliantly against Tech the year before, was nursing an injury. When word reached Atlanta that he would not be able to play, Tech officials displayed guarded optimism. They felt that Heisman was trying to fool them a second time. What they didn't know was that Heisman had an extremely capable substitute in Gil Ellison. Although Ellison wasn't as fast as Sitton, he was bigger and stronger and his play against Tech helped fashion an easy 73–0 victory. The win brought an extra reward to Clemson. The University of Georgia team had made a deal with the Clemson players, offering them a bushel of apples for every point they would defeat Tech above the score Clemson made against them, which was 29. The Tigers ended up with 44 bushels of apples that fall.

They also lost Heisman. Georgia Tech was determined to get him as coach. They lured him with an offer of $2,250 a year, plus 30 percent of the gate receipts after expenses. The financial possibilities far exceeded the $1,800 Heisman was making at Clemson. But Heisman had stamped an indelible mark on Clemson football. He compiled a 19–3–2 record, winning 83 percent of his games. It still ranks as the highest winning percentage in Clemson history.

The Golden Age that had begun with Heisman lasted until 1907, and Clemson became a gridiron force. In seven years the Tigers won 33, lost only 12, and tied seven games while outscoring their opponents, 987 to 249. Shack Shealy followed Heisman in 1904, and in one year he coached the team to a 3–3–1 mark. In 1905, Eddie Cochems went 3–2–1. Bob Williams coached in 1906 and turned in a 4–0–3 record. In 1907, young Frank Shaughnessy, who later went on to become one of the nation's most respected coaches, had a 4–4 record.

After that season, Clemson's football fortunes sank into what has been descried as the Dark Ages. During a span of almost two decades, Clemson posted a 69–82–10 record.

6 Memorial Stadium

Clemson's Memorial Stadium is aptly known as "Death Valley." With a seating capacity better than 85,000, the stadium is one of the largest on-campus venues in the country and by far one of the noisiest. Opposing coaches hate to bring their teams into Death Valley and understandably so. The Tigers are practically unbeatable there. After the 2013 season, Clemson's home record had a 72 percent winning rate.

It was because of the thunder of the crowd in a sea of orange that the NCAA rules committee passed a new amendment in 1982 to its 1978 rule governing crowd noise. Instead of two warnings per snap, the rule was changed to two warnings per game with a violation resulting in a penalty on the home team. In the ACC, the rule is referred to as the "Clemson Rule."

"Our crowd is a very good crowd, noisy sometimes, but good," Coach Danny Ford offered. "Everybody will have to adjust. Maybe some people aren't used to playing before noise. We played at Notre Dame and they had crowd noise. It was loud but it was fun to play in that atmosphere."

The Death Valley frenzy wasn't always that way. Before 1942, before the stadium was erected, Clemson crowds were small. The Tigers played their home games on Riggs Field, which had a capacity of some 9,000, hardly enough noise to scare a rabbit. During Jess Neely's nine years at Clemson, the Tigers never played more than four home games. In six of those years, Clemson played a minuscule two games.

Before he left for Rice in 1940, Neely told Frank Howard, who was one of his assistants, that there was no need to expand the stadium. He also confided to Howard that Clemson couldn't build a winning program for big-time football because there isn't enough money to support it.

Nevertheless, Howard was determined. He laid out plans for a 20,000-seat stadium. But building it wasn't easy. With low funds, the labor consisted of scholarship athletes and little mechanized equipment. But Howard, an Alabama farm boy, was out on the field with them. It was a slow process week after week and took two years to build.

"About 40 people and I laid the sod on the field," Howard revealed. "After around three weeks, I remember it was July 15, we had only gotten halfway through. I told them that it had taken us three weeks to get that far. But I would give them three more weeks pay for however long it took to finish.

"I also told them I'd go over to the dairy barn and get 50 gallons of ice cream when we got through. You know, it didn't take 'em but three days to finish the rest of the field, and we sat down in the middle of the field and ate that whole 50 gallons of ice cream."

At the beginning of the construction, Hoard left his own mark as only he could. When each of the four corners of cement was poured, Howard took a chew of tobacco out of his mouth and tossed it in the wet concrete, a little Howard legacy enmeshed in each corner of the stadium.

There wasn't another major expansion of the stadium until the 1958 season when 18,000 sideline seats were added. That year, Howard reached a milestone in a 26–21 hard-fought win over a strong North Carolina team. It was Howard's 100th victory, earned on a hot September day before a record crowd. It was so hot that hundreds were overcome by heat stroke and the concession stands ran out of cups in the third quarter and ice early in the fourth period.

Clemson's success brought on additional seats. More than 5,000 were added for the 1960 season. An additional 8,900 were in place 19 years later and the capacity increased to 60,000. By 1983, the seating numbered 79,575. The original part of the stadium was built for $125,000 or $6.25 per seat. The upper deck that was finished in 1983 cost $13.5 million or $866 per seat, and crowds of 80,000 are not uncommon. Clemson leads the ACC in attendance yearly, with a season ticket rate of 60,000.

In 1974 the playing surface was named Frank Howard Field in honor of the legendary coach, and it has more private boxes than any other college stadium. The largest can accommodate 44 people, and a double deck press box is well received by all media.

"We go to a lot of great venues for college football but it doesn't take a back seat to any place in terms of the atmosphere, stadium noise, and facilities. This is a special place on a Saturday night," ESPN commentator Todd Blackledge said.

He never gave an opinion of the food served in the press box...

7 1940 Cotton Bowl

January 1, 1940
Dallas, Texas
Clemson 6, Boston College 3
The news that Clemson had been selected to play in the 1940 Cotton Bowl was received calmly, even though it was the first bowl bid the college had received. Daily life in the sleepy town was undisturbed.

However, the mention of Clemson College created a shock in staid old Boston. The cosmopolitan city people had never even heard of Clemson. They wondered where it was located and who the upstarts might be who would play mighty Boston College. There was so much mystery regarding Clemson that the *Boston Post* dispatched one of its sportswriters, Gerry Hern, to the campus to whip up a series of articles about the school. The only knowledge he had about the football team was that they had finished the season with an 8–1 record, were coached by Jess Neely, and had a triple-treat All-American tailback named James "Bonnie Banks" McFadden who could run, throw, and kick with unrivaled skill.

Hern was surprised to learn that Neely's office was on the second floor of the old fertilizer building. Neely wasn't exactly a talkative person. He was deeply involved with the football team and spent most of his time on the field or in his office. In fact, whenever he dropped by one of the stores in town, he spoke so slowly that a local wag remarked, "You could roll a cigarette by the time Jess asks you how you're feeling."

Meanwhile, Neely created an air of mystery by going to Atlanta for several days. Of course, he refused to comment on the reasons for the trip. The speculation around town was that he either went to see Clark Gable in *Gone With The Wind*, or that he had held a secret meeting with Josh Cody, who had coached Clemson before Neely took over. Cody was now coaching Florida, which was the only team that had defeated Boston College that year, and there were suspicions that Neely was getting some scouting reports on the Eagles from the former Clemson coach.

Hern spent a week in Clemson. He seemed impressed with the town and its people, whom he found to be friendly. The quiet setting of the college was quite different from the hustle and bustle of Boston. He mentioned in one of his articles that although the team was nicknamed the Tigers, the players prefer to be known as the Country Gentlemen. When Neely returned from Atlanta, he spoke to Hern in his office.

"Well, I'd rather Boston knew our offense so we could try a lot of trick stuff," Neely told him. "The boys love fancy plays. In fact, every now and then they make one up on the field; and if I don't recognize a play, I'm sure Boston coach Frank Leahy won't.

"That McFadden put a lot of these gray hairs on my head. I don't discourage him any. He's a right smart tailback, and if he feels like he has worked the team into a bad spot, I like to see him get reckless. We've scored a few touchdowns on plays I've never seen before."

There was no question that "Bonnie Banks" McFadden was the local hero. He was an All-American, and he was idolized by all the youngsters in town. They called him "Banksie." The previous year he was also named an All-American in basketball and quite possibly was the first college athlete to achieve such status in two sports. He was thin and willowy, standing about 6'3" 174 lbs., and he had an engaging personality to accompany his good looks. He claimed he could catch rabbits by hypnotizing them, simply by wiggling his ears.

McFadden grew up in a small town in South Carolina called Great Falls.

"Why, there's no such place," said McFadden one day to Hern on the steps outside the barracks. "It's kind of a crossing. Everybody is kind of a colonel there. Every time an auto goes through Great Falls, the colonels line up on the sidewalk and shake their heads, muttering, 'Heavens to Betsy, what'll they think of next?' I don't know how many people are there, but I'm sure that every one of them is living."

A friendly type with a fine sense of humor, McFadden would stop between classes to talk to anyone who called to him. One day one of the yard men stopped him. He didn't even talk football. Instead, they discussed whether or not a local widower with seven sons should marry a widow with 13 sons and daughters, which was the big social topic around town. Until it was settled, the widower would do his courting on Sunday evening. McFadden couldn't help solve the problem.

Not only was McFadden a local hero, he had earned a reputation around the state, as well. Once, when he was a sophomore in high school, he got off a punt that traveled so far that the officials stopped the game to measure it. A short time after he was named an All-American, Governor Burnet R. Maybank gave a speech in Clemson to honor McFadden.

"Banks," the governor said, "you're making the All-American team is worth $10,000 to the state of South Carolina."

"Gov," McFadden shouted, "you just put that in writing—on a check."

A crowd of 20,000 may seem small today, but that many people came to the Cotton Bowl on a cold afternoon in Dallas to see little Clemson go against the big eastern power, Boston College. It was the largest crowd that Clemson had ever played in front of.

After a scoreless first period, the Eagles scored in the opening minute of the second quarter. Alex Lukachik kicked a 26-yard field goal to push Boston College in front 3–0. After McFadden put the Eagles in the hole with a quick kick, the Eagles didn't hesitate to punt the ball back to Clemson. Starting on their own 43-yard line, the Tigers mounted a drive. McFadden led the way with a 12-yard run and a 16-yard pass. Timmons crowned the drive by plunging for a touchdown from the 1-yard line. Bryant missed the extra point, but Clemson led 6–3. Nobody expected that the halftime score would be the final score, as well. McFadden played brilliantly on defense, knocking away Boston quarterback Charlie O'Rourke's passes time and again while averaging 43 yards on his punts.

"Clemson is every bit as good as they were cracked up to be," Leahy praised. "We lost to a great team, one of the best I have ever seen. I have the satisfaction of knowing that while we were beaten, the game wasn't lost on a fluke."

Yet Clemson didn't get to fully savor its victory. There were reports after the game that Neely had been offered a five-year contract to coach Rice. Neely wouldn't comment. Several weeks later, he did indeed leave Clemson to take the Rice job.

CLEMSON	0	6	0	0	6
BOSTON COLLEGE	0	3	0	0	3
BC Lukachik 34 FG					
CU Timmons 1 run (Kick failed)					
Attendance: 20,000					

8 1948 Season—11–0

The 1948 season was one of the most talented in Clemson history, especially when considering it was a unit with just 37 players on the travel squad. Eight players on this club are in the Clemson Hall of Fame. The team was a perfect 11–0, including a school-record seven wins away, and a No. 11 final Associated Press ranking.

Clemson was one of three undefeated, untied teams and had the most wins in the nation that year. Michigan and Notre Dame were also undefeated, but neither team played in a bowl game.

Clemson was a club that was dominating on defense (allowing just 76 points) and a precision single-wing offense that performed in the clutch. Five of the 11 wins were recorded by a one-touchdown margin or less—more "close" wins than any team in Clemson history. It might have been the greatest squad in school history in terms of special teams.

The perfect season of 1948 was as much a surprise to Clemson fans as the perfect season of 1981. Both years, the Tigers were

Clemson went undefeated in 1948. (Photo courtesy of the Clemson University Sports Information Department)

coming off mediocre seasons. In 1947, Clemson was just 4–5 and had to win the last three games to do that.

"Entering the 1948 season, we didn't think we would be as good a team as the previous year before Henry Walker decided not to come back," recalled Phil Prince, captain of the 1948 Tigers. "He had been our leading receiver the previous year and would have been one of the top payers in 1948. He had already earned one degree from Virginia and then got another from Clemson in the spring of 1948. He was offered a job in the textile industry and decided to take it. He went on to become the president of the company."

Many teams in recent Clemson history have had a formula that featured talented youth and wise veteran players. According to Prince, that was one of the reasons for the success of the 1948 Tigers.

"We had an interesting mixture of seniors and sophomores. The difference in the 1948 team compared to 1947 was the sophomore class. That group of sophomores was the greatest group of athletes Clemson had in one class up to that point. At the same time, we had some experienced players in the senior class. It just seemed that the leadership of the seniors jelled with the athletic talent of that sophomore class."

Fred Cone, a sophomore in 1948 who is among just six football players in the Clemson Ring of Honor, agrees with Prince. "We had a lot of great athletes on that team. Bobby Gage, he could run, he could pass, he did everything. He called the plays, he ran the team, he gave everyone confidence.

"Frank Gillespie, Phil Prince, Gene Moore, they were all great team leaders who set an example for the sophomores. We were lucky to have such a group of leaders.

"We also had an outstanding coaching staff," continued Cone. "Coach Howard was our leader, but the assistants were very good. I remember Goat McMillan drilling us on how to hide the ball when we were practicing the spin for the single-wing offense. He taught us all the tricks of hiding the ball from the defense."

Prince summarized another important team characteristic. "Vince Lombardi once said, 'To be a successful team, you have to love each other.' We were always there for each other. To go undefeated and untied, we had to stay together. We had a lot of cliff hangers in that season, and we had to stay together to pull them out. We didn't have any quit in that team."

The 1949 Gator Bowl is still considered one of the most exciting games in the bowl's history.

"From a spectator's standpoint, I still think it is the most exciting game I ever saw a Clemson team play," Coach Frank Howard said. "We couldn't stop them and they couldn't stop us. That's the reason we went for it on fourth down late in the game.

"I was afraid to let them have the ball back. I guess we were fortunate, but we had some good players and they came through for us."

For Clemson, it jump-started an era that saw the football program go to six bowl games in 12 years, including two trips to the Orange Bowl and one Sugar Bowl appearance.

"I don't think that I have ever had more satisfaction out of one season than I did in 1948," Howard said.

Frank Howard

Most colleges would give a coach a gold watch at a testimonial dinner and wish him well in the years of his retirement, but Clemson made a place for Frank Howard, and deservingly so. Howard and Clemson have been synonymous through the years when the school was struggling to gain an identity. He, more than any other coach, created the mania that is Clemson football. Certainly, no other coach has been at Clemson longer, and it is reasonable to assume that no other coach ever will.

"If there wasn't a Frank Howard, Clemson would have had to create one," remarked Dick Ensley, the manager at the town's Holiday Inn. "That's how much he's meant to the school. He just loves to sit around and tell stories. I've heard some of them many times, but I don't mind hearing them again because most of them are so funny."

The Holiday Inn is just a 3:00 ride from Clemson. Howard stops there regularly for his morning coffee before driving to his office at the Jervey Athletic Center. It was his way of keeping in touch with the local gentry, which he enjoyed doing so much. One morning he had his coffee with a couple of state troopers. Another time he would sit with several local businessmen. Even early in the morning, Howard is awake enough to crack a few jokes, which is his style.

"Bob Hope came here a few years back and asked me to give him the grand tour," Howard told a visitor who stopped by his table. "Well, I picked him up, and we drove down to the first stoplight. Then, we went on down to the other one. Ol' Bob turned to me and said, 'Frank, I thought you were going to show me around town?' Well, I just looked at him and told him, 'Good Lord, Bob. If you want me to, we'll go back up and I'll show you again.'"

There wasn't a better storyteller either than Howard. Told with pure country charm, he often repeated some of Clemson's football lore hundreds of times, and people still liked to hear the tales. He is still referred to as the coach; he would sit and talk about Clemson with anyone who asked him, including people he's met for the first time. That's how much Clemson has meant to Howard all these years. He had a genuine love affair with the school and the town itself.

Howard was an assistant on Neely's staff for nine years. When Jeff Neely left to become head coach of Rice Institute in Houston, Texas, in 1940, Howard was named as his successor. His appointment was unique. Howard's name was placed in nomination by Professor S.R. "Slim" Rhodes at an athletic council meeting that had been scheduled to hire a replacement for Neely. Howard, who was seated in the back of the room, supposedly waiting to be interviewed as a prospective candidate, seconded the nomination. The other council members took it from there and voted for Howard as Clemson's 17th head football coach. Howard received a four-year contract, which he ultimately misplaced several years later on a business trip. It was the only contact he received during the 30 years at Clemson. Every year after that Howard's acceptance to an offer to continue as coach was formalized by a handshake.

"I never asked for another contract, and they never offered me one," Howard remarked. "I guess I'm the only coach who ever wore

Legendary coach Frank Howard. (Photo courtesy of the Clemson University Sports Information Department)

out three college presidents. I never will forget that first one, Dr. Sykes. When he hired me he said, 'Coach, there's only one request I want to make.' I said, 'Doc, what's that?' He replied, 'I don't want you to go round telling people what I pay you.' I said, 'Heck, you don't need to worry none 'cause I'm as ashamed of it as you are.'"

Under Howard, along with his humor, Clemson began to generate national exposure. Mostly, it was though the bowl appearances. Before Howard took over as head coach for the 1940 season, Clemson had appeared in only one major bowl game, the 1940 Cotton Bowl, which was Jess Neely's final game as coach before he went to Rice. Beginning with the 1949 Gator Bowl, Howard led the Tigers to six postseason bowl games—the 1951 Orange

Bowl, 1952 Gator Bowl, 1957 Orange Bowl, 1959 Sugar Bowl, and the 1959 Bluebonnet Bowl that was played in December of that year. His teams won six Atlantic Coast Conference championships, more than any other school, and two Southern Conference championships.

Howard's 1948 team went 11–0 and made its first bowl appearance under him. Yet, Howard doesn't consider that team the best he ever coached. "That was the best record one of my teams ever had," Howard said, "but that wasn't my best team. The best I ever had was either in 1958 or '59."

In 1958, Clemson finished with an 8–3 record. The following season they improved to 9–2. Following the '58 campaign, Clemson was matched against LSU in the Sugar Bowl on New Year's Day. Clemson lost in a thrilling game 7–0 when Heisman Trophy winner Billy Cannon threw a touchdown pass in the third quarter and then proceeded to kick the extra point before 82,000 fans.

"Cannon was a good player, but they didn't hurt us the rest of the time," Howard recalled. "We hurt ourselves with fumbles and other mistakes. I remember we ran a screen pass that coulda won the game, but it was dropped. That's the kind of day it was."

When his 1959 team went 9–2, Clemson was invited to play TCU in the Bluebonnet Bowl that December. Clemson became the first college to appear in two postseason bowl games the same year. The Tigers took advantage of the opportunity to defeat a good TCU team 23–7, overcoming a 7–3 deficit in the process.

Howard's teams weren't fancy. They played hard-nosed football. Howard was a strong exponent of the single wing, which had always been described as "three yards and a cloud of dust." However, the evolution of the T formation made the single wing obsolete. After Clemson was blanked 14–0 by Miami in the 1952 Gator Bowl, Howard had to yield to the changing trends of college football and install the T formation. It wasn't all that easy.

"We were one of the last teams to change from the single wing," Howard said. "That was the only offensive I know anything about, and that's the way I recruited my players. I had to go out and learn the T formation, so I went to Bud Wilkinson, one of the best teachers I know of. That plus talking to other coaches and watching films was all I did."

It was during Howard's long coaching tenure that Memorial Stadium became more familiarly known as Death Valley. Howard devised a ritual for his players at every home game. They would leave the dressing room high behind the east end of the stadium and run down the hill through the goal posts onto the field as the enthusiastic Clemson fans stood and applauded. Psychologically, the scene created a feeling of invincibility. Through the years, Clemson had dominated games played in Death Valley.

Back in the early 1950s, S.C. Jones, a 1919 Clemson graduate, was traveling through Death Valley, California. He stopped his car long enough to pick up a rock that weighed about 10 lbs. and place it in the trunk of the car. He brought it back to Clemson and presented it to Howard, saying that since Memorial Stadium was known as Death Valley, it was only appropriate that he should have a rock from the real Death Valley.

The rock sat around Howard's office for several years. Finally, Howard got tired of looking at it. He told Gene Willimon, who had played for Clemson in 1932–33, to take the rock and put it on the field somewhere. Willimon had a better idea. He had the rock mounted on a cement pedestal and had it placed on top of the hill at the east end of the stadium. From that day on, the players would touch the rock as they ran down the field.

"On the first Friday we had it," Howard said, "I turned to my team and said, 'Lookie here, boys. If any of you boys are gonna go out and give me 120 percent, I'll let you rub my rock, and it'll give you supernatural powers.' Well, the rock story got in the papers. Then I got a letter from a woman. She said no wonder I didn't

Howard's Record

In his 30 years as head coach, all at Clemson, Howard produced a 165–118–12 record. Howard won six ACC championships in the conference's first 15 years (1956, 1958, 1959, 1965, 1966, 1967). In 1948 he was voted Southern Conference Coach of the Year and was named ACC Coach of the Year in 1966. Howard died in January 1994 at the age of 86. Fittingly, he was buried, as he wished, on a plot of land behind Death Valley, "Where I can hear the roar of the crowd cheering for my beloved Tigers on Saturdays in the fall."

How Frank Howard Became Head Coach

When Jess Neely left Clemson to become head coach at Rice, Frank Howard told him that he wasn't going with him. Neely responded by saying, "I didn't ask you." Howard never really thought about going to Rice. What he wanted was the vacant head coach position that Neely left at Clemson.

When the Clemson Athletic Council met after the 1940 Cotton Bowl to name Neely's replacement, Professor Sam Rhodes, one of the council members, placed Howard's' name in nomination for the vote. Howard was standing at the back of the room. He never left after being interviewed. When his name was nominated, Howard shouted, "I second the nomination."

The council members didn't hesitate in approving Howard. He was only given a one-year contact, which he admitted losing three months later. He never got another one in the 43 years he was at Clemson. While he was there he was presented with the Order of the Palmetto, the highest honor that the governor of South Carolina can bestow. Clemson also recognized Howard with the presentation of the Clemson Medallion, which is the highest public honor bestowed by the university to a living person who exemplifies the dedication and foresight of its founders.

Biggest Achievement

Frank Howard maintained that Clemson's 23–7 victory over TCU in the 1959 Bluebonnet Bowl was the biggest achievement by a Clemson team. His argument was that appearing in two bowl games in the same year established Clemson as the first team to do so. The

Bluebonnet Bowl was played on December 19, 1959, some 11 months after the Tigers faced LSU on January 1, 1959, in the New Orleans Sugar Bowl. By beating TCU, the Tigers improved their bowl record to four wins in seven games. In all seven of their bowl games, the Tigers were rated as underdogs.

win more games. I believed in rocks instead of God. She said if I'd believed in God instead of rocks, I would've been a lot better coach."

The fierce South Carolina–Clemson rivalry flourished in Howard's time. The game was played on Thursdays to commemorate State Fair Week. The Thursday meeting finally ended in 1959 when the game was moved back to Saturday and played subsequent years as a home game by the respective schools. Howard never appreciated the treatment Clemson received during the Thursday games at the Columbia Fairgrounds.

The 1969 season was Howard's final one as coach. When he stepped down, he had recorded 165 victories, which was 19th on the list of active or retired coaches. Even on his retirement, Howard managed to express his humor.

"I was in it long enough," he remarked. "I felt these people deserved to see another kind of football. They looked at me long enough."

President Robert C. Edwards released the following statement regarding Howard's retirement on December 10, 1969:

"As he announces his own decision, reached on his own initiative, to retire as head football coach and devote his full time to responsibilities of athletic directorship, I salute Frank Howard for all he is and all he has meant to Clemson.

"He is big time in every way. He has brought national recognition to Clemson, to the state of South Carolina, and to the Atlantic Coast Conference. He has been a stimulating force among the alumni and friends of Clemson. His lifetime record as a coach speaks for itself."

Howard remained on as athletic director for two years. In 1971, Bill McLellan was named as athletic director. It allowed Howard more time for banquet speeches and public appearances, which he always loved. Howard purchased a cemetery plot on Cemetery Hill, which is on a hill overlooking Memorial Stadium.

"That's where I'll spend all eternity, listening to the cheers for my Tigers," Howard said.

10 Danny Ford

If Norman Rockwell ever needed a gothic model for a college football coach portrait, Danny Ford would have been an ideal one for the iconic American artist. The soft-spoken Ford, with a country-boy look in a baseball cap behind the wheel of his pick-up-truck, would appeal to Rockwell. Or perhaps the image of Ford trolling Lake Hartwell for hybrid bass with a wad of Levi Garrett firmly in his cheek.

First and foremost, Ford was a football coach and one of the best in the annals of Clemson football. The Ford years were the golden ones, far beyond what anyone could have imagined, and he remains one of the most popular figures in the school's history.

Ford, the 21st coach in Clemson history, was ushered in under a cloud. Just after Clemson completed a 10–1 season and was preparing to meet Ohio State in the 1978 Gator Bowl, Charley Pell, who had restored Clemson's football program in the two years he was head coach, announced he had accepted the head coaching position at the University of Florida. The abruptness of Pell's move caught Clemson officials by surprise, created indignation among the school's followers, and sent shock waves across the tranquil

Ford at Clemson

Bob Bradley remembers an incident from the first year Ford came to Clemson as an assistant in 1977. The *Atlanta Constitution* had a story about the young assistant coach and intended to describe him as the "highly regarded Danny Ford." However, because of a typographical error, the phrase came out "highly retarded Danny Ford." After reading the story, Ford showed the article to Bradley.

"Can I sue 'em for that?" Ford asked.

Bradley pondered the question, leaned forward on his desk and dispatched a stream of tobacco juice into a paper cup. Then he looked seriously right at Ford.

"Danny, you're gonna have to prove 'em wrong first," Bradley drawled.

Clemson campus. The popular support that Pell had received during his two winning seasons evaporated as quickly as the dew under the South Carolina sun. Clemson fans became more vocal when Pell left. One banner that hung from a building in downtown Clemson read, "To hell with Pell."

"One thing Pell said was that one reason he was leaving and going to Florida was that he didn't think Clemson would ever have a chance to win a national championship," recalled Brian Clark, who was a senior offensive guard back then. "He thought the school was too unknown."

Before he left, Pell recommended to the athletic board that Ford replace him. After only 23 games at Clemson as an assistant coach, Ford was to be the new head coach. It took the athletic board just 48 hours to appoint Ford. On December 5, after just two extraordinary meetings with the athletic committee, at age 30, Danny Ford became the youngest Division I coach in the nation.

"When the committee was interviewing, the biggest item was my age," Ford said. "They talked about fear and awe. I told them, 'I don't fear anybody. The only thing I'm afraid of is snakes. If I see a snake, I take off running.'"

Danny Ford's first game as Clemson's head coach was the 1978 Gator Bowl.
(Photo courtesy of the Clemson University Sports Information Department)

Ford was stepping into a pressurized situation. He had less than three weeks to prepare for the Gator Bowl. Nevertheless, the players responded and went out and defeated Ohio State 17–15. Because of the Woody Hayes incident, more publicity was given to the Ohio State coach than the fact that Ford had won a bowl game in his first game as head coach.

Ford had never been a head coach before, not even in a Pop Warner League. He began as a graduate assistant at Alabama in 1970 and 1971. The next two years he was a full-time assistant. Ford then became an assistant coach at Virginia Tech for three years before Pell brought him to Clemson as his assistant in 1977. Yet Ford knew what winning was all about. At Alabama, he played on three bowl teams. Later, as a graduate assistant and as an assistant coach, he participated in four more bowl games.

"Being a head coach was something I always knew I'd do," Ford said. "I didn't know whether it would be in high school or a small college or what, but I knew I wanted to do it."

In his first full season as a head coach in 1979, Ford produced an 8–4 record despite having lost 15 starters from the 1978 team. The fourth loss occurred in the 1979 Peach Bowl against Baylor 24–18. Two of the three regular season losses were by only three and four points. It was quite a rewarding season for Ford. One of his biggest wins occurred against Notre Dame when Clemson overcame a 10–0 halftime deficit to defeat the Irish 16–10. It marked only the third time in Notre Dame's colorful football history that the Irish lost their season's home finale.

Clemson football appeared to be on the way back after three consecutive winning seasons. The Tigers' reputation grew because of their appearance in three nationally televised bowl games. However, in 1980, the program suffered a temporary setback when Clemson finished with a mediocre 6–5 record. Once again Ford's integrity prompted him to shoulder most of the blame for the team's lackluster performance after winning four of its first five games. Ugly whispers were heard about him being too young to be head coach and that perhaps he wasn't really qualified for the job. Ford admitted that he was still learning from his mistakes, but he refused to be discouraged. His goal was to be successful.

"I can look back and see I made some kind of mistake just about every day," Ford said. "Not big-time things necessarily, but things like not stressing a point or not talking enough to a particular player. There were times during the 1980 season when I overreacted."

Bowl-conscious Clemson fans were looking for bigger things in 1981. If there was any pressure on Ford, he didn't show it, although he realized his critics would be quick and vocal. After just two full seasons of coaching, Ford had reached a crossroad early in his career. He was aware he had to win, and win big, and he did a lot of soul searching in the lonely months before fall. The only sweet memory he had remaining from the 1980 season was a 27–6

Bigger Than Alabama-Auburn

Clemson coach Danny Ford also learned how much a rivalry meant to Tiger fans. Ford had played at the University of Alabama and was caught up in a deep-rooted rivalry with Auburn. After three years as Clemson's coach, he realized that this was bigger.

"This is a game that's not always won by the best football team or by who's supposed to be the best football team," Ford said. "But on that Saturday, you prove who has the best football team. Now, Alabama-Auburn is a great, great rivalry and they get after it. They have their land-grant jokes and their doctor and lawyer jokes, and there are the books of 100 Alabama jokes and the 100 Auburn jokes—just like it is here. But they let it die about the end of February.

"The Clemson–South Carolina rivalry, they don't let die. For 365 days a year, there's somebody at every function you go to who's talking about Clemson or South Carolina against each other. It's simply the biggest and the best rivalry in football."

triumph over nationally ranked South Carolina in the final game of the year.

"In planning for the 1981 season, it was the first year that we could say we had enough people to be a pretty good football team before the freshmen came in," Ford said. "We didn't have to turn to the new players for help."

Neither Ford nor anyone on his coaching staff anticipated just how successful Clemson would become in 1981. The team swept through the ACC and finished the season unbeaten with an 11–0 record, the first time that had happened since 1948. By season's end, the Tigers were voted the No. 1 team in the nation, an honor they had never received before. They secured their ranking when they defeated Nebraska in the Orange Bowl 22–15. Even Ford couldn't believe it.

"I wouldn't have bet on all this happening," Ford said. "No one could have imagined it either way. Not too many folks could have imagined we would have the type of year we had, being No. 1. Then it's very unusual for somebody who's been in coaching the short time I have to get that award. I just hope our staff and administration took a lot of pride in the honor because it's theirs more than mine."

Ford coached the team from 1979 until 1989, finishing with a 96–29–4 record. He won three ACC titles between 1986 and 1988. From 1981 to 1983, Ford was 30–2–2, the best in the nation. After the unbeaten 1981 season, he was voted Coach of the Year. He remains one of two coaches in ACC history with a 76 percent winning percentage.

11 Jess Neely

Perhaps one of Clemson's most beloved coaches was Jess Neely.

Neely's influence as inspiration is still present today as the IPTAY Scholarship Club was founded during his coaching tenure. IPTAY is the lifeblood of the Clemson Athletic Department. It provides funds for athletic scholarships and capital improvements.

Thousands of athletes have benefited through the IPTAY Scholarship Clemson fund since its inception in 1934. That first year of IPTAY, Neely and his staff convinced 160 people to pay $10.00 a year to Clemson, for a grand total of $1,600 (not bad during the middle of the Great Depression).

Neely was head coach at Clemson from 1931 through 1939 and spent the next 27 years at Rice University in Houston.

Neely coached Clemson to its first bowl game, the 1940 Cotton Bowl, where the Tigers capped a 9–1–0 season by beating Boston College 6–3. Clemson ended the season ranked No. 12 in the final AP poll, its first top 20 season in history.

Neely could only manage a 1–6–2 record in 1931. The weak record was further magnified by the realization that Clemson had scored only three touchdowns the entire season. Undismayed, Neely told Captain Frank Jervey that if he could get about $10,000, he could field a competitive football team. It took seven years for Neely to upgrade Clemson's football program. The breakthrough came in 1938 when Clemson went 7–1–1. In Neely's last season the following year, Clemson was 9–1, losing only to Tulane by a single point 7–6.

Boston College was ranked No. 11 going into the game, and it was Clemson's first win over a top 20 team in its history. The team featured the play of Banks McFadden, Clemson's first AP

All-American. Clemson had a 43–35–7 record during Neely's tenure.

Neely coached Rice to four Southwest Conference Championships and six bowl appearances, the last being a trip to the Bluebonnet Bowl in 1961. During 40 years of college coaching, he compiled a record of 207–176–19. Neely was ranked 12th in college football history in victories by a Division I-A coach when he

IPTAY was founded during Jess Neely's tenure as Clemson's football coach.
(Photo courtesy of the Clemson University Sports Information Department)

retired. For his accomplishments, he was inducted into the College Football Hall of Fame in 1971.

Neely graduated from Vanderbilt in 1923 after lettering for three years in football and serving as captain of the 1922 football team. He coached a year of high school football before returning to his alma mater to obtain a law degree. But he never practiced law.

He coached for four years at Southwestern College in Clarksville, Tennessee, and then went to Alabama in 1928. It was there that he met Frank Howard. Neely brought Howard to Clemson as line coach in 1931. Howard replaced him in 1940 and remained as head coach for 30 years. In 1967, Neely returned to his alma mater as athletic director. He officially retired in 1971 but continued to coach golf at Vanderbilt until 1981, when he moved back to Texas.

"If I didn't look in the mirror every day, I wouldn't know how old I am," Neely once said. "Working with the boys makes you feel young. I feel that in athletics the boys learn a sense of loyalty and sacrifice and values they don't learn anywhere else. They learn to compete and that is what life is all about...its competition.

"If they make good in football, chances are they'll be successful elsewhere. I like to see that those boys make something of themselves. That is my reward. The boys go to college to study and get that degree. Playing football is a side activity. When fellows go to a school first to play football, they get an entirely wrong sense of values. And when you start them off with the wrong sense, it isn't difficult for them to go astray."

"He was a good southern gentleman, but he worked us like dogs. The workouts were always twice as hard as the games," Dick Moegle said. "There were no superstars, no victory that was better than all the other victories. To him, football was a team game and we were all team players." Moegle was the player tacked in a famous episode in the 1954 Cotton Bowl, when frustrated Tommy Lewis of Alabama came off the bench to stop a certain touchdown. Rice won that game 28–6.

Neely died at the age of 85 in 1983, but his landmark accomplishments in the 1930s at Clemson contributed significantly to Clemson's outstanding football tradition.

12 Steve Fuller

Every once in a while a truly well-rounded individual comes along.

Steve Fuller was a scholar, an athlete, and a fine representative of his community. That combination made him one of the most decorated athletes in school history and the reason he was inducted into the Clemson Ring of Honor in 1994. He was also the first Tigers football player in history to have his jersey (No. 4) retired.

Fuller, a native of nearby Spartanburg, South Carolina, graduated from high school with a perfect 4.0 GPA in a class of more than 800, crowning him class valedictorian. He had offers to play professional baseball out of high school and had basketball scholarship offers from Division I schools, as well.

Fuller produced a preview of what Tigers fans should expect from him over the course of the next four seasons. He was named ACC Rookie of the Week in his first collegiate game, gaining 194 yards of the total offensive against the Tulane Green Wave. During his sophomore season, Fuller gained further recognition by being named ACC Back of the Week after the Tennessee game. He was also named to the All-ACC Academic Team in 1976.

Fuller demonstrated exceptional leadership during his junior and senior years, both on and off the field. Highlights on the field included leading the ACC in total offense for both years and being selected twice as the ACC Player of the Year, the only two-time selection in Clemson history.

Equally impressive were the team accomplishments, as Fuller quarterbacked Clemson to two consecutive Gator Bowls, the Tigers' first bowl appearance in 18 seasons. In 1978, Clemson posted an 11–1 record and was ranked No. 6 in the final AP poll, then the highest final national ranking in Tigers history.

Fuller earned the Gator Bowl MVP honors during his senior season (1978). He was the South Carolina Amateur Athlete of the Year during his junior season. The Atlanta Touchdown Club named Fuller the Back of the Year in the South in 1978, and he was also named the South Carolina Player of the Year during his junior and senior seasons.

At the conclusion of his senior season, he was also an AP Third-Team All-American. Another great athletic feat for Fuller included finishing seventh in the Heisman Trophy balloting, the highest finish for a Tiger in history. Likewise, he set several Clemson records. It is no wonder he was a first-round draft pick (No. 23 overall) by the Kansas City Chiefs.

He played eight years in the NFL and won a Super Bowl Championship ring with the Chicago Bears in 1985.

Off the field, Fuller illustrated his joint dedication to academics and community service. He was named the All-ACC Academic Team for three years and twice named to an Academic All-American, including a first-team selection during his senior season.

Fuller is one of just three football players in Clemson history to be named on-field All-American and Academic All-American in the same season. He majored in history (pre-law), which was not an easy route to take, and maintained a 3.93 GPA. Fuller's constant push for excellence earned him an NCAA postgraduate scholarship, the Jim Weaver Award from the ACC, one of the NCAA'S top five awards. Fuller delivered the acceptance response for himself and the four other winners.

Fuller was also presented with the National Football Foundation and Hall of Fame Scholar Athletic Award, a double that only

Quarterback Steve Fuller.
(Photo courtesy of the
Clemson University Sports
Information Department)

Kyle Young has accomplished since. His extracurricular activities included being a member of the Blue Key, Mortar Board, Tiger Brotherhood, Block "C" Club, Sigma Alpha Epsilon, Phi Beta Sigma, Phi Beta Kappa, and Phi Kappa Phi.

Fuller's honors may have collected dust once he left Clemson, but his fame did not. In 1979, he became the first football player and the second athlete in Clemson history to have his jersey (No. 4) retired. He also became a member of the Clemson Athletic Hall of Fame in South Carolina Athletic Hall of Fame. In September 1994, Fuller was inducted into Clemson's Ring of Honor along with legendary Coach Frank Howard and all-purpose back Banks McFadden.

Clemson bestowed another honor upon the former Tigers quarterback great. On April 6, 1996, the Clemson Centennial team was announced and Fuller was named the starting quarterback for this team. In 2002, he was named one of the 50 greatest players of the ACC's first 50 years.

He left behind a legacy that few can dare to touch. No doubt, Fuller remains one of the greatest student-athletes in Tigers history.

13 Banks McFadden

"Bonnie Banks." "The Great." These are two of the accolades that accompany Banks McFadden. He could have been given more because he was considered the greatest athlete in Clemson history lettering in three sports: football, basketball, and track. Of all the honors he received, the biggest one was when the Associated Press voted McFadden Athlete of the Year in 1939 because of his excellence as a runner, passer, punter, and for his defensive prowess, especially in defending passes. McFadden was also the only Clemson Tiger named an All-American in both football and basketball the same year.

The year 1939 was magical. On the football field he led the Tigers to a 9–1 record and Clemson's first ever bowl selection. McFadden starred in Clemson's 6–3 victory over favorite Boston College in the Cotton Bowl.

On the basketball court, McFadden took the Tigers to the Southern Conference Tournament Championship, the only post-season title in the school's history. As a center, he finished his career with a then team record 810 points.

Finally, in track, McFadden won three events in one afternoon in the State Track Championship, establishing records in all three of them. Earlier in the year, he finished first in five events in a dual meet, registering 25 points himself while the opposing team's total score was 28 points.

McFadden grew up in the small hamlet of Great Falls, South Carolina, which isn't even a dot on the map. When he reported to Clemson in 1937, he raised eyebrows his first appearance on the practice field. He was a lanky 6'3", 150 lbs. and looked anything but a football player. Frank Howard, who was an assistant coach at the time, looked at McFadden with dismay.

"I can remember the first time I saw him," Howard recalled. "He looked like one of those whooping cranes. I thought sure that Coach Neely made a mistake by giving him a scholarship. If McFadden drank a can of tomato juice, they could have used him as a thermometer. But he proved me wrong."

NFL scouts were nevertheless impressed by the skinny McFadden's career. He was taken by the Brooklyn Dodgers with the fourth pick in the 1940 draft. It is still the highest draft choice in the school's history. Even though he was second in the NFL in yards per carry as a rookie, he missed Clemson and returned to coach the defensive backs under Howard.

McFadden didn't hesitate to join the Army Air Force after Pearl Harbor in 1941 and spent four years in North Africa and Italy. He excelled so much during that time that he returned home as a colonel and coached Clemson's defensive backs for the next four years.

The popular McFadden earned a long list of honors throughout life. In 1966, he was presented with Clemson University's Distinguished Alumni Award. He was a charter member of the Clemson Athletic Hall of Fame and the South Carolina Hall of Fame. In 1987, both his uniform numbers, in football (No. 66) and basketball (No. 23), were retired. In 1994, he was inducted as a charter member of the Clemson Ring of Honor. The following year, the Banks McFadden Building at the Jervey Athletic Center was dedicated in his honor.

Boston College recognized McFadden's greatness. In October 2008, the O'Rourke-McFadden Trophy was introduced as a reward to the winner of the annual game between both schools in honor of the historic meeting between Charlie O'Rourke and Banks McFadden in the 1940 Cotton Bowl.

"Banks McFadden is one of the legendary figures of Clemson history," former Clemson coach Tommy Bowden praised. "His accomplishments on the field as an all-around athlete are second to none."

Of all the honors McFadden received as an athlete, he said the 1939 Football Team Award was the highest honor. "To me, when your teammates vote you something, then you feel pretty good," he remarked. "That award meant more to me than anything else."

Banks McFadden. (Photo courtesy of the Clemson University Sports Information Department)

14 Jerry Butler

Coaches from all over the ACC area gathered for the North-South All-Star Game in Columbia, South Carolina, in late July 1975. Ninety percent of the participants were highly recruited signees who were ready to join Division I schools from all over the Southeast. But at one juncture of the game, a wide receiver who had not signed a football scholarship with any school took over the game.

Jimmy Kiser threw a pass over the middle to a wide receiver named Jerry Butler of Ware Shoals High School. Butler turned on the speed and raced untouched 70 yards for a score. The college coaches, who were not familiar with the track star, took notice and collectively asked, "Who is that guy?"

That included the Clemson coaches. Much to their glee, they discovered by the end of the evening that Jerry Odel Butler was in fact coming to Clemson...on a track scholarship.

Butler went on to star at Clemson, earning first-team AP All-America honors and leading Clemson to uncharted team accomplishments. In 1999, Butler became the sixth member of the Clemson Football Ring of Honor, the highest honor accorded a Tiger gridder. He was named to the ACC 50-Year Anniversary Team in the fall of 2002.

Statistically, Butler's accomplishments are countless. He was a model of consistency, as shown by his 36-game streak of making at least one reception, a streak he set between 1976–78, a record that is still intact today. He concluded his career with 139 receptions for 2,223 yards and 11 touchdowns, a 16-yard-per-catch rate. All those figures are still in the top five in Clemson history. Butler set the Clemson single-game reception yardage record with 163 against

Georgia Tech in 1977. His 58 catches in 1978 stood as a record until 1997.

The honors certainly followed, especially after his senior year. Butler appeared on the *Bob Hope Christmas Special* in 1978 thanks to his selection to the AP All-American team, the only AP First-Team All-America receiver in the school history.

While Clemson fans will always remember his considerable statistics and honors, one play stands out. At South Carolina in 1977, Clemson trailed the Gamecocks 27–24 in the final minutes. The Tigers needed a victory to clinch a Gator Bowl berth, a selection that would be Clemson's first bowl invitation since 1959.

Steve Fuller quarterbacked Clemson to the South Carolina 20-yard line. With just 49 seconds left, Fuller lofted a ball to the right corner of the end zone toward Butler. Using every ounce of his exceptional athletic ability, Butler made a leaping backward diving reception, giving Clemson a 31–27 victory.

Track star Jerry Butler became one of Clemson's most accomplished wide receivers. (Photo courtesy of the Clemson University Sports Information Department)

That season, that game, that catch launched the program on a 20-year run that saw Clemson return to the national ranking, bowl selections, ACC championships, and a national championship. Many Tiger supporters wonder how fate would have dealt with the program had Butler not made that catch.

Given these heroics at Clemson, Butler was chosen as the No. 5 selection of the entire 1979 NFL draft by the Buffalo Bills. That is still the third-highest draft choice by a Clemson football player in history.

Butler made Buffalo's front office look smart, as he set NFL rookie records for touchdown receptions (4) and reception yardage (255) in a 1979 contest against the New York Jets.

"That was the best single-game performance I've ever seen from a wide receiver," NBC broadcaster and former NFL quarterback John Brodie said. "I played the game for 16 years, but I've never seen anything like that."

Butler ended his rookie year with 48 receptions for 834 yards, four touchdowns, and was named the AFC Rookie of the Year by *The Sporting News.* The following year, he increased his reception total to 57 for 832 yards and was named to the Pro Bowl.

By the end of his nine-year career with Buffalo, Butler had 278 catches for 4,301 yards and 29 touchdowns. He missed two seasons due to knee injuries, 32 games that certainly could have enhanced his career numbers.

After his years at Clemson, Butler took community service to another level at the professional level. In 1981 and 1982, he was named the Bill's NFL Man of the Year. He was one of five finalists for the award nationally in 1981. In 1983, he was honored with the Jackie Robinson Award for community service by the YMCA of Greater Buffalo. In 1986 he was a finalist for the Byron "Whizzer" White Award for outstanding community service from the NFL Players Association.

Upon completion of his football career in 1987, Butler became Director of Players/Alumni Relations for the Buffalo Bills' organization. A position he held until 1999 when he became an assistant coach with the Cleveland Browns. He is currently working in the front office for the Denver Broncos.

15 Fred Cone

Fred Cone is living proof that recruiting services and all their accompanying hype aren't what they are cracked up to be. Cone was inducted into Clemson's Football Ring of Honor in the fall of 1997, just the fourth Clemson football player in history to receive the honor.

But he came to Clemson without having played a down of high school football. It is perhaps the most unusual story concerning an athlete's journey to Clemson. Cone was visiting his sister in Biloxi, Mississippi, far from the haunts of his hometown, an obscure place called Pineapple, Alabama.

Unknown to Clemson head coach Frank Howard, Cone's sister lived next door to Howard's sister, Hazel, in Biloxi. On years when Clemson would play Tulane in New Orleans, Howard would send Hazel a pair of tickets.

"One year she sent the two tickets back," Howard remembered, "and she said she'd like to have four tickets because she wanted to take the next-door neighbors to the game."

That was in 1946, Cone's senior year in high school. After Cone graduated, Hazel wrote him a letter.

"Brother, I have you a good football player, but he's never played football."

Howard recalled that he had told the Clemson registrar to save him 40 beds in the barracks and that he would turn in that many names on September 1.

"When Hazel wrote me about Fred Cone, I had 39 names on that list," Howard remarked. "So I just wrote 'Fred Cone' in as the 40th name. And that's how I got probably the best, in not the best, football player I ever had."

Cone graduated from Moore Academy in Pineapple and came to Clemson in 1947 as a freshman, but first-year players were not eligible to play then. It was probably best for Cone because he had not played high school football. He needed a year to get acclimated. When Cone became eligible for the varsity in 1948, the football program took on a different air.

In the second game of his career, against N.C. State, Cone had the first of his eight 100-yard rushing games, leading Clemson to an important victory. He was Clemson's top rusher (635 yards and seven touchdowns) that season, a regular season that saw Clemson compile a perfect 10–0 record and an invitation to the Gator Bowl in Jacksonville, Florida, against Missouri.

Clemson ended up on the long end of a 24–23 game. Cone rushed for 72 yards and scored twice in the first quarter, but it was his efforts on a fourth-down play that was the difference in the game.

Clemson held a one-point lead and faced a fourth-and-3 at the Missouri 45. It was either gamble for a first down or punt and give Missouri another chance to score. As Howard would say later, "We hadn't stopped them all day, so I took my chance with a running play."

Cone hit a stone wall at left tackle but kept digging and slid off a little more to the outside, found a little wiggle room, and mustered six yards and a first down at the Missouri 35. Clemson retained possession those few remaining minutes and ran out the clock. Years later Howard said it was the most memorable play of his 30-year career.

Despite a down year in 1949, Cone gained more yards (703) rushing and scored more touchdowns (9) than his sophomore year. However, 1950 was to bring about another undefeated season.

After the expected win over Presbyterian College to start the season, Clemson faced preseason No. 17 Missouri on the road. Cone gained 111 yards in 21 attempts, one of three Tigers over the 100-yard mark that day.

The victory over Mizzou ignited Clemson. The Tigers enjoyed another undefeated season; the only scar was a 14–14 tie with South Carolina. Cone had his third game with 100-plus yards rushing (in four games) and scored twice against the Gamecocks, but Steve Wadiak was unstoppable that day, out-gaining the entire Clemson team with 256 yards rushing.

However, Cone played most of the game with a busted lip after taking a shot to the face by a USC defender. In those days, there were no facemasks on helmets and just before halftime he was hit on the right side of his mouth as he went to cut.

At halftime the team doctor sewed him up without the help of any Novocain, stitching him up with just a needle while Howard was talking to the team.

"It wasn't too painful because I was too excited about the game," Cone said. "In this game, you just didn't feel pain."

In 1950, Clemson scored 50 points in three games, but Cone saved his best until his last regular season game against Auburn.

Rumor had it that if Clemson scored over a certain number of points on Auburn that the Orange Bowl bid was in its pocket. The Tigers won big 41–0. Cone gained 163 yards, two shy of a five-yard average, and scored three touchdowns on the ground and one on a 28-yard reception.

Icing on the cake this time came against Miami in the Orange Bowl. Although Sterling Smith's tackle of Frank Smith in the end zone for a safety brought a 15–14 victory Clemson's way, Cone gained 81 yards on the ground, scored once, punted four times, and returned one kickoff. It put a great climax on Cone's career.

The 1948–50 era is the only time in Clemson history that has seen the Tigers football program record two undefeated seasons in a three-year period. Cone and Ray Mathews were the only common denominators in the starting lineup on those two teams.

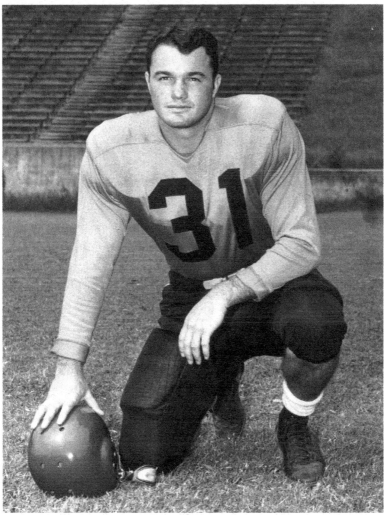

Fred Cone had never played football before attending Clemson. (Photo courtesy of the Clemson University Sports Information Department)

Cone's senior season numbers (845 rushing yards, 15 touchdowns) were school records at the time. He also set career records for rushing yards (2,183) and touchdowns (31). He was Clemson's first 2,000-yard rusher, and his 31 career touchdowns and 189 points were a school record at the time.

A seven-year hitch with the Green Bay Packers was so impressive that he was inducted into their Hall of Fame in 1974. One year he led the NFL in field goals. He was also a member of the Dallas Cowboys in their first year of existence in 1960. Later he returned to Clemson as its chief recruiter for 10 years beginning in 1961.

16 Terry Kinard

Terry Kinard is the most decorated football player in Clemson history. Those honors grew in 2001 when he was inducted into the College Football Hall of Fame and Clemson Ring of Honor.

Kinard was inducted into the College Football Hall of Fame in December 2001 at the annual National Football Foundation ceremonies in New York City. He was also honored at the College Football Hall of Fame in South Bend, Indiana, in August 2002.

Kinard, who played for the Tigers from 1979–82 and was named National Defensive Player of the Year by CBS Sports as a senior, was just the second Tiger in history to be honored by the College Football Hall of Fame and the first since Banks McFadden in 1959.

Ironically, Kinard burst onto the national scene in South Bend against Notre Dame in 1979. Starting as a freshman, Kinard had two fourth-quarter interceptions and seven tackles overall to lead Clemson to a 16–10 victory over the Fighting Irish. Twenty-two years later he was inducted into the College Football Hall of Fame, which is located just two miles from Notre Dame Stadium.

"This is a dream come true," Kinard stated. "It's something you don't expect, but when it does happen, you are thrilled. It is a great honor when you consider that only one other Clemson player has been named to the Hall of Fame. To be alongside a legend like Banks McFadden means a great deal to me.

"Clemson gave me the opportunity. I was very fortunate. I could not have picked a better place to go to school. I played with a lot of great players at Clemson, especially guys on our defense like Jeff Davis, Jeff Bryant, and many others. I certainly could not have made it to the Hall of Fame without the great players we had at Clemson at the time.

"I also have to thank Coach [Danny] Ford and the other coaches. I especially have to thank Coach Willie Anderson who recruited me. Years later, he gave me the opportunity to go to Oklahoma and serve on his [high school] coaching staff. He impressed upon me the importance of finishing my degree, which I did [from Langston University in Oklahoma]. It has made a world of difference. I am sure it made a difference in me getting into the Hall of Fame. He cared about me many years after I left Clemson, and it says a lot about him and the people at Clemson."

A native of Sumter, South Carolina, Kinard was an AP First-Team All-American in 1981 and 1982, the only two-time AP First-Team All-American in school history. He was, in fact, a unanimous selection in 1982, the only unanimous First-Team All-American in Tigers history.

Kinard recorded 17 interceptions during his Clemson career, still the high mark in school history and second in ACC history. He was in the top 15 in the nation in interceptions in 1981 and 1982, and he was a major reason Clemson had a combined record of 21–1–1 during those two years. Clemson's defense finished in the top 10 in the nation in scoring defense each year. He was Clemson's

Terry Kinard tackling Georgia's Herschel Walker. (Photo courtesy of the Clemson University Sports Information Department)

second leading tackler in the 1981 National Championship team and led the 1982 squad that finished eighth in the final AP poll.

At the conclusion of his Clemson career in 1982, Kinard was chosen in the first round of the NFL draft by the New York Giants and was the No. 10 overall pick of the draft. He played seven years for the Giants, including in the team's 1986 Super Bowl championship season. Kinard was named to the NFL All-Rookie team in 1983 and the Pro Bowl in 1988, as well.

Since his retirement from football, Kinard was named to *Sports Illustrated's* All-Century team of college football. In 2000, he was named Clemson's top player of the 20th Century by CNNSI.com. He was also chosen to the *USA Today* All-Decade team for the 1980s.

In 1996, Kinard was named to Clemson's Centennial team and received more votes than any other defensive player. In 2003, he was named one of the 50 greatest male athletes in ACC history and was also named to the ACC 50-Year Anniversary team.

"Terry Kinard was a dominating player because he was a great tackler who also could break on the ball and make the interceptions," said Ford, who was Kinard's head coach during his entire career at Clemson. "I haven't seen a player who could dominate a game from the secondary like he could. He covered a lot of ground and made a coach feel secure about the secondary.

"He had the ability to be a dominant player from the time he was a freshman. You don't see a lot of freshmen safeties take over a game in Notre Dame Stadium, but he did that when we defeated Notre Dame in 1979.

"When you look at what Kinard accomplished initially at Clemson and what Clemson did as a team during his career, you can see that he is most qualified to be in the College Football Hall of Fame."

17 Jeff Davis

Even though Clemson's football heritage is over 100 years old, it does not take long to determine the most significant accomplishment in the program's history...the 1981 National Championship. And along the same lines, it does not take long to single out the most significant team leader of that great accomplishment...Jeff Davis.

When examining Davis' contribution to Clemson athletics in terms of leadership, citizenship, and athletic records and awards, it is no surprise that he became just the fourth member of Clemson's prestigious Ring of Honor prior to the opener of the 1995 season. He was also inducted into the College Football Hall of Fame in 2007.

"It is hard to express my feelings on being inducted to the Clemson Ring of Honor and College Football Hall of Fame," Davis said. "These honors would be spread among my coaches and teammates and all of Clemson who had an impact on my life during my career."

The Native of Greensboro, North Carolina, registered a then Clemson record 175 tackles in leading the Tigers' 1981 defense that set a school record for turnovers forced (41) in a single season. He still holds the Clemson career record for caused fumbles (10) and recovered fumbles (8), and his 24 tackles against North Carolina in 1980 are second-most in school history.

He played 40 games for Clemson between 1978 and 1981 and had 469 career tackles, 16 pass breakups, 18 tackles for loss, four sacks, and four interceptions. He started all 35 games for the Tigers between 1979 and 1981. He was a model of consistency, having registered at least double-figures in tackles in 22 of his last

Jeff Davis was selected as the fourth member of the Clemson Ring of Honor in 1995. (Photo courtesy of the Clemson University Sports Information Department)

23 games. Overall, he had 30 double-figure tackle games in his 40-game career and led the team in tackles 25 times.

For his accomplishments in 1981, Davis was named the MVP of the ACC, just the third defensive player in league history to win the award. He concluded the season in grand style with a 14-tackle performance in the 22–15 Orange Bowl win over Nebraska that clinched the National Championship for the Tigers, Clemson's first national title in any sport. Davis was named defensive MVP of the contest, as well.

At the conclusion of the season, Davis was named a First-Team All-American by UPI, the Football Coaches Association, Football Writers Association, Walter Camp Foundation, and *Football News*. He was named the Lineman of the Year by the Atlanta Touchdown Club, as well.

"We had purpose," Davis recalled. "We took everything one game at a time and did not get caught up in the chase for the

National Championship. When we started the season, the championship was not a [realistic] goal. We were coming off a 6–5 season in 1980 in which we all thought we could have done much better."

After clinching the ACC title with a win over Maryland and the state championship with a convincing victory against South Carolina in Columbia, Davis and his Tigers teammates prepared to meet No. 4 Nebraska in the 1982 Orange Bowl, a game that would determine the National Championship.

"We just knew we were going to win that night," said Davis, who was nicknamed "The Judge" by then assistant sports information director Kim Kelly. "I think the first possession of the game was the key because they fumbled and William Devane recovered the ball. That led to a score and that was something we had been doing all year, forcing turnovers and taking over the game. That just told us that this game was not going to be any different than any of the others."

Perry Tuttle, Davis' roommate for four seasons and also an All-American on Clemson's 1981 National Championship team, recalled that season and Davis' passion for the game.

"When we were in the room at night, he would talk about the defense and what it was going to do until I fell asleep. As the season went on, we started dreaming about what could happen with this team, and as we went along, everything stated to come true."

Davis was a fifth-round draft pick of the Tampa Bay Buccaneers in 1982, but he proved the NFL scouts wrong by posting impressive numbers during his six-year NFL career. The inside linebacker played 83 games, including 72 as a starter, between 1982–87. He led the Buccaneers in tackles three of the six years, including a career-high 165 stops in 1984. Davis served as team captain for four seasons, as well.

Davis has been just as successful in life after football. During the spring of 1999, he returned to Clemson as field director of the Call Me Mister Program within the Department of Education,

Health & Human Development. In April 2001, he received the Use Your Life Award from Oprah Winfrey's Angel Network for his work in the Call Me Mister Program.

Davis is a member of Dabo Swinney's staff, working as assistant athletic director for player relations and external affairs.

"One of my main goals in life is to touch the lives of other people and touch them in a positive way," he promised. "Any time you receive an award like this, it means you've been surrounded by great people."

18 C.J. Spiller

The superlatives for C.J. Spiller began in high school and continued throughout his four-year career as one of Clemson's greatest running backs.

"C.J. was just a little guy, but he had a burst that nobody else had," Spiller's high school coach Buddy Nobles said. "It was like he was playing touch football and wouldn't let people touch him. He was definitely the talk of the town."

Spiller was also the talk at Clemson. From the first time he touched the ball, it was easy to see the burst Nobles was talking about. In Spiller's freshman year against Boston College, he took a swing pass in the flats and cut back to the middle of the field where he made one would-be tackler miss and raced 82 yards for his first career touchdown.

Later that year against Georgia Tech on ESPN, with *College GameDay* in the house, he got the entire country's attention when again he caught a pass in the flats and jumped over two Yellow Jacket defenders within a two-yard radius of tackling him. Twice he faked going inside and then cut back outside while racing down the sideline 50 yards for the score. It didn't even look as if he moved.

He also had a 50-yard touchdown run in the 31–7 victory, the first player in Clemson history to score two touchdowns of 50 yards or more in the same game.

"He is the fastest kid I've coached," Nobles said. "The reason he is the fastest kid is because within two steps he is full speed, where it will take me and you eight to 10 steps and by that time he already has 10 or 12 yards on you and then with him being God-given fast, he is leaving you and making you look like a crazy fool for even trying to run after him."

That's what Spiller made Auburn look like in the 2007 Chick-fil-A Bowl. He took a handoff at his own 17, made one move, bounced it outside, and he was off to the races. Three Auburn players gave chase and when Spiller saw one might catch him while looking at the big video board in Georgia Dome, he turned up the speed another notch.

"I just love seeing him on the field, I really do," Sammy Watkins said. "Just talking about him puts a smile on my face. He is something."

"Graduating was my main goal when I came to college," Spiller said. "That's one that I can take off [my list] and it's something no one can take from me. In football, sooner or later you will have to put the cleats up and put them in the closet, but you will always have your degree. Nobody can take that away from you. So all the hard work I have put in had paid off."

There were some who doubted Spiller's decision to come back to Clemson when he was a shoo-in first-round selection in the NFL draft. But Spiller firmly believed he was sent to Clemson for more than just being a football player.

He put his trust in God and let his faith guide him. To him, earning his degree was more important than anything he accomplished on the football field. He also wanted to be a good role

The speedy C.J. Spiller was one of Clemson's greatest running backs.
(Photo courtesy of the Clemson University Sports Information Department)

model to his younger sister, LaShey Mitchell, and his daughter, Shania.

"I'm the type that I don't want to tell someone else to do something if I have not done it," Spiller said. "I could not go out and speak to people about getting an education and getting their college degree if I had not finished.

"Of course I also wanted my daughter [Shania] to understand that money can get you a lot of things, but it cannot buy you happiness or anything like that. It would have been a joyful time to play in the NFL, but I'm pretty sure the NFL isn't going anywhere anytime soon, so it will always be there. But to come back and play one more season with your friends and then play in this great stadium, which I think is the best one in the country, and then having Coach Swinney as my head coach. There were a lot of things that played into me coming back."

But none of it was more instrumental than his faith.

"My faith has always paid off," Spiller said, "You just have to believe. That's the thing Coach Swinney always talks about, and that's something that I kind of learned from him. He always believes in his faith and it plays a role in every decision he makes, and it should.

"Your faith is never going to let you down. Like I have said, my faith and every decision that I make always goes to The Man Upstairs. He always has the right answer for you. Whether you like it or not, he is going to have the correct answer."

Spiller's faith guided him on one of the most prolific individual seasons in Clemson football history. His 2,680 all-purpose yards in 2009 were a single-season record, as was his 20 touchdowns. His numbers, including 1,212 rushing yards, 503 receiving yards, and five kick returns for touchdowns, allowed Spiller to become a unanimous First Team All-America player, the third in Clemson history at the time.

He also was named ACC Player of the Year, and after rushing for 233 yards in the ACC Championship Game, he was named the game's Most Valuable Player.

Spiller established more than 30 Clemson game, season, and career records, as well as several ACC records and NCAA records. He is the first player in college football history to eclipse 3,200 rushing yards, 2,000 kickoff return yards, 1,000 receiving yards, and 500 yards in punt returns.

"C.J. is very talented, but he just doesn't get by with his talent," Swinney said. "There are a lot of guys who have talent, he is a rare guy.... It is such a rare thing to see a guy have this kind of ability and that kind of talent and then you get the best out of him. I mean he can notch it down quite a bit and still be pretty good.

"There are a lot of talented guys in the NFL that are good but could be great if they had that kind of commitment all the time."

Spiller's commitment isn't just admired by his head coach. As he walked across the Littlejohn Coliseum stage to receive his degree, members of the Clemson Board of Trustees in attendance rose in near unison to give Spiller a standing ovation. No one in the Clemson athletic department can remember a time when the Board of Trustees gave a student-athlete a standing ovation at a Clemson University graduation ceremony.

The act by the Board of Trustees, which was spontaneous, triggered a louder ovation from the nearly 10,000 students and family members in attendance.

"It was a very humbling honor," Spiller said. "You don't realize how many lives you really touch or who is watching everything you are doing both on and off the field, so that's why I'm very careful in what I do and how I present myself."

In 2010, the Buffalo Bills drafted him No. 9 overall in the NFL draft. He has not disappointed them, either. In 2012, he rushed for 1,244 yards and scored six touchdowns while also catching 43 passes for 459 yards and two more scores on his way to being named to the AFC Pro Bowl roster.

19 The Early Years

Clemson first opened its doors in 1893 as a small land-grant college. Two strong-willed individuals were responsible for its start. One was Ben Tillman, who was governor of the state throughout most of the 1890s. A colorful, suspenders-wearing individual, Tillman was more popularly known as "Pitchfork Ben" because of his deep sentiments for the country and farm people of the state. He looked upon South Carolina University in Columbia, which was then nearly 100 years old, as a center of vanity and snobbery, and he made his feelings known around the state. His spirited speeches attracted the support of Tom Clemson, the son-in-law of John C. Calhoun, who had been vice president of the United States for eight years, 1825–32, under President Andrew Jackson.

Originally from Abbeville, South Carolina, Calhoun had an 800-acre plantation called Fort Hill. After Calhoun's death in 1850, Tom Clemson acquired the plantation and used it to create the college campus. Spurred by Tillman's criticism of South Carolina University, Clemson generously offered not only to provide land but money as well for a new state school for agricultural and military education. Clemson was granted military status by the federal government. Students completing their military requirements would receive a lieutenant's rank and could join the army as a regular or maintain a reserve commission should they decide to remain in civilian life. Those pursuing the military curriculum would be required to attend class in uniform.

It was all that Tillman needed. With the legislature's approval, he removed Carolina's agricultural and mechanical schools and reestablished them at Clemson. He practically reduced South Carolina University to a shell, and it was then reorganized as South Carolina College. When Clemson opened its doors in 1893, 466 students enrolled, while South Carolina's student body dwindled to 72 the same year. Thus, the bitter seed of the Clemson–South Carolina rivalry was sown and never forgotten by supporters of South Carolina.

Clemson fielded its first football team in 1896. That September, a group of 30 students met in the barracks to organize the Football Association. An early supporter of their efforts was Professor W.M. Riggs, who had played the sport as an undergraduate at Auburn College in Alabama. Riggs coached the football team that year;

surprisingly, Clemson won two of the three games they played. They opened with a 14–6 victory over Furman, lost to South Carolina, 12–6, and then ended the season with a 16–0 triumph over Wofford. Riggs was assisted by another professor, R.V.T. Bowman, in whose honor Bowman Field was named several years later.

The next year though, in 1897, the students felt that Riggs, who had coached without any remuneration, should devote his entire time to academics. It was also agreed that a full-time football coach should be hired. W.M. Williams coached Clemson that year and finished with a 2–2 record. In 1898, J.A. Penton, an assistant coach at Auburn, was hired as coach. After an opening defeat to Georgia, Clemson finished with three straight victories.

However, due to a lack of funds, Riggs was back coaching in 1899. There was no lack of victories. Clemson won its first four games before losing to Georgia and Auburn. In only four years, while football was still in its infancy on the peaceful rolling campus,

Clemson's first football team took the field in 1896. (Photo courtesy of the Clemson University Sports Information Department)

Clemson had done well. Tillman was proud of the team. He referred to the students as "horny-handed sons of toil." Most of the student body had labored as farmers before entering college. They were rugged individuals, playing without headgear and only a little padding at the elbows and knees. Few had nose or shin guards. The uniforms were tightly fitted and made of canvas fabric. Since they didn't have helmets they wore their hair long, the players could have been called Lions. However, the orange-and-purple-striped jerseys and stockings that they wore resembled Tigers, which they were nicknamed.

Riggs, however, was still primarily needed for his ability as an administrator and faculty member. He was, in fact, in later years to become president of Clemson. So after the 1899 season, a larger meeting was held on December 7 that resulted in the creation of the Football Aid Society. The Society was the forerunner to the Clemson College Athletic Association. Its sole purpose was to aid the football program, and its primary objective was to secure a coach for the 1900 season. B.H. Rawl was elected the Society's first president and W.G. Hill, secretary-treasurer. When the Society met a second time, it generated its first monies. A total of 132 people pledged $372.50 within an hour. A ways and means committee was also appointed with the objective of raising additional funds. The Society had the full support of Riggs. He spoke at the meeting:

"So long as the game of football helps to make better men of our students, stronger in body, more active in mind—men full of energy, enthusiasm, and an indomitable personal courage; men not easily daunted by obstacles or opposition; who control their tempers and restrain their appetites, who can deal honorably with vanquished adversary and can take victory moderately and defeat without bitterness.

"And as long as football properly controlled and regulated helps the student in his college duties instead of hindering him; gives zest and pleasure to college life, makes name and fame for the college on account of victories won, not only by skill and prowess of the team on the gridiron but by their gentlemanly conduct in the streets of the town they play, in the hotels where they quarter, and on the trains."

20 The Rock

The Rock that sits majestically on a pedestal on a grassy knoll at the top of the east end zone where the players run down to the field had its origin in California. Legend has it that S.C. Jones, a Clemson alumnus, brought the white flint rock, almost the size of a bowling ball, all the way back from Death Valley, California, and delivered it to Clemson.

"Here's a rock from Death Valley, California, to Death Valley, South Carolina," Jones told Howard.

In all the years that went by, nothing was known about the rock until 1966. One day, when Frank Howard was cleaning out his office, he instructed Gene Willimon, who played for Clemson in 1932–33 to do something with it, as Howard was busy preparing for the opening of the football season.

"Throw it over the fence or out in the ditch, do something with it, but get it out of my office," Howard barked.

Willimon, who was the executive secretary of IPTAY at the time, came up with a better idea. He saved The Rock and had it mounted on a pedestal. The day The Rock made its public debut in 1967 at the Tigers opening game against Wake Forest, Howard seized the moment and used it as a motivational tool.

"Looka here boys, if any of you boys are gonna go out and give me 100 percent, I'll let you rub my rock," Howard shouted. "Any of you who isn't going to give me 100 percent, keep your filthy hands off my rock. Don't touch it."

Clemson defeated Wake Forest 23–6 and the tradition began. Howard built on it. The next day he made reference to it in a speech about The Rock on his television show. It didn't impress one lady in North Carolina. She mailed Howard a note that read:

"Dear coach: If you'd believe more in God and less on that rock, you'd be a better football coach."

Rubbing The Rock has left an indelible memory on any number of former Clemson players. Some almost mystical, like Michael Dean Perry, who was a six-time Pro Bowl star with the Cleveland Browns and Denver Broncos.

"The Rock has strange powers," Perry believes. "When you rub it and run down the hill, the adrenaline flows. It's the most emotional experience I've ever had."

The Rock was cherished and glorified over the years for its motivational power until 1962 when someone chipped off a piece of the symbol. However, it wasn't until the summer of 2013 that The Rock was brutally vandalized by a young 18-year-old Clemson fan from North Carolina. The fan had a Clemson sticker on his 1993 Ford pick-up and all sorts of Clemson memorabilia in his home in Pisgah Forest and never attended Clemson. An unlikely suspect indeed.

Clemson University security charged him with breaking The Rock's plastic case and breaking off a chunk of stone on the night of June 2. Witnesses identified the subject and the truck from surveillance footage taken from outside the stadium. Yet, the stone was never found.

"It is very disappointing that someone would disrespect our unique tradition to this extent," Dabo Swinney said. "It is one of the iconic images of the game. I know our coaches and players look forward to rubbing Howard's Rock, running down the hill, and furthering one of the great traditions of college football."

Coach Frank Howard with The Rock. (Photo courtesy of the Clemson University Sports Information Department)

Former Clemson linebacker Jeff Davis claims the power of The Rock comes from knowing how others before you worked hard to make the Tigers a success year after year.

"The power comes from the individual touching The Rock. You understand the numerous athletes that paid the price for you to be there," Davis contends.

Clemson athletic director Dan Radakovich said the school has increased security around The Rock to prevent any future vandalism. He believes Clemson fans will sleep better knowing the school was able to catch the perpetrator.

It is now a tradition for the Clemson Ranger Club to protect The Rock during the 24 hours preceding the Clemson–South Carolina game when it's held in Death Valley. ROTC cadets keep a steady drum cadence around The Rock prior to the game, which can be heard across campus.

The only time The Rock left the stadium was for a two-month period before the 2000 season when John Fernandez's granite company worked to fit it on a new pedestal. Fernandez claimed that The Rock was only out of his sight while he slept. He even held a cookout with The Rock as the guest of honor.

The Rock sits on a black granite base with the inscription: "Howard's Rock. From Death Valley, CA to Death Valley, South Carolina."

21 Historic Riggs Field

With the overuse of Bowman Field and the need for a seated stadium, Clemson embarked on building its first Athletic facility, Riggs Field.

Perhaps one of the first big stepping stones in helping make Clemson successful in athletics today was the construction of Riggs Field, named after one of the most beloved university leaders of the early years. What made Riggs Field so significant to the school at the time it was built in 1915 is that it was the first major facility on the campus dedicated to intercollegiate athletics.

Riggs Field gave the football team a place to play and practice on its adjunct fields. The baseball field was constructed where the tennis courts are now, and the track encircled the football field.

Construction of Riggs Field started in the early summer of 1914. Approximately $10,000 was appropriated for the construction of the facility that covered almost nine acres. Before its completion the Clemson Board of Trustees unanimously agreed to name the new athletic complex Riggs Field in honor of Clemson's first football coach and originator of the Clemson Athletic Association, Dr. Walter M. Riggs.

Riggs was the first football coach at Clemson in 1896. He stepped down as head coach in 1897 to devote full time to academics, as he was an engineering professor. He also coached the team in 1899 because the athletic association was low on funds. However, in 1900, the search for a new coach must have been serious, as Riggs hired John Heisman to coach the Tigers.

Although no longer the head coach, Clemson athletics and Riggs could not be split. While he did not hold the title, Riggs was also the equivalent of an athletic director, managing the money and making contracts with other teams. The well-respected Riggs also held many positions over the years in the Southern Intercollegiate Athletic Association (SIAA), an early conference preceding the Southern Conference. Riggs later became the president of Clemson on March 7, 1911. He served in his capacity until his death in 1924.

Riggs Field was dedicated in grand fashion on October 2, 1915. The band, corps of cadets, along with faculty and alumni marched from Tillman Hall to the new field. The group formed a "C" formation on the field and poured forth a thrilling volume of patriotic Tiger yells and songs. Professor J.W. Gantt, president of the athletics association, introduced Dr. Riggs as "the man who has done more for the athletics at Clemson and probably more for southern athletics than any other man."

In presenting the field to the corps of cadets, Dr. Riggs said, "This magnificent field is a token of recognition by the Trustees of Clemson College of the importance of military and athletic training for the cadets. It is to be a place for the teaching of principles of teamwork and fair play. This large and beautiful athletic field is to stand for the development of the physical man, and whether in real work or in play, it is hoped that this field will be used as an agency in the development of high and honorable men. Whether victorious or defeated, may the men of this field always be gentlemen of the highest type."

A few minutes later, Dr. Riggs made the initial kickoff in the first football game played on the new field. While on the field, he wore a new orange and blue sweater he had just received from Auburn, his alma mater, as they too wanted to congratulate Clemson and Dr. Riggs for their accomplishments. Clemson and Davidson played to a 6–6 tie that day.

Clemson's football team compiled a 57–16–6 record during its 27 years at Riggs Field. The baseball team won better than 70 percent of its games there when the diamond was part of the complex.

Riggs Field today is considered to be one of the top (if not *the* top) soccer facilities in the nation. Clemson started playing soccer at Riggs in 1980. The 1987 NCAA Men's Soccer Final Four was contested there, and Clemson won the national championship before a record crowd of 8,332.

As one looks from Riggs Field and sees the grand clock tower of Tillman Hall guarding that part of campus, it is only appropriate that these two symbols of the university are so close in proximity as both have played such a significant role in Clemson history.

The original configuration of the track and former football stadium and bleachers, was featured in a long scene in the latter portion of the 1974 Burt Lancaster movie, *The Midnight Man*, filmed in part at Clemson University in 1973.

Riggs Field was named in honor of Clemson's first football coach, Dr. Walter M. Riggs. (Photo courtesy of the Clemson University Sports Information Department)

Historic Riggs Field is the fifth oldest continuously used college athletic facility in the nation.

The Hill

It might not have the historical significance of the Battle of Bunker Hill in the Revolutionary War or the battle for San Juan Hill of Colonel Teddy Roosevelt and his Rough Riders in the Spanish-American War waged in Cuba, but don't tell that to any Clemson fan.

The worst mistake that Coach Hootie Ingram made that infuriated Tigers fans was that he did away with the tradition of the players running down The Hill in Memorial Stadium that had been established since 1945. It had been a time-honored tradition that fans had cheered in seeing the players running down a 100' grassy knoll at the east end of the stadium.

Bob Bradley, who was Clemson's Hall of Fame sports information director, had a reason for it. Bradley was a close confidant of Frank Howard during the 43 years the colorful coach had been idolized at Clemson.

"I guess Ingram was trying to get rid of anything connected with Howard," Bradley reasoned. "There was so much pressure put on him that Ingram finally gave in the last three games of the 1972 season."

The pressure on Ingram was evident. In those three years, when the players did not run down The Hill, Clemson's record was 6–9. The players decided they wanted to run down The Hill before their game against South Carolina in 1972. Despite a freezing rain that day, Clemson fans had plenty to cheer about, a 7–6 victory.

The Hill spectacle is well coordinated. After the Tigers' final pregame warm-up, the team returns to the dressing room under the west stands for a final meeting. Ten minutes before the scheduled kick-off, players board buses and ride around the north stands to the east end zone and assemble behind while the band plays the "Tiger Rag" as the players stream onto the field.

Placekicker David Treadwell never forgot the experience. He was an All-American player on the 1987 team.

"Clemson's record at home is not a coincidence," he maintained. "Running down The Hill is part of that record. You get inspired, and so much of college football is about emotion. You get out of that bus and you heard the roar of the crowd and it gives you chills up and down your spine."

Wide receiver Jerry Butler feels the same way. He, too, was an All-American on the 1987 squad.

"Running down The Hill is still talked about everywhere I go," he said.

Fred "Doc" Hoover, Clemson's head trainer for 40 years before he retired in 1999, was in charge of directing all the essentials involved with The Run.

"You have to allow time for the players to leave the locker room, board the busses, and not get caught in any traffic," Hoover detailed. "But you have to time it so you're not in one place too long. You hate to have the players sitting around."

The Hill's popularity became an opening for television broadcasts prior to the kick-off. That gave Hoover another responsibility in that the players had to run down The Hill exactly at the prescribed time.

"If it's a 12:10 kick-off, they want you at 12:03," Hoover disclosed. "But sometimes the players aren't ready, and then you're hanging around again."

The Hill could present some other pitfalls. Hoover is one of a handful who have fallen down while coming down The Hill, but others are unknown. "I'm the only one who will admit it, that's why," Hoover confessed. "It was on film, so I had to. Television gave me a 10 for my recovery.

Years Later, Clemson coach Tommy Bowden avoided such a debacle. Because he had no cartilage in one knee, it would present a danger for him to run. He decided to walk down from the side. "If I get in front, I'll get trampled," Bowden remarked. "I want to walk, not roll."

Popular TV broadcaster Brent Musburger is one who is rolls with The Hill. "It's the most exciting 25 seconds in college football," he believes.

Clemson faithful agree.

23 Alma Mater

After almost 30 years of borrowing another university's tune, a group finally decided that Clemson should create its own. The Tiger Brotherhood society (formed in 1928 and still active today) sponsored a contest for a new tune. On May 5, 1947, an article in *The Tiger* announced the winner of the contest as Robert E. Farmer of Anderson, an architecture student and member of the glee club. Since Farmer could not read or write music, he sang the melody to a musician friend who wrote it down. Hugh McGarity, the director of Clemson's glee club and band, was commissioned to write an arrangement.

A short article in the September 21, 1950, issue of *The Tiger* stated that:

New music composed last year by Professor H.H. McGarity is now the official music for the Clemson Alma Mater. A petition for the change circulated by Tiger Brotherhood last spring was signed by a majority of the student body. Upon the recommendation of Dr. Poole, the new music was presented to the alumni association at its annual meeting June 3. The group voted its approval and Dr. Poole proclaimed it the official Alma Mater at graduation exercises on June 4, at which it was sung officially for the first time.

Nineteen years later, in a letter to Dr. John Butler (then director of bands) dated March 28, 1969, Walter T. Cox (the vice president for student affairs) stated:

Dean Hurst has advised me that the Faculty Senate, at their meeting on March 11, 1969, passed a Resolution recognizing the services of Dr. Hugh H. McGarity, now retired after 21 years as a member of the faculty of Clemson University.

The resolution expressed the appreciation of the Senate and resolved that Dr. McGarity be given credit, when appropriate, as the composer of the music of the Clemson Alma Mater. The Resolution was passed unanimously. It is the interpretation of Dean Hurst and Dr. Eugene Park, President of the Faculty Senate, that it would be appropriate to give the name of the composer of the music whenever the words of the Alma Mater is printed in programs of athletic events and other University affairs.

In the early 1970s, James Copenhaver (now director of bands at the University of South Carolina) came to Clemson as the interim director of bands while Clemson band director Bruce Cook was on a leave of absence. Copenhaver commissioned his former college band director, Robert Hawkins of Morehead State University, to write a new band arrangement of the Clemson Alma Mater. It is that arrangement that is played by the Tiger Band to this day.

On March 20, 1989, Robert E. Farmer, then an architect in Greenville, wrote a letter to *Clemson World News* in which he recounted the Tiger Brotherhood contest. After being named the winner, he said, "For about a month, I basked in the warm glow of local fame.... About a year after the contest, the present alma mater tune emerged. It only used the middle section of my tune, and that was altered and re-harmonized."

Farmer was asked to re-construct his winning alma mater tune. Farmer's music and the tune which we now know as the Clemson Alma Mater by McGarity were taken to a professional music teacher (Mrs. Sybil McHugh) for her opinion. She observed that the chorus was similar ("Dear old Clemson, we will triumph..."), that the value of the notes was the same, but that the two versions were in different keys. "I would add from my own observations as a composer and arranger that the melody of the two choruses is identical. Robert Farmer's tune is beautiful, but it has inherent flaws in melody and harmony. This is what Hugh McGarity must have realized, and set out to fix. The part of the mystery that may never be solved is why McGarity altered the tune of the verse so drastically and why Mr. Farmer was not given proper credit." (Clemson band archives)

In the outcome of the 1989 investigation, headed by Walter Cox, it was deemed that all future copies of the Clemson Alma Mater should bear the following heading:

Music by: Robert E. Farmer '49 and Hugh H. McGarity
Adopted: June 4, 1950
Words by: A.C. Corcoran '19
Adopted: January, 1919
Arranged by: John H. Butler

The Clemson Alma Mater that emerged on June 4, 1950, is certainly one of the great college hymns. Robert E. Farmer said it best in his 1989 letter to the *Clemson World News*:

"An Alma Mater tune, by tradition, should be a rather solemn, stately affair that commands quiet attention and certain reverence. The cheers should cease, the hats come off, and the hand placed over the heart so that for one moment, memories and sentiments are expressed."

24 1903 Game with Cumberland

Clemson's archives assert that the first Bowl Game ever played by its football team occurred on November 26, 1903, in Montgomery, Alabama. At the turn of the century the South was developing into a hot bed of college football, and Clemson's meeting with Cumberland College was billed as the "Championship of the South."

It was a battle of heavyweights. Clemson was considered the best in the Central Division of the SIIA by defeating Georgia, Georgia Tech, North Carolina State, and Davidson. A loss to North Carolina marred a perfect season. The Clemson powerhouse had vanquished its opponents 156–11, highlighted by a 73–0 drubbing of Georgia Tech.

Cumberland was just as impressive. It dominated the Western part of the South by beating bigger schools such as Tennessee, Vanderbilt, and Sewanee with a dynamic offense that produced 297 points.

The contest was a big one for the Tigers. It was only the eighth year of Clemson football, and the team relished the opportunity to establish itself as a southern powerhouse under Coach John Heisman.

It was looked upon as a battle of Cumberland's giant backfield attacking the Tigers' line with Clemson relying on its smaller but quicker backs to get to the outside for long runs.

Cumberland was the heavier team, averaging 5'11" and 172 lbs., while Clemson measured 5'9" and 163½ lbs. Clemson's largest player was J.A. McKeown at 6'2", 194 lbs.

Cumberland dominated the opening half as the Bulldogs scored twice to bring the score to 11–0. A touchdown was worth five points and an extra point one.

Following a 10-minue halftime break, Cumberland kicked off to Clemson for the deciding second half. John Maxwell received the kick on the 10-yard line and never stopped running. He sped 100 yards (the field was 110 yards back then) to get Clemson back in the game. However, the Tigers missed the extra point and Cumberland led 11–5.

Clemson had time for one play, and the Bulldogs were braced for a trick play that Heisman liked to use. They got fooled simply because Fritz Furtrick took the snap and instead of veering to the outside, he ran straight up the middle for a touchdown. It was left to Jock Hanvey to kick the tying point, and he did to tie the game 11–11.

But a quandary. The winning team is awarded the ball, but no one won! Captain W.W. Suddarth of Cumberland wanted Captain Hope Sadler of Clemson to have the ball. But Sadler insisted that Suddarth should have it. For some 10 minutes the conversation didn't produce an answer for both deserving teams.

The solution that was agreed upon was to give the ball to patrolman Patrick J. Sweeney. He was rewarded for his effort for efficiently manning the sidelines by warning the media, fans, and substitutes to stay down in front and allow the spectators to view the game.

It was Heisman's last game as coach of Clemson. Later that night, when the team returned to Clemson, he began preparations to make another trip to Atlanta to become the coach of Georgia Tech.

25 The Probation

A stench still remains over the town of Clemson from the two-year probation period inflicted on Clemson football by the NCAA during the 1983–84 seasons and further magnified by an additional one in 1984 by the ACC. During those years, Clemson's scholarships were reduced, it was banned from any television and bowl games for two of those years, but it was allowed to keep the 25 wins it accumulated, including the NCAA title.

The transgressions that were found occurred during Charley Pell's final year at Clemson in 1978. The large Clemson cognoscenti to this day feel it shouldn't have been applied to Danny Ford's first year as head coach in 1979 after coaching Clemson in only one game, the 1978 Gator Bowl.

On November 6, 1981, John Feinstein, the prize winning author, was a sportswriter with *The Washington Post*. He documented the ongoing 18-month probe that was being conducted by the NCAA.

"On this idyllic campus where the trees are just now beginning to turn color, there is a darkening cloud on the horizon, one that threatens to engulf Clemson at the very moment when it should be celebrating its greatest athletic achievement."

The recruiting violations centered around two high school players from Knoxville, Tennessee, linebacker James Cofer and quarterback Terry Minor. After signing ACC letters to attend Clemson, the two requested releases from their scholarships. Clemson refused. The players revealed that they were offered money from boosters. Minor confessed to $1,000 and Cofer $500.

Spontaneous joy should have been enjoyed on the Clemson campus because at the time the story broke the Tigers were ranked No. 2 in the AP poll and No. 3 in UPI with an 8–0 record and postseason bowls waiting. Clemson football was flourishing again. Instead, the reported NCAA probe created worry.

Clemson acknowledged that the NCAA did indeed appear twice in the off-season to interview players and coaches. Sources were saying at least 100 charges were on the NCAA docket going back to Pell.

Athletic director Bill McLellan admitted the NCAA presence on campus. "We haven't received any letter informing us of any charges," McLellan said. "We haven't had any contact with the NCAA since the investigators were here. I'm concerned about the investigators. We all are. If probations come, we'll adjust to it. I'm not assuming the worst though. We'll have to wait and see."

Ford did all he could to keep focused on an unbeaten season and quelling any fears from his players.

"I don't see any cloud hanging over this program," he remarked. "We haven't done anything wrong."

Tennessee, a member of the Southeastern Conference, honored an ACC commitment letter. It meant that the players involved could not enroll at Tennessee without a release from Clemson. Ford admittedly said no. He had reason to.

"If they had told us early on that they wanted a release or that they had some kind of problem with us, it would have been different," Ford explained. "We've already turned down other kids because we had made a commitment to those players. We were shocked. It came out of nowhere. I had to think something funny was going on."

Ford's refusal to release the players caused them to publicly accuse Clemson of having offered them money in return for staying. Ironically, Minor and Cofer enrolled at Louisiana Tech but dropped out.

"Guys who go around making accusations behind your back are the worst," Ford vented. "If they got a problem with things I'm doing, let 'em call me. I guarantee you all that those guys got something in their closets they wouldn't want getting out."

Yet, it was Clemson's closet that the NCAA was rummaging through. At a time when he should be taking bows, Ford was now looking over his shoulder. McLellan, too. "I would never say flatly that we're lily white because I can't keep track of every move made in this department," McLellan claimed.

Months later Ford did disclose that the NCAA had built up a huge file rife with complaints from Clemson's competitors. "You don't get investigated until you get turned in by so many people and you get a file so thick," he said.

The files said a lot—more than enough to impose the sanctions on Clemson. The day after the NCAA's decision was announced, Ford held a press conference in Greenville. He contended he wouldn't have resigned had he been made aware what the NCAA's ruling would be. With the condemnation, he felt he had no choice but to do so.

"It was a situation where a separation was wanted, and it was done," he announced. "I don't think I have the option of being the coach at Clemson. I deny any wrongdoing on my part. I am confident that impartial review of the facts will do prove. My era is over."

If there is any consolation derived from this sordid mess, it was attributed to Clemson officials. Three times they appealed to the ACC for removal of the one-year ban. They were rejected all three times. Yet Clemson continued to persist on removal of the penalty and finally got a reversal.

In August 1984 it was discovered that the appeals process was mishandled by ACC commissioner Robert James and the conference itself. According to the bylaws, the appeal of any penalty should have been rejected and referred to the ACC's executive committee. James was the only one who admitted that the entire process had been mishandled by the league office.

"This should not have been the same group and will not be in the future," James promised. "We will now ensure that the same group that will determine the initial punishment for a school in violation of the rules will not hear the appeal."

Despite the pain, the Clemson community can take solace in knowing that it caused the ACC to revise its by-laws.

26 1949 Gator Bowl

January 1, 1949
Jacksonville, Florida
Clemson 24, Missouri 23
Although Clemson finished with identical 4–5 records in 1946 and 1947, Coach Frank Howard must have suspected the future would be brighter. He scheduled 10 games for Clemson in 1948, and the Tigers went out and won all of them. No college team in the state of South Carolina had produced an unbeaten season in 48 years, and it was such a momentous accomplishment that the Tigers were toasted at a gala banquet in Eppes Restaurant in Greenville that was attended by 300 guests and chaired by the governor of South Carolina, J. Strom Thurmond. Since the governor was himself a Clemson alumnus, the occasion was that much more meaningful to him.

"I am proud of Frank Howard," Thurmond began in his after-dinner speech. "I'm glad that he was named Coach of the Year, an honor he deserved. The fame will last for years."

But Coach Howard was only hoping it would last long enough to beat Missouri in the Gator Bowl. The experts around the country didn't think it was likely. Despite the fact that Clemson, Michigan, and California were the only undefeated teams in the nation, the forecasters established Missouri as a one-touchdown favorite. The analysts were convinced that Missouri had played a much tougher schedule. In addition they felt Missouri's coach, Don Faurot, was more of a household name than Howard and his squad of Tigers, who had more often been called "country gentlemen." The experts were not impressed with the knowledge that Clemson had scored 250 points while yielding only 53 to its opponents.

Howard had put together a fine backfield. As usual, the defense was powerful, but it was the offensive punch of the Tigers that was the team's strongest point. Tailback Bobby Gage had gained more than 1,000 total yards during the season, most of it with his passing. Fred Cone was a young, hard-running fullback, and Bob Martin, the team's captain, was a veteran quarterback.

The star of the backfield was wingback Ray Mathews. He had led the Southern Conference in scoring with 78 points and had beaten out North Carolina's highly heralded "Choo Choo" Justice, who had 66. Only a sophomore, Mathews had gained 573 yards rushing and had caught 13 passes for 363 yards. He capped the regular season by scoring all three touchdowns in a 20–0 victory over The Citadel.

In truth, Missouri represented a stern test for the Tigers. They had easily won 8-of-10 games. Faurot, who had invented the Missouri Split-T, had produced an explosive offense. More impressive, Missouri had averaged a little better than 36 points a game in its victories, and its line outweighed Clemson's by 5 lbs. per man. Other than the Buckeyes game, Missouri's only loss was to Oklahoma, the Big Seven champion, and Missouri had finished in the runner-up spot behind the Sooners.

"As soon as I knew we'd be playing Missouri, I went over to Duke to visit my ol' buddy Wallace Wade," Howard said. "We didn't know much about the Split-T, and Duke had played Missouri the year before and got beat 28–7. I spent the whole day learning about the formation from Coach Wade. When I was ready to leave, he asked me if I was going to use his defense. When I told him I wasn't, he wanted to know why I had wasted his time and mine. I told him that it hadn't been a waste at all, that I had learned plenty, especially what defense not to use.

"Honestly, before the season began I thought maybe we might win six; and again I thought maybe we might lose six. I probably chewed more tobacco that year than ever before. If I had to guess why we had such a good season, I'd say it was because we all pitched in with the material we had, worked hard, and played hard."

Almost all the seats, except the ones in the end zone, were filled by game time. A crowd of 35,273 was in the stands, which was the largest crowd ever to see a football game in Jacksonville. Clemson went to work quickly by recovering a Missouri fumble on the 19-yard line and scoring five plays later on a one-yard plunge by Cone. Later in the period, Cone scored again from a yard out to give Clemson a 14–0 lead.

In the second quarter, Missouri struck back. It scored early in the period; and then with five minutes remaining in the half, it tied the game at 14–14. Nothing appeared to be going right for Clemson at this point. The halftime ceremonies ran too long, and the Clemson drill platoon had to shorten its presentation.

However, Clemson took the second-half kickoff and marched straight down field. The touchdown that put it back on top again 21–14 came on a tricky pass play from Gage to Johnny Poulos that fooled Missouri completely. Near the end of the quarter, Missouri added a safety when Gage threw a pass that landed incomplete in his

The 1949 Gator Bowl was one of the most memorable bowl performances in Clemson's history. (Photo courtesy of the Clemson Sports Information Department)

own end zone. The two points trimmed the Tigers' lead to 21–16 when the third quarter ended, and the stands were in pandemonium.

Midway through the final quarter, Clemson added to its lead. Jack Miller booted a 32-yard field goal that stretched the Tigers' edge to 24–16. They needed it, too, because Missouri moved quickly after taking the kickoff and scored on a 20-yard pass play. In the closing minutes of the game, however, Clemson hung on to its 24–23 lead and ran out the clock with three first downs.

"This is the best team I have ever coached," Howard said.

CLEMSON	14	0	7	3	24
MISSOURI	0	14	2	7	23
CU	Cone 1 run (Miller kick)				
CU	Cone 1 run (Miller kick)				
UM	Entsminger 2 run (Dawson kick)				
UM	Entsminger 1 run (Dawson kick)				
CU	Poulos 9 pass from Gage (Miller kick)				
UM	Safety, Gage pass grounded in end zone				
CU	Miller 32 FG				
UM	Bounds 20 pass from Braznell (Dawson kick)				
Attendance: 35,273					

1981 Georgia v. Clemson

September 19, 1981
Clemson, South Carolina
Clemson 13, Georgia 3

During Danny Ford's first two years as Clemson coach, the Tigers had recruited prep sensation Herschel Walker as hard as he went after anyone. He was a sculpted 6'1", 222-lb. running back who reportedly ran a 4.25 in the 40-yard dash.

"We wanted him pretty bad out of high school," Ford confessed. "We recruited him hard and often, and Georgia did, too. He had great size and great speed. He was well put together."

Clemson captain Jeff Davis wasn't the least bit intimidated by Walker's notoriety. He took pride in Clemson's defense.

"I'm anxious to go up against the top back in the nation. Last year, Herschel was a freshman who played like a senior. But it's going to be different when he comes to Death Valley. He'll find that he won't be able to do as well against this senior."

Davis showed his teammates he had the confidence to beat the defending national champions, a team that had never lost with Walker in its lineup. In fact, Clemson's 13–3 victory that September 19 afternoon would be the only regular-season loss of Walker's three-year career with the Bulldogs.

Once again, it was the defense that carried the day for Clemson. The Tigers forced nine turnovers (five interceptions and four fumbles), which is still the team record for turnovers forced in a game. The nine takeaways were recorded by nine different players, the best stat that shows this was an all-around team effort. It gave Clemson 16 forced turnovers in two games, the best back-to-back takeaway totals in school history.

Buck Belue threw five interceptions and lost a fumble for six of the nine turnovers. Walker had lost just one fumble his entire freshman season when he gained more than 1,600 yards and set the all-time NCAA freshman record. He had three fumbles in this game, two that were recovered by the Tigers defense, including one by William Perry when he seemingly just shoved Walker aside to scoop up the ball.

Walker would get 111 yards rushing on 28 carries, but he never reached the end zone. In fact, he would play three games against the Tigers in his career without scoring a touchdown, joining Heisman Trophy winner George Rogers of South Carolina with that career note against Clemson's defense.

This was a true rock-em-sock-em game from the outset, as the two teams combined for only 491 yards of total offense. Clemson had just 236 yards on the day but still won by double digits. Field position was a big issue, and Dale Hatcher was an unsung hero as he averaged 43 yards on seven punts.

Clemson scored 10 points in the second quarter, and it held up. An interception by Tim Childers set up the only touchdown of the day, an eight-yard pass from Homer Jordan to Perry Tuttle. Donald Igwebuike kicked two field goals, one in the second quarter and one in the fourth quarter. Georgia's only points came on a Kevin Butler field goal on the Bulldogs' first drive of the second half.

The Bulldogs had won 15 consecutive games, the longest active winning streak in college football at the time. Their No. 4 national rating was the highest-ranked team Clemson defeated in Death Valley during the first 107 years of Clemson football, and was only eclipsed when Tommy Bowden's Tigers beat No. 3 Florida State in 2003.

When Rod McSwain intercepted a pass in the end zone with 1:08 left to clinch the win, the defense came off the field whirling their index fingers. They were giving notice that they had defeated last year's No. 1 team, and that Clemson was No. 1 on this day.

CLEMSON	0	10	0	3	13
GEORGIA	0	0	3	0	3
CU Tuttle 8 pass from Jordan (Pauling kick), 2nd, 7:13					
CU Igwebuike 39 FG, 2nd, 0:11					
UGA Butler 40 FG, 3rd, 11:24					
CU Igwebuike 29 FG, 4th, 14:01					
Attendance: 62,466					

28 2012 Chick-fil-A Bowl

December 31, 2012

Atlanta, Georgia

Clemson 25, Louisiana State 24

Trailing 24–13 to No. 7 Louisiana State entering the fourth quarter, Dabo Swinney's team came off the mat to score three times in the final stanza against one of the nation's staunchest defenses. Chandler Catanzaro's 37-yard field goal as time expired lifted No. 13 Clemson to a 25–24 victory in the Chick-fil-A Bowl in the Georgia Dome.

After Clemson pulled within two points with 2:47 left in the game on a 12-yard touchdown strike from Tajh Boyd to DeAndre Hopkins, it was unable to pull even when Boyd's pass on the two-point attempt fell incomplete.

But the Clemson defense quickly got the ball back to its offense by forcing a three-and-out with 1:39 remaining, and Boyd, who was named Chick-fil-A Bowl Offensive Most Outstanding Player, engineered a drive that covered 60 yards in 10 plays and culminated in Catanzaro's game-winner.

In the opening quarter, Jeremy Hill of LSU burst off tackle and cruised into the end zone for a 17-yard touchdown run and a 7–0 lead. Making matters worse, Sammy Watkins was lost for the night after suffering an injury on the play.

With things already looking bleak, the ACC Tigers mustered a big-time response against the vaunted Louisiana State defense, marching 75 yards in 11 plays and finding the end zone on an 11-yard run by Boyd to tie the score 7–7.

Louisiana State jumped back on top early in the second quarter, however, as it capped an eight-play, 65-yard drive with a six-yard touchdown pass from Zack Mettenberger to Jarvis Landry, and led 14–7.

Later in the quarter, Clemson marched the ball 70 yards in eight plays and found the end zone on an 11-yard touchdown pass from Boyd to Hopkins to make the score 14–13 before Catanzaro's point-after attempt was blocked.

As badly as the first half started for Clemson, the second half followed suit. Michael Ford returned the second kickoff 43 yards, and on the next play, Hill ran 57 yards to paydirt and a 21–13 lead just 17 seconds after halftime.

Clemson's defense continued to do its part and got the ball right back to its offense, and Malliciah Goodman and Grady Jarrett combined for Clemson's sixth sack of the game on third down.

The offense took advantage of the opportunity as Boyd engineered an 11-play, 77-yard drive and hit Hopkins in the back of the end zone for a 12-yard touchdown pass to make the score 24–22 with 2:47 left in the game.

The two-point try failed, but Clemson's defense once again did its job by forcing a quick three-and-out. A touchback on the ensuing punt gave Clemson the ball at its own 20 with 1:39 left in the game.

At that point, Boyd worked his magic, hitting Hopkins for a 26-yard strike on fourth-and-16 to get the drive rolling. He eventually completed his last five passes of the game to set up Catanzaro's game-winning kick.

CLEMSON	7	6	0	12	25
LOUISIANA STATE	7	7	10	0	24
LSU Hill 17 run (Alleman kick), 1st, 14:04					
CU Boyd 11 run (Catanzaro kick), 1st, 9:46					
LSU Landry 6 pass from Mettenberger (Alleman kick), 2nd, 13:12					
CU Hopkins 11 pass from Boyd (Catanzaro kick failed), 2nd, 13:12					
LSU Hill 57 run (Alleman kick), 3rd, 14:43					
LSU Alleman 20 FG, 3rd, 4:49					
CU Catanzaro 26 FG, 4th, 9:26					
CU Hopkins 12 pass from Boyd (Boyd pass failed), 4th, 2:47					
CU Catanzaro 37 FG, 4th, 0:00					
Attendance: 67,563					

29 2014 Orange Bowl

January 3, 2014
Miami Gardens, Florida
Clemson 40, Ohio State 35

Clemson defensive coordinator Bret Venables bristled a bit earlier in the week when he was asked about the Orange Bowl against No. 6 Ohio State being billed as a shoot-out. While the final score, 40–35 in favor of No. 11 Clemson, may have indicated that was the case, Venables could smile afterward knowing his unit made the plays that were the difference.

The Tigers forced four second-half turnovers, including interceptions on the Buckeyes' last two possessions, to rally from a

110

halftime deficit for a BCS bowl win and a second straight 11-win season, both firsts in school history.

"It means we're one step closer to our goal, which is to be the best in the country," head coach Dabo Swinney said. "Ohio State...what a great football team. You don't luck up and get to BCS games. You earn your way there. And you don't luck up and win them. You have to earn it on the field."

Stephone Antony's interceptions with 1:18 left sealed the win after Clemson had turned the ball over on the previous possessions to give Ohio State an opening. That came after a Spencer Shuey recovered fumble on the previous Buckeyes' drive that put the Tigers in the driver's seat.

"That was fun to watch," Venables said. "Just as you draw it up, those guys go out and execute it. To see those guys do that on back-to-back series, it was special."

It was not all defense for Clemson as Sammy Watkins set Tigers and Orange Bowl records with 16 receptions and 227 receiving yards to garner MVP honors, and Tajh Boyd accounted for 505 yards of total offense and six touchdowns.

"The biggest thing going into this game was that we were going to win or lose the game through Watkins or Boyd," Swinney stated. "That was the plan."

Watkins, who had eight catches for 130 yards in the first half, passed Aaron Kelly to become the school's all-time leader in receptions with his first grab of the second half, which gave him 223 for his career.

"The offensive line and the coaches put me in the best situation to make plays," Watkins said. "I have been blessed with great coaches and a great quarterback the past three years. It's an honor to break all those records, but it's great to do it with the team and have success with the team."

Boyd moved into a tie with Rodney Williams (1985–88) for most wins in school history by a starting quarterback with 32 and

Looking Ahead

During practice for Clemson's 2014 Orange Bowl game against Ohio State, Coach Dabo Swinney took time to look ahead to the upcoming season. He rambled out newcomer names RB Wayne Gallman, Tyrone Crowder, Scott Pagano, and LB Dorian O'Daniel that could make an impact. Swinney was already thinking about spring practice.

"Gallman, wow," Swinney shouted. "Dorian O'Daniel, those are two guys who just jump out." The pair was redshirted in the 2013 season.

Swinney and his staff were excited about getting a long look at some of his younger players that brought a smile to his face as they took part in drills with the varsity. A couple of defensive linemen, Tyrone Crowder and Scott Pagano, also caught Swinney's eye.

"I'm excited about those guys," Swinney added. "And the walk-on kid from Daniel, Adrian Dunn. It's great. It was fun to see the guys respond. We've got some young guys that have some bulldog in 'em. It's going to be a fun spring around here."

Credit Herbstreit

ESPN's Kirk Herbstreit had it right. Before the 2014 Orange Bowl, he predicted the outcome of Clemson's game against Ohio State: "This game has 45–42 written all over it. So it may come down to who has the ball last. I don't see the defenses playing well at all in this game. I'd be shocked if Tajh Boyd doesn't have one of his better games."

also set the record for most wins over top 25 ranked teams with eight, including five victories over top 10 foes.

"This is a very special night," Boyd said. "Just the significance of the game, not for me, not for this team, but for the university, for the fans that support us day-in and day-out, has been unbelievable. It's a very special evening. I couldn't pick a better way to go out as a senior."

The first half had the feeling of missed opportunities for Clemson. In the second half, the Tigers made sure they did not miss another.

Was Herbstreit ever right. Clemson won 40–35, and Boyd threw for 378 yards and five touchdowns.

2014 Recruits "One of the Best"
Nobody could be happier than Coach Dabo Swinney about Clemson's incoming 2014 recruits. Swinney didn't hesitate in claiming that it will prove to be "one of the best if not the best" he's recruited since taking over the program in 2009.

Looking back, Swinney pointed out that four consecutive classes were rated in the top 15 in the country by ESPN that have produced three consecutive 10-win seasons. In the *USA Today's* Coaches Poll, Clemson ranked seventh for the 2013 season.

Swinney's "best" correlation is supported by the fact that ESPN rated Clemson's 2014 class as No. 12 in the nation. The group of 25 includes four four-star receivers and three three-star running backs.

Clemson appears to have a replacement for quarterback Tajh Boyd in Deshaun Watson who was the state of Georgia's career passing leader while only a junior. He was considered one of the top quarterbacks who turned down offers from the big three Florida colleges along with Ohio State and Tennessee early on to shut down all other potential offers to sign with Clemson.

"We certainly lost a good group of seniors, but this is a good group coming in here," Swinney beamed.

That was thanks in part to an array of miscues that included an interception near the goal line, a turnover on downs that led to a touchdown, a Buckeyes drive that was extended twice after Clemson forced fourth down, a safety for intentional grounding in the end zone, and a missed extra point.

But the Tigers cashed in on two third-quarter turnovers by the Buckeyes as Watkins and Martavis Bryant made acrobatic catches in the end zone to put Clemson on top entering the fourth quarter.

Things looked bleak for the Tigers after Ohio State stretched its lead to 29–20 and got another stop on third down to open the second half.

Clemson finally got the break it had been so desperately seeking, after its offense had been forced to punt on the next drive, as Corey Brown muffed a punt and Robert Smith was there to recover the loose ball at the Ohio State 33.

"The spark was the punt return fumble," Swinney explained. "We were down. We were minus-one in the turnover margin, and that was a huge thing. When we win the turnover margin, we win. That's just the way it is for us."

The Tigers cashed in three plays later as Watkins went up and made an acrobatic catch in the end zone for a 30-yard touchdown that narrowed Ohio State's lead to 29–27. Watkins tied Clemson's career record for touchdown catches with his 27th on the play.

The Tigers defense kept the momentum going on the ensuing drive. On third-and-8, pressure flushed Braxton Miller out of the pocket and his pass to the sideline was intercepted by Jayron Kearse to give Clemson the ball at the Ohio State 38.

Four plays later, Boyd and Bryant hooked up on a fade route again as Bryant hauled in a juggling catch in the corner of the end zone to put the Tigers back on top 34–29 with 32 seconds left in the third quarter.

The Buckeyes regained the lead on a 14-yard pass from Miller to Carlos Hyde to make the score 35–34 with 11:35 left in the game.

The Tigers went back in front on a five-yard grab by Seckinger, who Boyd found wide open for the touchdown. The score put Clemson on top 40–35 with 6:16 remaining.

With the Buckeyes facing third-and-13 on the ensuing drive, Breeland crashed in on a corner blitz and hit Miller, the ball popped loose, and Shuey snatched it out of the air at the Ohio State 47.

The Tigers gave the ball right back as Ohio State came up with an interception three plays later, but Anthony picked off Miller two plays later to get the ball back for Clemson to seal the win.

CLEMSON	14	6	14	6	40
OHIO STATE	9	13	7	6	35
CU Boyd 48 run (Catanzaro kick), 1st, 12:50					
OSU B. Miller 33 run (Basil kick), 1st, 5:44					
CU S. Watkins 34 pass from Boyd (Catanzaro kick), 1st, 4:56					
OSU TEAM safety, 1st, 2:25					
CU Bryant 3 pass from Boyd (Catanzaro kick failed), 2nd, 6:16					
OSU Heuerman 57 pass from B. Miller (Basil kick failed), 2nd, 3:39					
OSU B. Miller 3 run (Basil kick), 2nd, 0:12					
OSU Hyde 1 run (Basil kick), 3rd, 5:50					
CU S. Watkins 30 pass from Boyd (Catanzaro kick), 3rd, 2:47					
OSU Hyde 14 pass from B. Miller (Guiton pass failed), 4th, 11:35					
CU Seckinger 5 pass from Boyd (S. Watkins pass failed), 4th, 6:16					
Attendance: 77,080					

1978 Gator Bowl

December 29, 1978

Jacksonville, Florida

Clemson 17, Ohio State 15

The 1978 Clemson team was notable for many reasons, and not the least of which was a 17–15 win over Ohio State in the Gator Bowl. The team won 11 games (eight by convincing margins), had the nation's largest winning streak after the bowl game, changed head coaches 19 days before the bowl, and ended the coaching career of Woody Hayes.

The first quarter of new Clemson head coach Danny Ford's first game was scoreless.

The second quarter was unusual in that there were four possessions in the stanza and each team scored twice. Ohio State drove to the Clemson 9 on the passing of Art Schlichter, but the Buckeyes had to settle for Bob Atha's 27-yard field goal.

Quarterback Steve Fuller engineered an impressive 80-yard, 15-play drive after the kickoff. Staying mostly on the ground, Fuller ran around left end from four yards out to give Clemson the lead.

Schlichter duplicated Fuller's feat nine plays later, but Clemson right end Steve Gibbs blocked Vlade Janakiewski's extra-point try.

Clemson got the ball back with 1:15 remaining in the quarter, and Fuller passed his way to the Buckeye 30. With only five seconds left, Obed Ariri hit a 47-yard field goal that gave the Tigers a 10–9 lead at halftime.

Clemson scored the only points of the third quarter as the running combination of Fuller, Marvin Sims, and Warren Ratchford ground out 83 yards in 18 plays. Cliff Austin went the final yard for the score, and Ariri's conversion gave Clemson a 17–9 cushion.

With 8:22 left in the game, Schlichter scored his second touchdown to bring Ohio State within two points. Jim Stuckey tackled Schlichter on a sweep to prevent the two-point play, and Clemson led 17–15.

Ohio State mounted one final drive. Faced with third-and-5 at the Clemson 24, an interception by second-team middle guard Charlie Bauman (the only theft of his four-year career) killed the drive. Bauman was forced out of bounds on the Ohio State sideline, and Buckeye coach Woody Hayes swung at the Clemson player. Consecutive unsportsmanlike conduct penalties gave Clemson excellent field position, and Fuller was able to run out the clock, giving Clemson its first win over a Big Ten team.

Middle guard Charlie Bauman made the only interception of his Clemson career in the 1978 Gator Bowl. (Photo courtesy of the Clemson University Sports Information Department)

Bubba Brown led the Clemson defense with 22 tackles, still a school record for tackles in a bowl game. Jim Stuckey added 10 tackles.

CLEMSON	0	10	7	0	17
OHIO STATE	0	9	0	6	15

OSU Atha 27 FG, 2nd, 12:08
CU   Fuller 4 run (Ariri kick), 2nd, 5:03
OSU Schlichter 4 run (kick blocked), 2nd, 1:21
CU   Ariri 47 FG, 2nd, 0:05
CU   Austin 1 run (Ariri kick), 3rd, 2:16
OSU Schlichter 1 run (run failed), 4th, 8:11

Attendance: 72,011

31 Orange Pants and Shoes

Orange Pants I

Before the opening of the 1980 season, Coach Danny Ford was looking for something, anything, to create a spark among his players. He talked it over with the team's equipment manager and ordered him to order special pants. He was thinking about South Carolina in the final game of the year.

Ford was a bit on the hot seat. After losing the last two games in 1979 and then being only 5–5 during 1980, Clemson fans were becoming restless and there was talk around town from any number of critics who wanted Ford to be fired. Ford decided to break out the pants before the South Carolina game.

The Gamecocks were already Gator Bowl–bound, and they featured the best running game in the country, George Rogers, who went on to win the Heisman Trophy.

Knowing he would need to get a spark in the locker room, Ford called his two defensive leaders, cornerback Willie Underwood and linebacker Jeff Davis, into his office before a practice that week. That's when Ford pulled out a pair of burnt-orange pants. The pants took Underwood and Davis back a second, but they agreed to wear them.

Ford asked Underwood and Davis to keep it quiet because he was going to surprise the team after the player's meal the Friday night before the game.

"We knew something was up, but we didn't really know what," running back Cliff Austin said.

When dinner was done, Ford came up front where he said a few words about the game and then reached down and held up the orange pants.

"This is what we are wearing tomorrow," Ford said.

"When he did that, the room went crazy," Davis said. "That's all the guys could talk about was wearing those orange pants with the orange jersey and the orange helmet and how the fans were going to love it. Coach Ford was a master motivator. He knew how to push the right buttons.

"That moment relaxed us. All of a sudden, we weren't thinking about having to win this game to save his job or about how we were going to stop George Rogers or any of that. We were just looking forward to playing the game."

To surprise the fans, Ford asked his players to put their thigh pads in their orange pants to wear their orange jerseys over their white pants for pregame warm-ups. With the thigh pads already in place, it would make the transition of changing the pants faster when they got back in the locker room.

"We all knew we were going to change into the orange pants when we got back in the locker room, so we were pumped up and ready to go," Davis said. "We knew how excited the fans were going to get when they see us come to the top of the hill wearing all orange."

The fans saw the Tigers gather at Howard's Rock dressed in all orange for the very first time, and the sellout crowd of 64,000 in Death Valley became extremely loud. "When the fans saw us, they went absolutely crazy," Davis continued. "We knew we were going to win."

Orange Pants II

Woody McCorvey was in shock when he and the rest of the Clemson football team walked into the locker room in 1989 and saw the infamous orange pants sitting in each of the players' lockers.

The Tigers had just returned from pregame warm-ups as they prepared to play South Carolina at Williams-Brice Stadium in Columbia that night.

"That was something that was very uncharacteristic of what Coach Ford did because it was a tradition that we wore them at home," said McCorvey, who is now an associate athletic director at Clemson. "The only other time they wore them on the road was when they won the national championship in 1981."

Clemson had not worn orange pants since losing to Florida State in 1988 in a game that is known as "Puntrooski." Ford would only allow them to be pulled out for what were deemed special games. He used them as motivation, and it worked.

Clemson was 15–2 at the time in the orange pants, which first debuted in a 27–6 victory over South Carolina in 1980. The two losses were a one-point defeat by the Gamecocks in 1984, and a three-point loss to the Seminoles in 1988.

The Tigers would have to earn the right to wear orange pants by the way they practiced. The seniors would request to wear the special britches the Monday before a big game, but players never knew if they would get to wear them until they came in from pregame warm-ups.

McCorvey remembers the emotions in the locker room that night when the players saw the pants.

"When we went back into the locker room and saw that they were out, it went crazy in there," he said. "You could not believe the sense of the locker room when those kids saw those pants. We went back out there and played with a lot of enthusiasm and a lot of emotion.

"It was pretty much a complete ballgame by us that night."

The Tigers rushed for 335 yards and finished the night with 446 total yards in a 45–0 victory. The defense held the Gamecocks to 155 total yards while forcing five turnovers in the series' last shutout.

"Clemson played a perfect game," South Carolina head coach Sparky Woods said. "I think the turning point took place when we kicked off. We just got beat throughout the entire game."

The 15th-ranked Tigers scored on their first four possessions while totaling 302 yards before halftime. Running back Terry Allen scored on two first-quarter runs and had 97 yards before reinjuring his knee late in the second quarter. That was the last time he played in a Clemson uniform.

But Allen's injury was a sidebar to the kind of night it was for Clemson. The Tigers physically dominated the game on offense, defense, and special teams.

Some say that the 1989 game is still the best game a Clemson team has ever played against the Gamecocks.

"I was not here for the 63–17 game [in 2003], but during my seven years, that night in 1989 might have been our most complete ballgame that we played," McCorvey said. "We had a lot of good ballgames in those years, but I can't remember a one from the beginning to the end where our players played that way the entire game.

"You talk about playing four quarters on offense, defense, and special teams—that was a four-quarter football game."

And it all started because of a change in pants—special orange pants, that is.

"We had no idea and still to this day, I have never asked or talked to Coach Ford about it," McCorvey said. "I don't know what made him do it, a lot of times he would meet with the seniors and they would talk about things in there.

"Whether they talked about it that week, I don't know. We did it, though, and it was something I will always remember and I know those players will remember it, too."

Orange Shoes

On a windy November day in 1967, it probably was the shoes that enabled Clemson to upset 10th-ranked N.C. State 14–6 in Clemson's first-ever win over a top 10 team in Death Valley. N.C. State was ranked No. 1 in the ACC on defense coming into the Clemson game and was a big favorite to beat a 4–4 Clemson team.

The Wolfpack was enjoying a fabulous year, defeating its first eight opponents. After the Pack defeated Virginia in Charlottesville in the eighth game, Penn State and Clemson remained, both on the road.

Before the Nittany Lions game, there was talk that N.C. State had the Sugar Bowl bid wrapped up, provided there was at least a split in the last two games. The Wolfpack lost to Penn State 13–8, making the Clemson–N.C. State game even more crucial for the Wolfpack's New Year's Day bowl hopes.

N.C. State started wearing the white shoes on defense when left cornerback Bill Morrow noted a member of the Kansas City Chiefs wearing white shoes. Morrow, who scored the first touchdown for N.C. State in the new Carter-Finley Stadium when he intercepted a pass in 1966, went to co-captain Art McMahon with the idea. Linebacker Chuck Amato said he would paint his shoes white, and the idea spread throughout the Wolfpack defense.

Buddy Gore (44) was one of Clemson's greatest backs. (Photo courtesy of the Clemson University Sports Information Department)

A few of the Clemson players, the week before the N.C. State game, wanted to paint their shoes orange to counteract the perceived intangible advantage of the visitor's white shoes.

"I remember a lot of players got together and decided to paint our shoes orange," former Clemson tailback Buddy Gore recalled.

"Our trainer, Herman McGee, rounded up the orange paint needed for our idea, and we went to the dorm that week and painted our game shoes orange. I have no idea where he got the orange paint. Coach Howard did not know what we were doing until that Saturday morning. I think he liked our plan."

Gore was one of Clemson's greatest backs, and in 1967 he was named the Atlantic Coast Conference's Player of the Year.

Assistant Coach Don Wade was also involved in the scheme. "We got the paint from eight or nine different places," Wade explained. "It's tough to find orange paint that would be suitable for shoes."

N.C. State jumped ahead 6–0 after Gerald Warren hit two second-quarter field goals from 37 and 47 yards out with his back to a gusty 22-mph wind.

Gore scored what proved to be the winning touchdown for the Tigers early in the third quarter. With a third-and-11 situation facing the Tigers on N.C. State's 27, Clemson was obviously facing a throwing situation.

"N.C. State was in a defense that would provide double coverage on the wideouts and forced the linebackers to cover the man coming out of the backfield," Gore remembered.

"I was not the primary receiver by any means," Gore continued. "After all, I only caught seven passes my entire career. I was in the flats around the 12-yard line, and I was open after beating the linebacker. The cornerback and the safety were with our wide receiver. I will never forget when I was open in the flats. I looked at our quarterback, Jimmy Addison, and he stared right back at me and he threw me the ball and I went in for the touchdown."

Clemson went on to win the game 14–6, ensuring the Tigers at least a tie for the ACC crown. The Tigers defeated South Carolina the next Saturday to clinch the championship outright.

"How many tackles did those orange shoes make, Coach?" a sportswriter asked Coach Frank Howard after the game. "None," Howard replied in a word. "But I tell you, there is something about football that makes boys believe in something that will help them. When they believe they can do something, they usually do it."

On that particular day, it must have been the shoes!

32 Clemson's First All-American

O.K. Pressley may never be compared to Elvis Presley, but he claimed fame as Clemson's first All-American. The native of Chester, South Carolina, Pressley, who was the starting center and linebacker for three years, was named 3rd team All-American by Newspaper Enterprise of America in 1928, John Heisman and Walter Trumbull teams.

"O.K. Pressley was like his initials—O.K.," exclaimed Henry Asbill, an end for the Clemson teams in the late 1920s.

Nobody could account for his first name; it was strictly O.K. He was somewhat shy as a youngster. When he arrived at Clemson, he was too modest to relate his high school exploits. He began playing for the local YMCA team. Luckily, he was discovered by a Clemson coach one day at a YMCA campus and became an overnight sensation.

In his three years at Clemson, Pressley started every game at center and linebacker and was captain of the first Clemson team to win eight games, in 1928. Besides his All-American tribute that year, Pressley was named All-Southern and All-State.

One of Pressley's most memorable games occurred against South Carolina. A week before the game, Pressley suffered a head injury in the Auburn game. Coach Josh Cody decided against playing Pressley against the Gamecocks. O.K. insisted that he was able to play, but exercising caution, Cody refused.

At a critical part of the game, with Carolina on Clemson's 10-yard line, Pressley jumped off the bench and pleaded with Cody to let him play. Seeing the fire in his star's eyes, Cody relented and waved Pressley onto the field.

Pressley made his presence felt immediately—and did he ever. On the first play, he dropped a Carolina runner for an eight-yard loss. On the next play, he did so again, this time for seven yards. But he wasn't finished. On the next two plays he produced five- and seven-yard losses that discouraged Carolina for the rest of the game. Pressley's dynamic effort is considered the greatest one-player stand in Clemson history.

No one that afternoon could have imagined that Clemson, led by Pressley's heroics, would rout South Carolina 32–0. Both teams entered the game unbeaten at 5–0 with the Gamecocks stabled as the favorite.

Pressley, indeed, was every inch an All-American and deservedly inducted into the Clemson Hall of Fame in 1978.

1978 Season

The Tigers were coming off an 8–3–1 season in which they went to their first bowl game in 18 years and finished the year ranked 19th in the final Associated Press Top 20 poll.

Clemson began the 1978 season looking as if it was going to exceed its lofty expectations. The ACC's preseason favorite rolled over The Citadel in the season-opener as eight different Tigers scored in a 58–3 victory.

"It was easy because we worked hard for four weeks to make it look easy," fullback Marvin Sims said. "I wasn't surprised we did this well; I expected it."

The eighth-ranked Tigers expected to do the same thing in Week 2, when they rolled down the road to Athens, Georgia, to play unranked Georgia. The Bulldogs were still smarting from the 1977 matchup when Clemson knocked down a two-point conversion on the last play to sneak out of Athens with a 7–6 win.

But the Clemson players were confident and felt this was their year to shine. Georgia quickly brought them to earth. The Bulldogs forced six Clemson turnovers and kept the Tigers out of the offense, while holding the strong running game to 156 yards.

The defense held its own, holding Georgia to two first-half field goals, but the Bulldogs opened the second half with an 80-yard drive capped with a 13-yard Jeff Pyburn touchdown pass to flanker Carmon Prince. Georgia had seized control of the game and finished the afternoon with 205 rushing yards against Clemson's proud defense.

The Tigers were stunned. Just three hours earlier they were boasting about being unbeatable and being the best in the country, and suddenly they were left trying to figure out what went wrong.

"We learned our lesson quick," linebacker Bubba Brown said. "After The Citadel game, we were on top of the world, and when we went to Athens as the favorite, I think we were beginning to believe all the stuff people were saying about how good we were.

"The Georgia game brought us back down to earth. We learned that even though we had talent, we had to work for everything we got."

This was when arguably the best Clemson team ever assembled was born. A look to the final NCAA statistics from that season tells the rest of the story.

The Tigers of 1978 finished fifth in the nation in scoring offense at 32 points per game, and fifth in the nation in scoring defense, allowing just 10.5 points per game. Clemson was fourth in the nation in total offense at 436.7 yards per game. The Tigers were sixth in the nation in rushing, averaging nearly 300 yards per game, and fifth in turnover margin. The passing game, led by Fuller, completed 54 percent of its passes and threw just five interceptions.

Even the special teams were among the best, as the Tigers finished second in the nation in punt returns, and Obed Ariri was 12th in the nation in scoring.

A look at the future NFL stars on that 1978 team gives more evidence that this was the most talented team in Clemson history. No less than six players (Butler, Fuller, Jim Stuckey, Jeff Bryant, Perry Tuttle, and Terry Kinard) were first-round draft choices. Seventeen players on the team were drafted, and 18 played in the NFL. Eleven of the 18 played at least five years in the NFL.

The players on Clemson's starting offense that year played a combined 61 years in the NFL. Just look at the offensive line alone. Jeff Bostic, the center, played 14 years in the league. His brother, Joe Bostic, was starting guard who started nine years in the league and was an All-American player in 1978. Steve Kenney, a starting tackle, played for the Philadelphia Eagles and Detroit Lions for seven years.

Fuller played eight years in the league, while his favorite targets, Butler and Clark, were both All-Pros and played seven years and nine years in the league, respectively. That does not even include second team wide receiver Perry Tuttle, who was a first-round draft pick and All-American athlete in 1981.

The character of the team started to take over in the third game, and the result was a 31–0 victory over Villanova, a team led by future All-Pro Howie Long. A Clemson homecoming crowd enjoyed a 38–7 victory over Virginia Tech in the season's fourth game, as Fuller ran 75 yards for a touchdown on the game's second play from scrimmage—still the longest run by a Clemson quarterback in team history.

The offense continued its dominance of the offensive line in Week 5 when the Tigers gained 419 yards rushing in a 30–14 win over Virginia. Lester Brown, known as "the Rubber Duck," had 178 yards rushing, including a 59-yard touchdown run on Clemson's first play from scrimmage.

A 28–8 victory over Duke followed, led by Randy Scott, who had three takeaways out of Clemson's seven total forced turnovers.

The N.C. State game in Raleigh was a battle of the Browns. N.C. State was led by Ted Brown, a senior running back who had rushed for 227 yards and four touchdowns against Clemson as a freshman. The Tigers featured Lester Brown, who would end the season as Clemson's second 1,000-yard rusher in history who also had a record 17 touchdowns.

The key to the game was Clemson linebacker Bubba Brown, who earned National Player of the Week honors from *Sports Illustrated*. Clemson's all-time leading tackler finished the day with 18 tackles and almost personally limited Ted Brown to 70 yards on 21 carries and no touchdowns in Clemson's 33–10 victory.

Clemson rushed for 247 yards, including 118 yards and two touchdowns by Lester Brown. Rex Vain returned an interception 93 yards for a touchdown, his second 90-plus-yard return of his career. It was a big victory for Clemson over a team that would end the season with a 9–3 record and a top 20 final ranking.

"This was a great team victory," Coach Charley Pell said. "I can't express in words how much this victory means. It is the greatest team effort I've been a part of since I first put on a football uniform in 1958."

It was also a proud day for Clemson fans. In one of the most incredible showings of spirit in college history, the 5,000 or so

Clemson fans forced N.C. State quarterback Scott Smith to back away from the line of scrimmage and ask the referee for time because of crowd noise—noise caused by the visiting Clemson fans.

The winning streak continued the next week on Tobacco Road with a 51–6 scorching of Wake Forest. For the sixth time in eight games, the Tigers rushed for 342 yards and gained 208 yards passing. Lester Brown led the way with a 117-yard rushing performance, and Tuttle caught his first career touchdown pass in his hometown of Winston-Salem, on a 42-yard pass from Fuller.

The defense showed how much improvement it had made over the previous two years. In 1976, Wake Forest running back James McDougald had rushed for 249 yards against the Tigers. The entire Wake Forest team had just three yards rushing in 25 attempts on this afternoon.

The rivalry with North Carolina was one of the strongest in the ACC in the late 1970s and 1980s. Clemson was a heavy favorite against a young North Carolina team that featured a sophomore linebacker named Lawrence Taylor. The outside linebacker would go on to be considered one of the NFL's greatest defensive players of all time, as he helped lead the New York Giants to two Super Bowl Championships in the late 1980s and early '90s during his Hall of Fame career.

Clemson closed out the season by defeating Maryland and South Carolina.

1951 Orange Bowl

January 1, 1951
Miami, Florida
Clemson 15, Miami (Florida) 14

In 1950, the Tigers were undefeated once again. There weren't many other teams in the country that could match Clemson's 8–0–1 record, the tie having occurred in a 14–14 game against South Carolina that had been played on a rain-swept, muddy field at Columbia. In fact, some experts believed that Clemson had the best single wing attack in the country. The Tigers were ranked 10th in the final college poll, the highest position they had ever achieved. It should have brought them recognition and respect. Strangely, it didn't produce either.

The grapevine had it that the Miami populace was disappointed about playing little-known Clemson.

"Shucks, we've won the only two Coach Frank bowl games we've been in, which don't seem to mean much to some folks," Coach Frank Howard said. "They ought to read the AP poll if they want to know about Clemson."

The Orange Bowl was the only bowl to present two unbeaten teams. Miami, like Clemson, had an 8–0–1 record. (The Miami tie was in a game against the University of Louisville with a final score of 14–14.) While the selection committee for the Orange Bowl was unanimous in its selection of Miami, they were openly split regarding Clemson's appearance. Several of the members had voiced support for twice-beaten Alabama. Yet, Howard was gracious in accepting the invitation to participate, knowing, of course, that the Gator Bowl officials also wanted Clemson if the Orange Bowl had collapsed.

"I'm very happy that Clemson is to play in the Orange Bowl with such a worthy opponent as Miami," Howard said when the Orange Bowl committee finally made up its mind. "Our boys deserved all the credit. They have played for the team's success as a whole and not for individual glory. I believe we have more outstanding players than other teams."

One of the outstanding players Howard was referring to was fullback Fred Cone, who was playing his final year for Clemson. Cone not only enjoyed his best season, he was also the team captain. He had led the Tigers in rushing with 845 yards and in scoring with 92 points, and he was selected on the All-Southern Conference team. Howard believed that the 180-lb. Cone was the best fullback in the country.

And there was wingback Ray Mathews, who had topped the Tigers in rushing the previous two years, who was also ending his career. Howard also had a good-looking prospect in newcomer Billy Hair at tailback. Hair had passed for three touchdowns against Duquesne and ran for two more, and he also tossed two touchdown passes against Furman. The remaining members of Clemson's strong backfield were blocking backs Wyndy Wyndham and Dick Hendley and wingback Jackie Calvert. They had scored a total of 328 points, while the usually strong defense had limited the opposition to just 62 points during the season.

Despite all the pregame furor about Clemson, a crowd of 65,181 attended the contest. Once again, it was the largest crowd that any Tigers team had played before, and they were determined to perform well. They got as far as the Miami 37-yard line after the opening kickoff, but they stalled. After Miami was stopped, Clemson got the ball again but couldn't get a first down. After an exchange of punts, the first quarter ended scoreless.

Early in the second period, Hair was sent into the game. He immediately ran for seven yards and then threw a 45-yard pass to Bob Hudson on the Miami 4-yard line. On third down, Cone

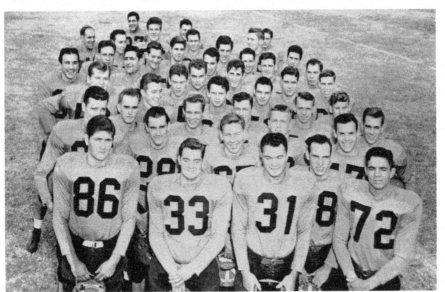

Clemson's 1950 football team defeated Miami (Florida) in the 1951 Orange Bowl 15–14. (Photo courtesy of the Clemson University Sports Information Department)

took it from the 1-yard line. Charlie Radcliff added the conversion to give underdog Clemson a 7–0 lead. Although the Tigers were in Miami's territory most of the second period, they couldn't score again by the end of the first half.

Hair ignited the Clemson offense once again in the third quarter. He completed three passes in a 75-yard drive, the last one for 21 yards to Glenn Smith for a touchdown. Radcliff missed the extra point, but Clemson led 13–0. Miami stuck back quickly for two touchdowns, and when the period ended, it had grabbed a 14–13 lead.

Clemson's big play came midway during the final period when Miami was backed up on its goal line. The Hurricanes' star runner, Frank Smith, tried to get some running room by taking a pitchout in the end zone. But Sterling Smith, an unheralded non-scholarship guard, broke through and nailed the Miami runner for a safety that gave Clemson a 15–14 lead. The game ended some seven minutes later with the happy Tigers carrying Smith and Howard on their shoulders around the Orange Bowl.

Howard said years later that he would never forget the crowd noise or what Sterling Smith had done that day.

"I thought the stadium was caving in from the noise," Howard said. "When Sterling ran off the field after getting that safety, his daddy came down out of the stands and started hugging and kissing him like crazy. That night he took his son's game jersey and wore it all over town. I never saw such a proud parent in my life."

CLEMSON	0	7	6	2	15
MIAMI (FL)	0	0	14	0	14
CU	Cone 1 run (Radcliff kick)				
CU	G. Smith 21 pass from Hair (kick blocked)				
UM	Mallios 5 run (Watson kick)				
UM	F. Smith 17 pass from Hackett (Watson kick)				
CU	Safety, F. Smith tackled in end zone by S. Smith				
Attendance: 65,181					

35 1989 Florida State v. Clemson

September 9, 1989
Doak Campbell Stadium
Clemson 34, Florida State 23

Two of the top winningest programs in the nation over the last three years met in Tallahassee, Florida, in Week 2. Clemson entered the game with a 29–6–2 record over the last three years for a .811 percentage, while Florida State was 29–7–1 for a .797 percentage. Clemson was ranked fifth and Florida State sixth in terms of winning percentage for that period of time. It also marked the duel of two of the winningest active coaches in college football. Danny Ford was fourth entering the game with a .754 winning percentage, while Seminoles Coach Bobby Bowden was eighth at .720.

Clemson exploded offensively in the first half and took a 21–0 lead in front of a stunned Florida State crowd. Terry Allen scored on a pair of one-yard runs on Clemson's first possession of the first and second periods. Wayne Simmons came through with a 73-yard interception return for a touchdown, the second longest interception return in Clemson history by a linebacker. Jimmy Quarles had a 90-yarder against Rice in 1951.

After a Florida State touchdown, Terry Allen showed his improved speed and went 73 yards for a score just 1:16 before halftime to give Clemson a 28–7 lead. Allen had 130 yards rushing and three touchdowns for the evening. It was the first time Florida State had given up 28 points in a half since the 1985 Florida game and, in general, Clemson surprised the nation via ESPN with a victory that would look better and better as the season progressed. Clemson entered the game ranked 10th in the nation but was an underdog against the 16th-rated FSU.

Chris Gardocki put the game out of reach with a pair of field goals in the fourth quarter as Clemson controlled the clock much of the second half behind the ball-handling expertise and passing proficiency of Chris Morocco. The native of Athens, Georgia, hit 8-of-9 passes for the evening for 134 yards, including four for 92 yards to Rodney Fletcher. He was a reason Clemson did not turn the ball over against Florida State for the second straight year. It was the 16th turnoverless game in Danny Ford's 119-game career but the seventh in the last 15 contests.

Clemson averaged 7.1 yards a play for the night, just the sixth time a Danny Ford–coached Clemson team had reached the 7.0 yards per play figure. Stacy Long was a key for Clemson as he had his first great game in an All-American junior season with an 85 percent grade and 10-knockdown block performance against Odell Haggins and the FSU front four.

Defensively, Doug Brewster was the top tackler with 12 stops, but a pair of Clearwater, Florida, natives also made great contributions in their home state again. Arlington Nunn had nine stops, while Vince Taylor contributed eight. Simmons had a sack to go with his 73-yard interception return. The Clemson defense held Florida State to 106 yards rushing. FSU scored a touchdown with just five seconds left to bring the margin to 11 points.

The victory over the 16th-ranked Seminoles gave Danny Ford a 6–0 record in the state of Florida, including 5–0 in bowl games. It broke a 10-game Florida State home winning streak and dropped Florida State to a 48–10–1 home record over the last 10 seasons.

CLEMSON	7	21	0	6	34
FLORIDA STATE	0	10	6	7	23

CU   Allen 1 run (Gardocki kick), 1st, 10:59
CU   Allen 1 run (Gardocki kick), 2nd, 14:57
CU   Simmons 73 interception return (Gardocki kick), 2nd, 12:57
FSU   Carter 1 run (Mason kick), 2nd, 1:34
CU   Allen 73 run (Gardocki kick), 2nd, 1:16
FSU   Mason 28 FG, 2nd, 0:00
FSU   Moore 1 run (Run failed), 3rd, 8:46
CU   Gardocki 29 FG, 4th, 14:13
CU   Gardocki 26 FG, 4th, 9:11
FSU   Parker 13 pass from Weldon (Mason kick), 4th, 0:05

1986 Georgia v. Clemson

September 20, 1986
Athens, Georgia
Clemson 31, Georgia 28

The Tigers ended an era of frustration when they upset No. 14 Georgia 31–28 on David Treadwell's second career game-winning field goal as time expired. Never before had Georgia lost a game in which it had scored 28 points or more.

The odds seemed stacked against the Tigers. Not only were they coming off a disappointing performance against Virginia Tech, Clemson's 18 seniors had never beaten Georgia, and only once in the last 17 tries had a Tigers club left Sanford Stadium victorious—a 7–6 win by the 1977 Gator Bowl Clemson team. Also, second games for the Clemson gridders had not been too kind, either, as the Tigers were 5–15–1 since 1965 in second games.

Before a regionally televised game on ABC, the Tigers had to rally three times for a 21–21 halftime tie. The 42 combined first-half points are the most markers scored by the two teams in the first two periods. As it turned out, the game ended as the highest scoring in series history, breaking a 66-year-old record.

Kenny Flowers carried six times for 72 yards, but an ankle sprain sidelined him the entire second half. Ironically, he registered his longest rush from scrimmage, a 57-yard romp, which set up his two-yard score when he suffered the injury. However, his departure marked fellow senior tailback Terrence Flagler's entrance. He began his All-American journey in this game by carrying 10 times for 90 yards and catching three passes for 58 yards. His scoring connection with quarterback Rodney Williams was the first time in six games that a Tigers signal caller had passed for a score.

137

Although the Tigers defense surrendered 383 yards, the defenders forced four turnovers, broke up five passes, and had three players rack up double-figure tackle totals. Defense tackle Raymond Chavous earned ACC Player of the Week for his 12 tackles, two for loss, in 49 plays. He caused a fumble late in the game that keyed the Clemson comeback. Athens, Georgia, native Norman Haynes had a career high 14 stops at linebacker, and cornerback Donnell Woolford finished with 10 hits.

CLEMSON	7	14	7	3	31
GEORGIA	14	7	7	0	28

GU   Tate 1 run (Crumley kick), 1st, 8:53
CU   Flowers 2 run (Treadwell kick), 1st, 6:18
GU   Henderson 32 pass from Jackson (Crumley kick), 1st, 3:23
CU   Flagler 9 pass from Williams (Treadwell kick), 2nd, 13:02
GU   Jackson 15 run (Crumley kick), 2nd, 8:45
CU   Johnson 1 run (Treadwell kick), 2nd, 3:12
CU   Williams 1 run (Treadwell kick), 3rd, 6:10
GU   Lane 78 pass from Jackson (Crumley kick), 3rd, 1:58
CU   Treadwell 46 FG, 4th, 0:00

2003 FSU Win

November 8, 2003
Memorial Stadium
Clemson 26, Florida State 10

Clemson ended 14 years of frustration by defeating No. 3 Florida State 26–10 in front of 79,826 fans in Death Valley. The win over the third-ranked Seminoles was the highest-ranked victory in Clemson history. It also marked the first time since 1989 that Clemson defeated Florida State.

Several landmarks occurred in the 16-point victory for Clemson. For Coach Tommy Bowden, it was his first win in five tries against his father, Bobby.

Aaron Hunt became Clemson's all-time scoring leader with 302 points, breaking Nelson Welch's previous record of 301. Derrick Hamilton became the school's all-time all-purpose yardage leader with 4,412, breaking Travis Zachery's record. Charlie Whitehurst broke Woodrow Dantzler's single-season record for passing yards (2,682) with two regular season games remaining.

Clemson set the tone in the game's opening moments. On its first offensive possession, the Tigers moved 65 yards in 11 plays before Aaron Hunt connected on a 23-yard field goal.

On Florida State's ensuing possession, Tye Hill notched his second interception of the season when he stepped in front of a long Chris Rix pass. The Tigers tacked on Hunt's second field goal minutes later, giving Clemson a 6–0 lead.

Clemson got the ball back with less than 3:00 to go in the first half. Whitehurst drove the Tigers from their own 35-yard line. The big play was a 51-yard hookup with Youngblood on third-and-10. Three plays later, Whitehurst rolled to the right and then scrambled back to the left for a one-yard touchdown run. His effort gave Clemson a 13–0 lead at halftime.

Florida State missed a field goal on its opening possession of the second half. Clemson took advantage by marching 63 yards in 11 plays. Hunt kicked his third field goal of the game from 32 yards away, giving Clemson a 16–0 cushion. The drive was set up by Whitehurst, who zipped a pass between three defenders as he was getting hit and found Curtis Baham for a 23-yard gain on third down.

The Seminoles responded with three points as Xavier Beitia made a 46-yard field goal. However, Clemson put the game away on the next two drives. First, Whitehurst executed a beautiful pump-fake to the right before throwing left to a streaking Hamilton. His 58-yard touchdown catch gave Clemson a 23–3 lead. Clemson kept up the intensity as Leroy Hill intercepted a Rix pass four plays later. The ball was tipped by Khaleed Vaughn. On the next Seminole drive, David Dunham sacked Rix 10 yards behind the line of scrimmage and forced a fumble. It was recovered by DeJuan Polk of Clemson. Hunt came on to nail his fourth field goal of the night, giving Clemson the 26–3 lead.

Florida State finally scored a touchdown in the final three minutes of the contest. Chauncey Stovall was able to get behind the Tigers secondary for a 71-yard touchdown, but it mattered little at that point in the game.

Whitehurst was outstanding in his first career start against Florida State. He finished 17-of-27 for 272 yards and the touchdown pass. He also rushed for 39 yards and a touchdown. His favorite target was Hamilton, who grabbed six balls for 123 yards and a touchdown.

Hunt came into the game needing 14 points to set the school record, and he did just that. He was 4-for-4 on field goals and 2-for-2 on extra points.

Defensively, the Tigers held Florida State to 11 rushing yards the entire game, the fewest total by Florida State in the Bobby Bowden era.

CLEMSON	3	10	10	3	26
FLORIDA ST	0	0	3	7	10

CU	Hunt 23 FG, 1st, 8:25
CU	Hunt 35 FG, 2nd, 14:56
CU	Whitehurst 1 run (Hunt kick), 2nd, 0:15
CU	Hunt 32 FG, 3rd, 6:39
FSU	Beitia 46 FG, 3rd, 3:25
CU	Hamilton 58 pass from Whitehurst (Hunt kick), 3rd, 1:21
CU	Hunt 37 FG, 4th, 8:29
FSU	Stovall pass from Walker (Beitia kick), 4th, 2:14

Attendance: 79,826

1979 Notre Dame Game

November 17, 1979
South Bend, Indiana
Clemson 16, Notre Dame 10

Clemson arrived in South Bend having won its last two games and looking for its eighth victory of the season in Danny Ford's first year as head coach. Notre Dame had glory and history and was only two years removed from its 1977 national championship, while Clemson was still growing on the national stage. Ford was only 31 at the time and if they could pull an upset, he would become the second youngest coach since 1934 to beat the Irish at home.

On a crisp sunny day in Indiana, Notre Dame won the coin toss and elected to receive. The Irish wanted to test Clemson's defense from the opening whistle. And they had a great opportunity from Clemson's 43-yard line. They found out in a hurry as three running plays failed to produce a first down.

Clemson didn't achieve much on its first possession by only reaching its own 45-yard line. However, the defense recovered a fumble on the Irish 40-yard line and gained a golden opportunity to produce the game's first score. Instead the offense went three and out.

Notre Dame got on the scoreboard first near the end of the first quarter on a 42-yard field goal by Chuck Male. When the period expired three minutes later, Clemson failed to score even though they had the ball twice. Playing conservatively, only three times did the Tigers call a pass play, one that went for a 27-yard completion.

The Tigers continued to experience trouble moving the football in the second quarter. They had the ball three times and got as far as the Irish 38 but failed to score any points. They never got close enough for Obed Ariri to try a field goal, which was discouraging.

Meanwhile, the first opportunity for Notre Dame resulted in a touchdown. The Irish drove 80 yards on 15 plays that took 5:17 minutes. Vargas Ferguson concluded the march with a two-yard run on second down that stretched Notre Dame's margin to 10–0 when time elapsed in the first half.

Notre Dame dominated the action. The offense erupted for 295 yards, while the defense limited Clemson to only seven first downs and 108 yards. Ferguson had a big first half, rushing for 95 yards as the Irish took control.

Clemson needed to make something happen with the second half kickoff but still couldn't perform. After making a first down, the Tigers had to punt. However, they did get a break when Notre Dame fumbled the ball and the Tigers recovered on the Irish 21. Yet, Clemson couldn't fully capitalize and had to settle for Ariri's 23-yard field goal that reduced the deficit to 10–3.

The Tigers got the ball back on their 33 with 8:00 remaining in the third period. Quarterback Billy Lott led them on a 42-yard drive that produced Ariri's 41-yard field goal to pull Clemson to 10–6.

Before the offense could get a breather, they were back on the field. Ferguson fumbled on Notre Dame's first play, and Bubba Brown recovered on the Irish 40.

This time they found the end zone. Lott ran a quarterback keeper that went for 26 yards. With a minute left in the period, Clemson went ahead for the first time at 13–10 and appeared to have the momentum.

It carried over into the final period. On Clemson's first possession, it moved 42 yards for another Ariri field goal—this one from 37 yards—and a 16–10 advantage. Clemson scored 16 straight points. With 8:30 left on the clock, could the defense, maligned in the first half, hold?

Terry Kinard gave the answer. He intercepted an Irish pass on Clemson's 3-yard line and got to the 25 before being tackled. His interception sparked the defense the remainder of the contest as linebacker Bob Grable had a monster game with a record 25 tackles. Notre Dame went three straight series without a first down as Clemson preserved a hard-fought 16–10 upset. It ranked as possibly the biggest road victory in Clemson's history. It was only the third time in 41 years that Notre Dame had lost its season home finale.

"We have voted on a bowl game, but I'm not going to announce it right now," a happy Ford said after the game. "We're going to enjoy this one right now."

CLEMSON	0	0	13	3	16
NOTE DAME	3	7	0	0	10

ND   Male 42 FG, 1st, 3:19
ND   Ferguson 2 run (Male PAT), 2nd, 5:53
CU   Ariri 20 FG, 3rd, 10:49
CU   Ariri 41 FG, 3rd, 3:47
CU   Lott 26 run (Ariri PAT), 3rd, 1:37
CU   Ariri 37 FG, 4th, 8:30

1977—The Catch

The 1977 Clemson–South Carolina game that ended the season at Memorial Stadium was a big one for both teams. The Tigers had their eye on a Bowl game, while the Gamecocks were determined not to have a losing season. Clemson was on a roll. After an opening loss to Maryland, the Tigers went on a seven-game winning streak that attracted the Bowl representatives.

What ignited Clemson was its exciting 7–6 victory over Georgia in Athens. As the Tigers were making the 70-mile trip back to Clemson, Coach Charley Pell instructed the bus driver to pull over, which surprised everyone. Pell had a reason. He wanted to savor the win because it was Clemson's very first victory at Georgia since 1914.

As the legend goes, Pell went into a convenience store and bought every player on the team a cigar to commemorate the win. The cigar celebration became a big part of the 1977 season, as the Tigers used the Georgia win to jump start a great run.

Pell and the Tigers went on to win seven straight games, and after each victory, they lit up a cigar. Well, sort of. Clemson wide receiver Jerry Butler chose not to smoke his cigar and instead he scribbled the score and date on each of his. There was just one place left in his collection back at his dorm—for the South Carolina game.

But South Carolina wanted no part of this so-called rite of passage. The Gamecocks were still smarting from the previous year's loss in Clemson when the Tigers, despite winning just two games prior to it, pounded USC 28–9, knocking it out of contention for a possible Peach Bowl bid.

The roles were reversed this time around. The Gamecocks were sitting at 5–5 and knew their season was over regardless of the outcome, but Clemson (7–2–1) was in the running for a Gator Bowl invitation and needed a victory over its archrival to secure the bid and go bowling for the first time since 1959.

During the first two-and-half quarters, everything was pretty much going according to plan. The Tigers had a veteran team that was hungry and a head coach that got them believing in themselves. The Gamecocks were young and unsure of what they could accomplish.

It is known simply as "The Catch." (Photo courtesy of the Clemson University Sports Information Department)

The Tigers jumped out to a 17–0 lead by halftime, thanks to a Warren Ratchford touchdown, a 30-yard field goal by Obed Ariri, and a Lester Brown touchdown from the 1-yard line. When fullback Ken Callicutt rumbled 52 yards midway through the third quarter, Clemson found itself up 24–0 and well on its way to victory.

"Dwight Clark and I did the unpardonable; we started talking about how great we had played," quarterback Steve Fuller said to *The (Columbian) State* newspaper back in November 2002.

145

It was about that time when South Carolina's Spencer Clark raced untouched for a 77-yard touchdown to cut the lead to 24–7. During the next eight minutes, the Tigers could do nothing right and USC could do no wrong.

On Clemson's next three possessions, it fumbled the ball, went three-and-out, and then shanked a punt 10 yards. USC took advantage of each mistake to crawl back in the game with two Steve Dorsey touchdowns to make the score 24–20.

With 7:02 to play, South Carolina again gained possession of the football and had a chance to take the lead for the first time all night as they moved the ball to the Clemson 40.

"We called a pass route we had not run all day," South Carolina receiver Phil Logan said years later. "The defense backpedaled, and I curled."

When Logan curled, quarterback Ron Ross delivered a strike. It was fourth-and-10 at the Clemson 40, and USC seemed desperate to make one last play to at least extend the drive. What Logan did not expect was to be so wide open.

"I expected to be hit, but nobody was there," he said. "I cut across the field, got some blocks, and I was never touched."

Logan's 40-yard touchdown gave the Gamecocks a 27–24 lead with 1:48 to play. Logan and his teammates were so confident the game was over that Logan was seen lifting his jersey to the crowd, revealing a game T-shirt underneath with white letters that read, "No Cigar Today."

It appeared to motivate the entire Clemson offense. Facing a third-and-7 from the Clemson 36-yard line, Fuller hit Rick Weddington for 26 yards to the South Carolina 38-yard line and a first down. After an incompletion, Fuller found Clark across the middle for 18 yards, setting up Clemson at the 20.

The Tigers quickly rushed to the line to run another play when Fuller noticed South Carolina's defense was confused and having trouble getting players onto the field. The play called for Butler to cut to the corner, but USC put pressure on Fuller and forced him to throw the ball earlier than he would have liked.

"I saw the ball headed toward the middle of the field," Butler said. "He was dumping the ball out of the end zone, but I jumped and got my hands on the ball, and I knew if I got my hands on the ball, I could catch it."

Butler made a leaping, twisting catch that no one else could have made in the game, and no one else has made since.

"It was a first-down play. We had plenty of time, and I threw it where he would catch it or it would be incomplete," Fuller said. "Nine times out of ten, it would have been incomplete."

Instead, it's a play simply known as "The Catch." The 20-yard pass play gave Clemson the lead, and with the extra point Clemson led 31–27 with 49 seconds left. The Tigers held on to defeat the Gamecocks.

The Catch II

Except for the 10,000 or so South Carolina fans that had made the trip up from Columbia, there was an eerie silence in Clemson Memorial Stadium in 2000 when tight end Tommy Hill fell on a Derek Watson fumble in the end zone to give the Gamecocks a 14–13 lead with 59 seconds to play.

For most of the 85,500 who were in attendance on that cold and damp evening, all had felt lost. But Clemson quarterback Woodrow Dantzler was not among them. As South Carolina set up to kick off, Dantzler gathered up the offense and sent them a message.

"I told them that this is not about to happen," he said to reporters afterward. "We're not going to let this happen to our seniors."

It took a controversial catch from one of those seniors, All-American Rod Gardner, to make the 98th battle of the Palmetto State's two biggest schools one of the best and most talked about games in the long-standing rivalry.

With only 19 seconds left, Dantzler led the Tigers back on the field following a timeout while staring at a third-and-12 situation from their own 42. When he took the shotgun snap, Dantzler rolled to his left, drawing the safety away from Gardner. He then stopped and threw a high, deep log to the right.

Gardner, who caught the decisive 29-yard touchdown the year before against the Gamecocks on a fourth-down play, ran a

It's known simply as "The Catch II." (Photo courtesy of the Clemson University Sports Information Department)

go-route down the far sideline. South Carolina had cornerback Andre Goodman underneath in coverage and safety Deandre Eiland deep as the ball went sailing through the air.

"It was in slow motion," Gardner said. "I wasn't even thinking about the defender. I just knew I had to make a play, and when it dropped into my hand, oh man."

Everyone in the stadium held their collective breaths as Gardner leaped high to haul in the 50-yard pass while falling backward. When he settled to the ground, Clemson had the football at the South Carolina 8-yard line with 10 seconds left and needed just a 25-yard Aaron Hunt field goal to win the game.

"I'm still trying to figure out what happened," Dantzler said.

Hunt was true on his kick, and Clemson celebrated into the night with a dramatic 16–14 victory.

"The rivalry, I didn't even really know about it until I got here," said Hunt, who was a freshman for Tennessee that year. "So it was all talk up until tonight. Now I know what it's really like. It's a privilege to have a chance like that, and it's awesome to make the kick."

The Gamecocks, on the other hand, were beside themselves and felt as if they were robbed of a victory by the officials. Goodman and Gamecock fans alike said Gardner pushed off to create separation.

"I looked at the ref and I know he was going to pull the flag," Goodman said. "He looked at me and smiled. I said, 'You had to see that.' He just smiled and shook his head. That rule is so funny. Sometimes it's called and sometimes it isn't."

Gardner saw it differently.

"I didn't touch him. I was playing the ball," he said.

Other than Gardner, everyone involved was surprised there was no flag thrown on what turned out to be the biggest single play in the history of the rivalry since Jerry Butler's leaping touchdown reception in the final seconds gave the Tigers a victory in 1977.

Prior to Gardner's catch, the two teams were flagged a combined 20 times for 188 yards. Clemson was called for four pass interference penalties that night, and former head coach Tommy Bowden admitted, by the way the game was being called, he was surprised he did not see one on that play.

"I know we probably had four interference calls and they had one. I was really surprised," he said. "From what I saw earlier, yeah, I was surprised. If it's up in the air, there was an interference call. Any time we threw a pass up. I thought there would be a flag called."

Former South Carolina head coach Lou Holtz was extremely angry following the game. He would later say Gardner's push-off was blatant. Because of the way the game was officiated, the Gamecocks coach never felt they had the game won when Hill landed on Watson's fumble in the end zone with 59 seconds to play.

"You never think you have it won. Not as long as there are 29 people on the field," he said.

The way Gardner saw it, it wasn't the officials who won the game; he just made a play when the opportunity came.

"I knew I had to make a play to win the game," he said. "We didn't want to lose the game like that."

Gardner finished his Clemson career as the all-time leading receiver in receptions (166) and yards (2,498) and was the first receiver in school history to record back-to-back 1,000-yard seasons. He was drafted 15th overall by the Washington Redskins in the first round of the 2001 NFL Draft.

41 1988 Citrus Bowl

January 1, 1988
Orlando, Florida
Clemson 35, Penn State 10

Everything went the Tigers' way as Clemson soundly defeated Joe Paterno's Penn State team by the score of 35–10. It is still the largest margin of defeat for a Joe Paterno–coached football team. Rodney Williams was selected as the Citrus Bowl's Most Valuable Player as he led the Tigers in a brilliant air attack that took the Nittany Lions by complete surprise, and the offense complemented it with a solid ground game.

The win was Danny Ford's fourth bowl victory in only nine seasons as Clemson's head coach. It also marked Rodney Williams' second bowl victory in his three-year playing career at Clemson and the second consecutive year that he was named the MVP of a postseason bowl. In 1986, Williams won the honor as the Tigers defeated Stanford in the Gator Bowl.

Williams, who was also named the Offensive Player of the Game, completed 14-of-24 passes for 214 yards. His primary target was wide receiver Keith Jennings, who hauled in seven passes for 110 yards, his best performance. Wideout Gary Cooper also added four receptions for 56 yards against Penn State.

The Tigers rushed for 285 yards against Penn State to go with the 214 yards passing. It was the first bowl game in which Clemson had at least 200 yards passing and 200 yards rushing. Terry Allen was the leading rusher with 105 yards and one touchdown. Fullback Tracy Johnson ran for 88 yards and three touchdowns. Joe Henderson added 54 yards on the ground and another touchdown.

Defensively, Clemson was led by James Lott's eight tackles. Safety Richard Smith also had seven tackles and one pass broken up. Strong safety Gene Beasley and linebacker Doug Brewster both had six tackles.

Linebacker Dorian Mariable was selected the Citrus Bowl's Defensive Player of the Game with his five tackles, including one for a loss. He also intercepted a pass in the end zone and returned it 46 yards in the third quarter.

CLEMSON	7	7	7	14	35
PSU	0	7	3	0	10
CU T. Johnson 7 run (Treadwell kick), 1st, 10:42					
PSU Alexander 39 pass from Knizner (Etze kick), 2nd, 12:51					
CU T. Johnson 6 run (Treadwell kick), 2nd, 9:14					
PSU Etze 27 FG, 3rd, 10:54					
CU Allen 25 run (Treadwell kick), 4th, 12:38					
CU Henderson 4 run (Treadwell kick), 4th, 0:25					
Attendance: 53,152					

1989 Citrus Bowl

January 1, 1989
Orlando, Florida
Clemson 13, Oklahoma 6

The Tigers rang in the New Year in fine fashion with a 13–6 victory over the Oklahoma Sooners, moving into the top 10 of the final AP poll for the first time since 1982 with a No. 9 ranking. The victory also gave Danny Ford a victory over the winningest active coach in Division I, Barry Switzer. Ford defeated the top three winningest

Clemson's Best Three-Year Stretch

In many ways, Clemson has had its best three-year stretch in school history. The Tigers have 31 wins in the last three years, the most in history for a three-year period. The same goes for the Tigers' 20 ACC regular-season wins in the last three years. Clemson has won 14 ACC games in the last two years, and all 14 have been by double digits.

The Tigers finished 10–4 in 2011 and won the ACC Championship, 11–2 and in the top 10 of the *USA Today* poll in 2012, the school's first top 10 finish since 1990, and 11–2 with a top 12 ranking in 2013.

Clemson has won 10+ games each of the last three years, a first for the program since the 1987–90 era when the Tigers had a four-year streak. Clemson is one of just seven schools nationally that had already clinched a third straight 10-win season. The others are Alabama, Northern Illinois, Oklahoma, Oregon, South Carolina, and Stanford.

In overall wins, Clemson is tied for eighth in the nation with 31. Ohio State is tied for 10th in the nation with 30.

Wins by FBS Schools (2011–13)

Rk School	2011	2012	2013	Total
1. Alabama	12–1	13–1	11–2	36–4
2. Northern Illinois	11–3	12–2	12–2	35–7
3. Florida State	9–4	12–2	14–0	35–6
4. Oregon	12–2	12–1	11–2	35–5
5. Stanford	11–2	12–2	11–3	34–7
6. Louisiana State	13–1	10–3	10–3	33–7
7. South Carolina	11–2	11–2	11–2	33–6
8. Clemson	10–4	11–2	11–2	32–8
9. Boise State	12–1	11–2	8–5	31–8
10. Ohio State	6–7	12–0	12–2	30–9
11. Georgia	10–4	12–2	8–5	30–11
12. Michigan State	11–3	7–6	13–1	31–10
13. Oklahoma State	12–1	8–5	10–3	30–9
14. Oklahoma	10–3	10–3	11–2	31–8

active coaches in the decade with wins over Switzer, Tom Osborne (Nebraska), and Joe Paterno (Penn State).

Although the Tigers faced a wishbone offense for the first time since Ford became head coach, the Clemson defense came through with flying colors, holding the Sooners to only 116 yards and no touchdowns on the ground.

The game was a defensive struggle, as the two teams failed to combine for 500 yards of total offense. The first five series of the first quarter ended in punts for both teams. Late in the period, the Sooners drove down to the Clemson 1-yard line, and the Tigers defense faced a first-and-goal situation. Outside linebacker Levon Kirkland stopped the ballcarrier for no gain on first down. On second down Jesse Hatcher sacked Jamelle Holieway at the 19. After an incomplete pass, the Sooners were forced to settle for a field goal.

Doug Brewster intercepted a pass early in the second quarter to set up the Tigers' first score, a 20-yard field goal by Chris Gardocki. With time running out in the first half, Gardocki put the Tigers up with another kick, this time a 46-yarder.

A fumble in the third quarter gave the Sooners the opportunity to take the lead, but the Tigers defense held and R.D. Lashar hit again from 30 yards. The Tigers responded on the next series, driving 80 yards in 15 plays for the game's only touchdown, as Terry Allen scored on a four-yard run. Allen, the game's Most Valuable Player, rushed for 25 yards and caught two passes for 17 yards on the drive.

Defensive MVP Jesse Hatcher caused and recovered a fumble on the Sooners' next drive, but the Sooners would have one more opportunity to score. After a punt, Oklahoma drove from its own 20 to the Clemson 14, as Hollieway put the Tigers' secondary to the test by putting the ball in the air. On the last play of the game, freshman Dexter Davis knocked down a pass in the end zone to seal the Tigers victory.

Terry Allen was named MVP. Allen rushed only for 53 yards, his season low, but scored the game's only touchdown and caught four passes for 47 yards to lead all Tigers receivers.

CLEMSON	0	6	0	7	13
OKLAHOMA	3	0	3	0	6

OKL   Lashar 33 FG, 1st, 0:00
CU   Gardocki 20 FG, 2nd, 7:10
CU   Gardocki 46 FG, 2nd, 0:00
OKL   Lashar 30 FG, 3rd, 2:17
CU   Allen 4 run (Seyle kick), 4th, 10:28

Attendance: 53,571

Head Coach Dabo Swinney

At 44 years old, Dabo Swinney is one of the youngest head coaches in the ACC and the country. However, his resume is already stuffed with many significant accomplishments on a school, ACC, and national level.

His mere appointment to the position was significant. In October 2008, he was named Clemson interim head coach, replacing Tommy Bowden, who had been his position coach as a player at Alabama and was Clemson's head coach since 1999. He led the Tigers to a 4–2 record over the remainder of the 2008 regular season, including a victory over Steve Spurrier's South Carolina Gamecocks in the regular-season finale that led to a Gator Bowl bid against Nebraska.

On December 1, 2008, the interim tag was removed from the title and he was named the program's head coach. At the time,

Dabo Swinney is the head coach of the Clemson Tigers. (Photo courtesy of the Clemson University Sports Information Department)

there had been 28 interim head coaches at the FBS level since 1970, and those coaches had a combined record of 26–86–2. Only one of those 28 interim coaches posted a winning record, and that was Swinney. When he was hired as the head coach, Swinney became just the second interim coach to be elevated to the head coach position at the same school during that time period.

In six years (five full seasons) as the Tigers' head coach, Swinney has directed Clemson to a 50–23 overall record (.685) and a 33–12 ACC regular-season mark (.733). He has also led the Tigers to the ACC Championship Game twice, won one ACC Championship, won or shared three ACC Atlantic Division titles, and has been named national Coach of the Year.

In addition to leading the program to six bowl games on the field in his young career, his players have excelled in the classroom. During the 2010–11, 2011–12, and 2012–13 academic years, the Clemson football program finished in the top 10 in the nation in APR scores.

Clemson has recorded double-digit victories for the third year in a row in 2013 (10–3) after finishing 7–1 in ACC regular-season games for the second year in a row. The Tigers had a 4–0 record in ACC road games, the first time that has happened since 1995.

The Tigers were No. 12 in the final 2013 BCS standings. It marked the third straight year Clemson finished in the top 15 of the BCS standings—one of only six schools in the nation that can make that claim. Clemson is also one of only five programs that has been ranked in the top 20 of every BCS standing each of the last three years.

For the fourth time in his first five full seasons as head coach at Clemson, Swinney was a finalist (top 10) for the Liberty Mutual National Coach of the Year Award in 2013. Swinney was also one of the 16 semifinalists for national Coach of the Year by the Maxwell Football Club Collegiate Coach of the Year Award for the second year in a row.

The Clemson offense has continued to put up record-setting numbers in 2013, as it has averaged 40.2 points and 502.0 yards per game. The Tigers defense is also in the top 25 in the nation in scoring defense, total defense, and turnovers forced.

The 2012 season was a groundbreaking year for the Tigers when looking at the overall consistency of the program. With an 11–2 overall record, including a 7–1 ACC mark, Clemson put back-to-back 10-win seasons together for the first time since a four-year streak from 1987–90.

The seven conference wins in the regular season set a school record. Clemson was co-champion of the ACC Atlantic Division and has won or shared the division crown three of the last five years. The school record for consecutive home wins (13) was also established, as was the record for consecutive wins by at least 14 points (7).

With Clemson's thrilling 25–24 win over No. 7 Louisiana State in the 2012 Chick-fil-A Bowl, the Tigers finished the season ranked No. 9 in the *USA Today* poll. It was Clemson's first top 10 finish in one of the two major polls since 1990. Clemson also reached the 11-win mark for the first time since its 1981 national championship season and for only the fourth time in school history. The Tigers finished No. 14 in the final BCS standing, as well.

The 2012 campaign featured a record-setting offense. Clemson had six of the 11 offensive players on the All-ACC first team chosen by media and set more than 80 school team and individual records.

Swinney was a finalist for the 2012 Liberty Mutual National Coach of the Year Award for the third time. He was also one of 16 semifinalists for national Coach of the Year by Maxwell Football Club Collegiate Coach of the Year Award.

Swinney's 2011 squad, which ended the season ranked No. 22 in the nation, captured Clemson's first ACC Championship

Three Claps

When a speaker comes to talk with the Clemson football team, Swinney will tell his players to give three claps as the distinguished guest comes in the room, out of honor and respect.

When Swinney walked into the meeting room at the McFadden Building on December 1, 2008, to tell the team he was going to be named Clemson's 25th head coach, safety Michael Hamlin asked the team to stand up and give Swinney three claps.

"I thought that was a great moment," Hamlin said. "That's a guy with great courage, and he always believes in himself and in the team. He always puts the players first, and that is what you want out of a coach."

It was an emotional day for Swinney, who somehow fought through the ashes of what looked like a season gone down in flames after Bowden's resignation and came out a winner. But in seven short weeks, Sweeney rallied the team, the school, and the community and persevered through it all.

in Charlotte, North Carolina. It tied for the highest-ranked team the Tigers have defeated in history. The victory, the Tigers' second over the Hokies in 2011, gave Clemson its first 10-win season since 1990. The Tigers' four wins over top 25 ranked teams established a school record, as well.

The Tigers jumped out to an 8–0 record and a No. 6 national ranking after being unranked in the preseason. Games 3–5 marked a tough stretch as Clemson hosted No. 19 Auburn, who entered with a national-best 17-game winning streak, and No. 11 Florida State along with a road game at No. 10 Virginia Tech. The Tigers were victorious in all three contests by scores of 38–24, 35–30, and 23–3 respectively, making the first time in history that an ACC team won three consecutive games over top 25 ranked (AP) teams. Clemson also held Virginia Tech without a touchdown for the first time in a game at Blacksburg since 1995.

Unique Swinney

Unique is another word to describe Dabo Swinney, and it has nothing to do with X's and O's. Swinney has a deal under Clemson's licensing program to sell merchandise with his name and a personal deal with Collegiate License Company. His deal with CLC is the only one of its kind with an active coach. "I think there's a value to Dabo's name and likeness, and it's to a point now where it can be broken out separately and compensated separately," Swinney's agent, Mike Brown, explained.

For his efforts, Swinney was named Bobby Dodd National Coach of the Year in 2011 to become the first Tigers head coach to win a national Coach of the Year award since 1981, when Danny Ford directed Clemson to the national title.

Swinney, who was also one of the five finalists for the Eddie Robinson National Coach of the Year Award, one of 10 finalists for the Bear Bryant National Coach of the Year Award, one of 10 finalists for the Liberty Mutual Coach of the Year Award, and received the Regional AFCA Coach of the Year Award in 2011, led the Tigers to their first Orange Bowl berth since 1981 with the help of five First Team All-ACC players.

Swinney became just the second Tigers coach to lead Clemson's program into a bowl game in his first two full years as head coach, joining his predecessor, Bowden. The 2010 schedule was one of the most challenging in school history, as nine bowl teams were on the regular-season slate and two of the four non-conference opponents were ranked in the top 25 when they played the Tigers, just the second time in 21 years the Tigers faced two top 25 conference opponents in the regular season.

The 2010 season included wins over bowl teams Georgia Tech, Maryland, and N.C. State. N.C. State was ranked No. 23 in the nation and was leading the ACC in scoring. But the defense held N.C. State and Russell Wilson to just one touchdown and 13 points. The team excelled defensively in 2010 and was third in the nation in scoring defense and in the top 25 in both total defense and passing defense.

In 2009, Swinney's first full year as head coach, he led the Tigers to their first championship of the ACC's Atlantic Division. The Tigers came just six points short of winning their first ACC title in 18 years. Swinney was named ACC Coach of the Year by *The Sporting News* and was a finalist for the Liberty Mutual Coach of the Year Award.

Swinney accumulated nine wins, second-most among all FBS coaches in their first full year behind Oregon's Chip Kelly. The nine wins tied for fourth-most in ACC history for a first-year head coach. He also led the Tigers to their first bowl win since 2005 in the 21–13 victory over Kentucky in the Music City Bowl.

Swinney hit the ground running in his first week as interim head coach, as he prepared for a 5–1 Georgia Tech team. He had to re-organize his staff and regroup his team and Clemson Nation in just five days. While the Tigers lost by four points, he accomplished many goals in that first week through his outstanding leadership. One of the most impressive demonstrations of unity came during the team's "Tiger Walk."

He has continued his community involvement through his foundation. His foundation made the first contribution to the cancer fund established for former Boston College linebacker Mark Herzlich. Many schools followed his lead the remainder of the season.

The Liberty Mutual Coach of the Year Award evaluates coaching performance in terms of coaching excellence, sportsmanship, integrity, academic excellence, and community commitment. It is easy to see why Swinney was a national finalist for that award in his first full season as head coach in 2009, and again in both 2011 and 2012.

2008 (4–3, 3–2 ACC)

Date	Opponent (Rank)	W-L	Score
10–18	***Georgia Tech**	**L**	**17–21**
11–1	*at Boston College	W	27–21
11–8	*at Florida State (24,24	L	27–41
11–15	***Duke**	**W**	**31–7**
11–22	*at Virginia	W	13–3
11–29	**South Carolina**	**W**	**31–14**
1–1	$ Nebraska	L	21–26

$ - Gator Bowl at Jacksonville, FL

2009 (9–5, 6–2 ACC)

Date	Opponent (Rank)	W-L	Score
9–5	**Middle Tennessee**	**W**	**37–14**
9–10	*at Georgia Tech (15,13)	L	27–30
9–19	***Boston College**	**W**	**25–7**
9–26	**TCU (15,14)**	**L**	**10–14**
10–3	*at Maryland	L	21–24
10–17	***Wake Forest**	**W**	**38–3**
10–24	*at Miami (FL) (8,9)	W	40–37
10–31	**Coastal Carolina**	**W**	**49–3**
11–7	***Florida State**	**W**	**40–24**
11–14	*at N.C. State	W	43–23
11–21	***Virginia**	**W**	**34–21**
11–28	at South Carolina	L	17–34
12–5	# Georgia Tech (12,12)	L	34–39
12–27	$ Kentucky	W	21–13

- ACC Championship game at Tampa, FL; $ - Music City Bowl at Nashville, TN

2010 (6–7, 4–4 ACC)

Date	Opponent (Rank)	W-L	Score
9–4	**North Texas**	**W**	**35–10**
9–11	**Presbyterian College**	**W**	**58–21**
9–18	at Auburn (16,15)	L	24–27
10–2	***Miami (FL)**	**L**	**21–30**
10–9	*at North Carolina	L	16–21
10–16	***Maryland**	**W**	**31–7**
10–23	***Georgia Tech**	**W**	**27–13**

10-30	*at Boston College	L	10-16
11-6	***N.C. State (23,25)**	**W**	**14-13**
11-13	*at Florida State	L	13-16
11-20	*at Wake Forest	W	30-10
11-27	**South Carolina (18,17)**	**L**	**7-29**
12-31	$ South Florida	L	26-31

$ - Meineke Car Care Bowl at Charlotte N.C.

2011 (10–4, 6–2 ACC)

Date	Opponent (Rank)	W-L	Score
9-3	**Troy**	**W**	**43-19**
9-10	**Wofford**	**W**	**35-27**
9-17	**Auburn (21,19)**	**W**	**38-24**
9-24	***Florida State (11,14)**	**W**	**35-30**
10-1	*at Virginia Tech (11,10)	W	23-3
10-8	***Boston College**	**W**	**36-14**
10-15	*at Maryland	W	56-45
10-22	***North Carolina**	**W**	**59-38**
10-29	*at Georgia Tech	L	17-31
11-12	***Wake Forest**	**W**	**31-28**
11-19	*at N.C. State	L	13-37
11-26	at South Carolina (14,13)	L	13-34
12-3	#Virginia Tech (5,3)	W	38-10
1-4	$ West Virginia (23,22)	L	33-70

- ACC Championship game at Charlotte, NC; $ - Orange Bowl at Miami Gardens, FL

2012 (11–2, 6–1 ACC)

Date	Opponent (Rank)	W-L	Score
9-1	Auburn	W	26-19
9-8	**Ball State**	**W**	**52-27**
9-15	**Furman**	**W**	**41-7**
9-22	*Florida State	L	37-49
9-29	*Boston College	W	45-31
10-6	***Georgia Tech**	**W**	**47-31**
10-20	***Virginia Tech**	**W**	**38-17**
10-25	*Wake Forest	W	42-13
11-3	Duke	W	56-20
11-10	***Maryland**	**W**	**45-10**

11–17	*N.C. State	W	62–48
11–24	South Carolina	L	17–27
12–31	$Louisiana State	W	25–24

*ACC game; $- Chick-fil-A Bowl—Atlanta, GA

2013 (11–2, 7–1 ACC)

Date	Opponent (Rank)	W-L	Score
8–31	Georgia	W	38–35
9–7	S.C. State	W	52–13
9–19	*N.C. State	W	26–14
9–28	*Wake Forest	W	56–7
10–5	*Syracuse	W	49–14
10–12	*Boston College	W	24–14
10–19	*Florida State	L	14–51
10–26	*Maryland	W	40–27
11–2	*Virginia	W	59–10
11–14	*Georgia Tech	W	55–31
11–23	The Citadel	W	52–6
11–30	South Carolina	L	17–31
1–3	$Ohio State	W	40–35

*ACC game; $- Orange Bowl—Miami Gardens, FL

44 Tajh Boyd

The dossier Tajh Boyd completed at Phoebus High School in Virginia didn't go unnoticed by a number of major colleges. Not when Boyd was rated the No. 3 prospect in the nation. Boyd twice led his team to the Virginia state football title while authoring a 43–2 record during four years. At any level of football that's big-time impressive and made Phoebus a big-time powerhouse in the state.

Clemson's chances of landing Boyd were slim at best. He originally committed to West Virginia but withdrew. He decided he would rather play for Coach Phillip Fulmer at Tennessee and received a verbal acceptance. However, when Fulmer was fired, new coach Lane Kiffin didn't want him. Boyd then sorted out the other offers he had.

"Ohio State and Oregon were after me pretty hard," Boyd disclosed. "I visited Clemson on a quiet weekend and had a chance to visit with Coach Dabo Swinney and liked what he had envisioned that could be built with the football program."

However, he had to wait a year before he could be part of the blueprint. Clemson had quarterback Kyle Parker around for another season, and he along with C.J. Spiller led the Tigers to their first ACC Atlantic Division crown in 2009 and a victory over Kentucky in the Music City Bowl.

In 2010, when Boyd saw his first action, it was in a backup role behind quarterback Kyle Parker. In limited action, he completed 33-of-63 passes for 329 yards and four touchdowns. Average at best.

As a sophomore, Boyd had a breakout campaign as the starting signal caller. He took the Tigers to three wins in a record-breaking style that raised eyebrows. The wins were over three ranked teams: No. 21 Auburn; No. 11 Florida State; and No. 11 Virginia Tech. It was the first time an ACC school won three straight victories against ranked teams.

Boyd established himself with a record-shattering season. He completed 59.7 percent of his aerials while grinding out 218 yards on the ground, 4,046 total yards, and a school record 38 total touchdowns. By the season's end, he had validated himself as a household name. He was named a first team All-American and the ACC's Player of the Year—the first Tigers quarterback to be so honored.

Tajh Boyd on the run. (Photo courtesy of the Clemson University Sports Information Department)

"What you like to see is Tajh growing," offensive coordinator Chad Morris said. "It means something to him. He's passionate about it. He wants to do good and sometimes he tries too hard."

It took Morris, in his first year as offensive coordinator, to bring the best out of Boyd. And Boyd's success continued to grow as a junior. In the first two games of the 2012 season, Boyd demonstrated how much. He completed 75 percent of his passes, 43-of-57, for 437 yards and four touchdowns.

"I feel like we're mature," Boyd observed. "But I feel like we're not close to our peak of what we can do."

Boyd continued to light up the scoreboard against Florida State but this time in a painful 49–37 loss. It bothered Boyd so much that when the Tigers reported for practice on Monday, he called a players-only meeting. He acted on his own with Swinney's permission.

"I'm glad he did," Swinney agreed. "Tajh isn't just the quarterback, he's the leader. That's what you want to see."

And lead Boyd did. The Tigers went on a seven-game winning streak, losing only to South Carolina at the end to finish 11–2 with a final victory over LSU in Atlanta's Chick-fil-A Bowl.

The only question that remained before Boyd's senior season was whether or not he would leave for the NFL. The last Clemson quarterback drafted was Charlie Whitehurst after the 2005 season. Boyd was rated higher but decided to remain on campus.

"I came back because I wanted to have fun and leave a legacy here," Boyd said. "The opportunity we have here this year to impact Clemson and change for the better is awesome."

Under Morris, Boyd thrived. He elevated his game to a high level and produced eye-popping numbers with 21 victories in the past two years. Going into his third season as a starter, Boyd was looked upon as a Heisman Trophy candidate.

And he had the statistics to merit the mention. Boyd had already established 51 school records and still had another year to embellish more. All but 11 of them came last season while playing in one less game the year before.

Boyd lit up the Clemson night sky in the opener against Georgia, an exciting 38–35 victory. He accounted for all five touchdowns with 312 total yards. With 11 games still remaining, Boyd was already first in school history in passing touchdowns, first in passing efficiency, and first in touchdown responsibility.

In the Tigers' fifth straight win against Syracuse, Boyd gave Clemson fans plenty to cheer about in a 49–14 romp. In one of his most dominating performances, he threw for 455 yards and five touchdowns. He was the face of the program and a strong Heisman contender with a shot at a national championship.

In a convincing 59–10 rout of Virginia a month later, Boyd manufactured four touchdowns and became the ACC's all-time leader in total touchdowns with 116.

Even though the regular season ended on a sour note with a 31–17 loss to South Carolina, Clemson still finished with an 11–2 record, an Orange Bowl victory over Ohio State, and ranked eighth in the AP poll.

Boyd had a prolific career, one that made him perhaps the best quarterback in the school's history. He has his name on 58 Clemson records, including ACC marks for career touchdown responsibility (133), passing touchdowns (107), and passing efficiency (155.2).

He started each of the Tigers' games, a record for consecutive starts in which Boyd won 32, tied (with Rodney Williams) for most career wins by a Clemson quarterback. He was also one of just three active FBS players with at least 1,000 passing yards and 1,000 rushing yards.

Boyd definitely left a legacy…

45 Sammy Watkins

The Florida schools were after him, Miami, Florida State, and Florida. But Sammy Watkins wanted Clemson ever since he was a sophomore star at South Fort Myers High School. He didn't speak out but kept it a secret between him and his mother. It was Clemson coach Brad Scott who influenced Watkins, a top 50 recruit, as a wide receiver.

Sammy Watkins holds several Clemson receiving records. (Photo courtesy of the Clemson University Sports Information Department)

"Coach Brad was the first one," Watkins remembered. "I liked him right away because he kept it real. He was always around. He came down every two weeks to watch me play. But it wasn't always about football. He came to my house and we went out to eat. My parents loved him."

It didn't take long for the coaching staff and the fans to love Watkins. The coaches were surprised to see the volume of notes Watkins compiled from just one meeting at preseason practice. At least six pages and then some. Watkins was determined to learn the offense quickly.

And he did. In his very first game he made an immediate impact against Troy in 2011. On the second play of the game, Watkins caught 33-yard pass from Tajh Boyd and ran untouched for a touchdown. He finished his debut with seven receptions for 81 yards.

That was only the beginning. There was more to come in what would be an electrifying freshman season by any Tigers player. Two weeks later against defending national champion Auburn, Watkins made it look easy with 10 catches worth 155 yards and two touchdowns.

Before the Florida State game the following week, Seminoles coach Jumbo Fisher was well aware of Watkins and paid him a high compliment.

"He's just a phenomenal player," Fisher praised. "He's the most impactful freshman maybe since Herschel Walker. Sammy made that kind of impact the day that he came in."

That became evident when the season ended. He established freshman records with 82 receptions, 1,219 yards, and 12 touchdowns, and he led the nation in reception yards per game, all-purpose yards, and touchdowns in breaking 11 school records.

"I thought I would have at least a decent season playing in Coach Morris' offense," Watkins remarked. "Coach Morris did a great job of pushing me to work hard, to stay in the weight room, and to watch film. I was able to take my play from practice to the game."

No one was more ecstatic about Watkins' first year than Coach Dabo Swinney. He knew Watkins was good but never realized how much.

"I knew Sammy was special, but he did some things that were shocking," Swinney exclaimed. "I never thought some of C.J. Spiller's records would be broken, but it took Sammy just seven games to break his single-season all-purpose yards when he had 345 yards at Maryland. That was quite a performance."

Watkins' sophomore season couldn't come soon enough. He expected more, and so did the coaches. Everyone expected his 2012 season to be even more spectacular. No one saw it, but it didn't come easy for him. He missed the opening two games because of an infraction. When he got back on the field, he was slowed by minor injuries and only showed flashes of himself like a 202-yard game against Wake Forest to set yet another school record.

Still, his numbers would be a model for other receivers. In 10 games, he produced 57 catches for 708 yards. When looking at it closely, he had more catches per game than his All-American freshman year.

"I wasn't in the same mindset from my first year," Watkins acknowledged. "Missing the first two games held me back. I didn't meet my expectations."

He did his junior season, which would be his final one. It was one of redemption—and did he ever achieve. In only half a season, Watkins stirred excitement with 36 receptions for 582 yards and four touchdowns, all team highs.

"My goal is to keep getting better every game," Watkins disclosed. "I want to keep being a leader for the team."

And lead he did. Watkins finished with 101 receptions for 1,464 yards and 12 touchdowns. He saved his best for the last game. He was named MVP of the Orange Bowl by setting a record with 16 catches for 200 yards. Watkins also set a Clemson record for career receptions with 240, and he had 3,392 receiving yards, another school record.

46 Brian Dawkins

One of the best memories strong safety Brian Dawkins has from his career at Clemson is an interception he made against North Carolina in 1995.

The Tigers were up 10–0 at the time, and the Tar Heels were threatening when he stepped in front of a North Carolina pass and took it back for a touchdown. It was his only touchdown of his four-year career at Clemson. And it turned out to be a big one, too, as UNC rallied to score the last 10 points of the game.

"That was a memorable play because of the significance of the game," he said. "At the time they were making a comeback on us and to make that play, it put the game away. That's something I will always remember."

That following week, the Clemson star had three interceptions in one half against Duke, which tied a Clemson record.

Dawkins finished the 1995 season with six interceptions and nine passes broken up. He also caused one fumble and recovered two while recording 60 tackles. At the end of the year his season was rewarded with All-ACC and All-American status.

He finished his career with 247 tackles and 11 interceptions. He earned his way onto three All-ACC teams, including first-team status during his All-American season in 1995.

Dawkins was named First Team strong safety on Clemson's All-Centennial team in 1996—the only active student athlete named to the team at that time—and was selected to Clemson's Athletic Hall of Fame in 2009.

Dawkins credited former Clemson defensive backs coach Charlie Harbison for helping him get to All-American status as well as prepping him for the NFL.

"When I got to the NFL, I knew the technique. I didn't have to learn as much technique-wise," Dawkins said.

Dawkins learned enough under Harbison to become one of the best and most feared safeties in the game. A second-round pick in the 1996 NFL Draft by the Philadelphia Eagles, he started 13 of the 14 games he played in, recording 75 tackles, a sack, and three interceptions. During his Eagles career, Dawkins earned seven Pro Bowl selections in 1999, 2001, 2002, 2004, 2005, 2006, and 2008. He played in five conference championship games and one Super Bowl, as well.

He was also a Pro Bowl selection in 2009 and 2011 as a member of the Denver Broncos. In all, he played in 224 games during his 16-year career. His 16 seasons in the NFL is tied with former kicker/punter Chris Gardocki for the most years by a Clemson player in the NFL.

"I don't know anyone that comes in this league and expects to play 16 years," Dawkins said. "There are some that say they are going to play that long, but that's not me. I wanted to make the team and have a successful career. The thing I always told myself is that I wanted to be a consistent player throughout the duration of my career.

"As you start to play a little bit, you start to research and you ask guys who have played a long time what do they do. You make your own plan from there."

That plan has helped Dawkins do many things in his career. In a 2002 game versus the Houston Texans, he became the first player in the NFL history to record a sack, interception, force a fumble, and catch a touchdown pass in a single game.

During the 2008 season he became the 10th member of the 20/20 interception and sack club and broke the Eagles' record for games played by surpassing Harold Carmichael, who had 180.

When he finished his career with the Eagles, he had started 182-of-183 games, recorded 898 tackles, 34 interceptions, and 21 sacks—good enough to almost assure a spot waiting for his bust in the Pro Football Hall of Fame.

If that happens, it will be an accolade no former Clemson player has ever had bestowed upon him.

"It has crossed my mind and, Lord willing if it does, that would be a tremendous accomplishment for myself and my teammates that have helped me along and believed in me from Little League all the way up to the NFL," Dawkins said. "To know that would be the case, with all the great athletes that have come through Clemson, and that I would be the one to hold that mantle up high for this university, that would be an honor.

"To know that I have played this long and accomplished the things I have accomplished, like all the Pro Bowls and playing 16 years and all of those things. That means it will all be worth it, and when they say 'Brian Dawkins,' and they say 'Clemson University' with it, that will be a special thing to me."

47 Anthony Simmons

When he first came to Clemson, Anthony Simmons wanted to be like the great linebackers that came before him. When he left after his junior year in 1997, he arguably could have been called *the* best.

In his three years at Clemson (1995–97) Simmons recorded 486 tackles, only 29 off the school record Bubba Brown recorded in 1976–79. The middle linebacker also recorded 52 tackles for loss, which is fourth all-time.

"Every player wants to be able to say, 'I left my mark here,'" Simmons said.

Simmons definitely left his mark at Clemson. He is just the second player in Clemson history to earn All-American status three straight years, including consensus first-team status in 1997 when he was a finalist for the Butkus Award, which is given to the nation's best linebacker.

During his last season in Tigertown, Simmons recorded 158 tackles, 25 tackles for loss, and had eight sacks. He even broke up four passes on those rare times he dropped back into coverage.

"He's the greatest pure hitter I've ever seen in college," defensive coordinator Reggie Herring said. "Against Maryland he hit a guy so hard on the goal line it was like a cannon had gone off."

Clemson had its fair share of great linebackers in the day, such as Bubba Brown, Jeff Davis, Levon Kirkland, and Ed McDaniel. But as good as they all were, none of them made the impact Simmons made from the moment he stepped foot on campus.

Just five days into fall camp, Simmons was in the starting lineup, one of the two true freshmen who longtime Clemson sports information director Tim Bourret can remember starting so soon.

During his freshman year, Simmons earned Third Team All-America honors with 150 tackles, including 11 tackles for a loss. In his sophomore year, he set a single-season record at the time with 178 tackles, including 16 for a loss, as he became a First Team All-American player.

After his junior season, he became the first Clemson player to be named First Team All-ACC as a freshman, sophomore, and junior.

One can only wonder what damage Simmons could have done had he not decided to enter the NFL draft after his junior season. Simmons was picked 15th overall by the Seattle Seahawks in the 1998 NFL Draft and had a seven-year career.

48 Fan-Mania and the Tiger Paw

The cars arrive early on football Saturday. At Clemson, it is a way of life. To a stranger, it is a phenomenon. On any one of six Saturdays during the football season, more than 80,000 Clemson fans pack Memorial Stadium to cheer their beloved Tigers. They come from all parts of the state, driving campers, panel trucks, station wagons, pick-up trucks, and just plain automobiles. Yet, the genuine love of these fans for Clemson reaches far beyond the boundaries of South Carolina. The cheering section arrives from the neighboring states of North Carolina, Georgia, Tennessee, and some even from as far as Virginia and Florida.

Their day begins early. They flock to any one of the downtown landmarks on Main Street, such as Mr. Knickerbocker, Ibrahim's Tiger Sports Shop, and a bit later, to Bob Higby's Esso Club. Mr. Knickerbocker is the biggest novelty store in town. It boasts that it sells more Clemson souvenirs than anybody in South Carolina. It probably does. The proprietor, James Spearman, is a long-time resident. Surprisingly enough, he was the town barber for more than

The Color Purple

Clemson's official colors are orange and purple. Clemson used to have purple and gold as the official colors. But football coach and athletic director Jess Neely (1931–39) changed that because he wanted uniforms that were more colorfast. It seems that the weather and constant washing were causing the uniforms to fade. So Neely worked with the Clemson school of textiles and developed deeper colors for uniforms, color that held up under the rays of the sun and the workings of the washing machines. Because of this, Clemson stated using orange and purple in the uniforms.

Annual Parade

The football season at Clemson kicks off each year with the annual Football Friday Parade. It takes place on the Friday afternoon before the first home game. It's a bit of a New Orleans Mardi Gras. Floats from a number of fraternities and sororities and other campus organizations compose the parade that travels down Main Street.

The colorful parade ends at the Amphitheater in the middle of the campus where the first pep rally of the season erupts. The Grand Marshalls of the parade are featured at the rally. Grand Marshalls over the years have ranged from golf professionals like Dillard Pruitt to Clemson Hall of Fame legends like Jess Neely and Frank Howard to television's Brent Musburger and College Hall of Fame coach Ara Parseghian.

20 years. However, when the postwar fad of crew cuts went out of style, he realized it was time to change professions. He then opened a clothing store but had enough vision to change to the novelty business when he saw the fanaticism of Clemson fans continue to grow over the years.

"Clemson people are a different breed," Spearman claimed. "We know that some of them will come out of the woodwork when the Tigers have a good season, but most are going to be there when their team plays. I think that the faithful Clemson football fans know football.

"I was talking to my banker. He was already asking me what bowl the boys were going to. Of course, they don't know that, but everyone it seems wants to know so they can get their reservations in. There are some people who have already made reservations at three or four different places where the big bowls are."

Down the road, Bob Higby is the well-known owner of the Esso Club, a filling station that anyone in Clemson will tell you isn't all that well known for pumping gas. Instead Higby rings up mostly beer sales on his cash register, starting as early as 9:00 in the morning.

"People have said that we sell more beer than gas here, and I think that we do on Saturdays," Higby said. "The place is so crowded that you can't get a car in here for gas, anyway. In the old days people would come by after the game and stay for a little while. Now I have trouble running them off at midnight. They all want to talk."

It is obvious Higby has a deep love for Clemson. His old gas station is truly a spa. A great many out-of-towners use it as a meeting place at night before the game. Thanks to another event entirely. Often, when Clemson plays a fierce rival such as Georgia, Higby's place becomes the home of Clemson Honky Tonk Sympathy Orchestra—a group that specializes in strictly country-bluegrass and square dance music.

"We just get them out there on the lot, and they promenade around the pumps," Higby said.

There seems to be some sort of happening for every Clemson home game. But the best one is the annual First Friday parade that takes place before the first home game of the season. Its aim is to get the student body and the town to be aware that the football season has arrived.

Chris Patterson, who was a senior at Clemson that year, was chairman of the First Friday parade. The march began on Main Street under a huge banner that bore the message, "Curb The Dawgs." The parade finished at the campus amphitheater where a giant pep rally took place.

"First Friday is more of a big party," Patterson explained. "You know, let's get behind the team and beat the hell out of everybody we play. It gets everybody's blood running orange. The parade we had before the Georgia game was the biggest in eight years. We had about 40,000 for the parade and pep rally."

Patterson was quite ambitious. He tried to get Woody Hayes, the former Ohio State coach, as grand marshal of the parade. There was no telling what the reaction would have been. Hayes

The Tiger Paw

The Tiger Paw was running rampant all over the state and beyond. Allison Dalton, Clemson's director of promotions and marketing and a former IPTAY official, was a visionary. In 1979 he saw the potential the Paw presented and began to harness a way that would benefit the university's coffers.

"I was surprised to learn that Clemson had no program to accommodate a new opportunity," Dalton observed. "The most defining evidence was that Clemson had chosen not to officially register the Tiger Paw, which was one of college athletics' most recognizable marks."

Within six months of joining the athletic department in his new position, Dalton sought to register the Tiger Paw with the federal government in Washington.

Clemson's athletic program, especially football, was rapidly gaining national recognition, and it was apparent that the unauthorized use of the Tiger Paw had become widespread.

It was a noble effort on Dalton's part. But it wasn't that simple—at least from a local standpoint. There were dissidents who felt a federal registration would generate negative publicity from merchants and fans who wantonly used the Paw without any restriction on financial gains.

Dalton faced a daunting task. Despite negative opposition, he pursued an arduous challenge in a three-year journey. Clemson's victory over Nebraska for the national championship in the 1982 Orange Bowl was the impetus that Dalton needed. In June 1984, he won approval for the Tiger Paw to become a registered trademark at the U.S. Patent & Trademark Office.

had resigned after the 1978 Gator Bowl in which Ohio State lost to Clemson 17–15.

That game attracted more national attention than any other bowl game that year when Hayes lost his temper and hit Clemson middle guard Charlie Bauman near the game's end.

"Woody Hayes called and turned us down," Patterson said. "He was really nice. He asked me if the rivalry was as big as Ohio

State–Michigan. I told him it was bigger because we're so close together."

There is no way to explain what makes Clemson fans so loyal, so intense. Howard, for all the years he had been at Clemson, couldn't offer an answer. He pondered the thought and just shook his head.

"I'll tell you the truth, I've never seen anything like it," Howard replied. "No other school comes close."

It was a spirit Clemson needed since it had always been known as "the other school in the state."

# Perry Tuttle

The one signature moment for wide receiver Perry Tuttle came in the last game of his Clemson career. It has lived for ages and may never be duplicated. It came at a tense moment in the 1981 championship game against a heavily favored Nebraska team in Miami's Orange Bowl, with Clemson holding a slim 12–7 lead in the closing minutes of the third quarter.

Quarterback Homer Jordan called Tuttle's number in the huddle. Jordan and Tuttle were close. They had developed a binding chemistry with each other, which made Tuttle Jordan's favorite receiver. They were going for the end zone, looking for a touchdown, one that would give Clemson control.

Tuttle raced there and at the precise moment spun, leaped high into the night air, and came down with the ball in his hands for an electrifying touchdown. It would become the clinching one in Clemson's 22–15 upset. The catch was enormous enough to appear on the cover of *Sports Illustrated*. It was the first time a Clemson player was highlighted on an *SI* cover. And, it's been the last.

All throughout the 1981 season, Tuttle lavished praised about Jordan being the focal point of the Tigers offense. He pointed out that every week for the last two years Jordan got better and better. But there was esteem for Tuttle, too. He was being compared to Clemson's all-time receiver, Jerry Butler.

"Tuttle's got a chance to be a great one," beamed coach Danny Ford before the season began. "By that I mean Jerry Butler's class or better than Butler. He's improved a lot."

Tuttle knew the comparison would come in which he was enjoying his best campaign. But he downplayed it.

"I don't think I'll ever be as good as JB," Tuttle intoned. "When I catch the ball, I just sort of razzle-dazzle my way to get a few yards. JB just outruns them. I think Butler is one of the best receivers to ever play college football.

"When I was a freshman, JB told me I could be good, but I don't know how much I believed that. He helped me a lot, not only as a receiver but with the academic side, as well. He pushed me hard on the books. I'm glad he was here then. It wasn't a very happy year for me."

In a run-oriented offense, Tuttle put up big numbers his senior year. He caught 52 passes for 833 yards and a school record eight touchdowns. But he almost never finished his stay at Clemson before it even began. He was a freshman under Coach Charley Pell and actually quit the team.

"The first day at practice, Pell had me lifting weights and running," Tuttle gasped. "It was like torture to me. I wasn't into that stuff. I just wanted to catch the ball. I got sick after the first day of practice. The next day I was more sore then I had ever been, and the third day I'm gone. Packed everything and I drove home."

After a day, Tuttle returned to Clemson and remained there for all four semesters. He finished as the all-time leader in career receptions, reception yards, single season yardage, and most yards receiving by a freshman, sophomore, and junior. Overall, Tuttle set nine records in receiving and caught at least one pass his last 32 games.

Tuttle was drafted in the first round by the Buffalo Bills. But he didn't like the cold and asked for a trade. He got his wish and was traded to Tampa Bay.

"I thought it was great," he smiled. "It was going to be 85 degrees the rest of my life."

On a Wednesday in September, Tuttle was told that he would be in the starting lineup. His joy only lasted for a day. On Thursday when he reported for practice, there was a note on his locker. He thought the coaches wanted to talk to him about starting.

"I walked into Coach John McKay's office and asked, 'Coach, what's up?' He said 'Perry, we've got some bad news. We don't need you anymore.'"

Tuttle left in tears. He went home and took the phone off the hook. He didn't want to talk to anybody. After a while he connected the phone. At that instant, it rang.

"I picked up the phone and this guy said, 'Can I speak to Perry Tuttle?' I said it was me. He said, 'I'm Coach Dan Henning of the Atlanta Falcons, and I've been trying to reach you all afternoon. We made a trade for you earlier today.'"

Tuttle finished the year with the Falcons. But that was his last season of NFL football. He went to the Canadian Football League where he got a chance to play with the Winnipeg Blue Bombers and starred. He earned All-CFL honors and played on the Grey Cup Championship teams. In his six seasons with Winnipeg, he caught 321 passes for 5,817 yards and 41 touchdowns and was elected to the team's Hall of Fame.

50 Terry Allen

As a youngster in Commerce, Georgia, Allen said he always wanted to attend Clemson. But Coach Danny Ford and running back coach Chuck Reedy never even saw him play in high school and didn't really know whether he was going to play offense or defense. In reality, Allen came to Clemson with relatively unspectacular credentials.

"I didn't do anything spectacular in spring practice, but I was consistent," Allen disclosed. "I found out that Coach Ford likes consistency, and I felt confident."

Allen was so confident that he had a record-setting freshman season after first going through a waiting period as a redshirt. Allen burst on the scene in 1987, leading the ACC in rushing with 973 yards on 183 attempts, an average of 5.3 yards a carry. His yardage total broke Kenny Flowers' freshman mark by more than 400 yards. His slashing running style and sure-handed ball carrying fit the Tigers' powerful ground game.

"I've always been that way," Allen disclosed. "I just tried to do what it takes to get some positive yardage. I was taught in high school to run north and south."

While Clemson fans were euphoric about Allen's frosh season, Allen remained low key and focused.

"It's a highly competitive environment here," Allen said. "You've got to love the competition to survive here because the talent at tailback is so high every year.

"I know that I'm going to have to bust it just as hard this year as I did as a freshman. But that's okay. It's the competition that makes you a better player."

Allen was just that. His improvement as a sophomore was evident by the 1,192 yards he produced in averaging 5.5 yards a run. He displayed his talents in the 13–6 Citrus Bowl victory over Oklahoma by being the game's MVP. Star status indeed.

But Allen wouldn't have anything of it.

"There's no way we can get the big head around here," Allen exclaimed. "Coach Ford will see to that. It's funny, but you can look at other teams and say that this guy's a star or that guy's a star. But here at Clemson, we don't see ourselves as having stars."

That was the way Allen approached his junior season. And he was more positive about not only his success but the team's as well after a 10–2 campaign. He was giddy one day at preseason practice when he did a 4.37 in the 40. It dispelled reports of a 4.7 clocking in high school.

"I never paid the 40-time any attention," Allen said. "You don't run like that in a game. It isn't that important. Getting from the tailback position to the line of scrimmage is the most important yards if any. I was always more consistent at getting what we needed rather than breaking the long play."

Allen took the phenomenal success at Clemson in the same stride in which he took practice. "The records don't mean a whole lot," he said. "When I played touch, I didn't think about winning. I didn't thing about much, but I always knew that the records would come. During my red-shirt year, I was talking to a friend one day and I told him we were going to rewrite the record books.

"But that didn't mean that I'm the best running back to have ever played here. The other guys might not have gotten as many chances as I had, or they might have played against better competition. Just because I had more years didn't mean I'm the best."

He played on five different teams in the NFL: Minnesota, Washington, New England, New Orleans, and Baltimore. In 130 games, he gained 10,215 combined yards and scored 73 touchdowns.

51 Joe Blalock

O.K. Pressley was indeed Clemson's first All-American, but Joe Blalock was the school's first two-time All-American. Like Banks McFadden, Blalock was a three-sport athlete. But he could have been more than that in the eyes of one of his teammates.

"Joe could have been a five-sport man had he had the time," Walter Cox believed. "He played football, basketball, and baseball but he could have been a heckuva track man or a boxer."

Blalock, a triple threat at end, was a big reason why Clemson emerged into national prominence during the 1940 season that placed him on the All-American stage. He did so with a fine performance against Wake Forest in a key Southern Conference battle between two unbeaten 3–0 teams. After a scoreless first quarter, Clemson, led by Blalock, caught fire on the way to a 39–0 rout.

First, he blocked a punt to position the Tigers in scoring distance, and he delivered on the very next play. He pulled back from his end spot and calmly threw a touchdown pass. Next, he scored a touchdown on and end around play. His third touchdown was electrifying 45-yard run with an intercepted pass. He finished the game with 105 yards on three receptions.

"Blalock was the best player we had at Clemson at the time," Frank Howard claimed. "I was a young football coach and hadn't had any experience. But Joe was a versatile player in the fact that he could come around from his end position and pass left-handed, and sometimes he wouldn't pass the ball but instead would keep it and run an end around. He was also a good pass receiver. I remember that he was a great football player—not good, but a great one."

Clemson great Banks McFadden also echoed praise for Blalock. Like Blalock, McFadden is one of Clemson's revered athletes.

McFadden played on the 1939 team with Blalock and admired his ability.

"He is one of the most outstanding athletes Clemson ever had," McFadden declared. "He was one of those natural-type people and could have played any number of positions. It didn't seem for him to take any effort in doing anything.

"Joe was exceptional. Boy, what a wingback he would have made on the old single wing formation. Like I said, he could have

Joe Blalock was Clemson's first two-time All-American. (Photo courtesy of the Clemson University Sports Information Department)

played anywhere except the interior line, and he may be able to do that, too."

While Joe DiMaggio was setting his incredible 56-game hitting streak in 1941, Blalock was ending his Clemson career with a 20.34 yards per reception record, one that remains a hallmark. In his career, Blalock had 38 receptions for 773 yards and 11 touchdowns. He was the first receiver in Clemson history to have a 100-yard receiving game.

52 Frank Johnstone Jervey

Frank Jervey wasn't around the Clemson campus quite as long as the clock tower of Tillman Hall, but the presence of his familiar face for decades rivals that of the ever-present tower clock as a symbol of what higher education and one's loyalty and service to his alma mater is all about.

It might be said that serving Clemson University with all his energy and earnestness has been a second career for "Captain Jervey," as he was fondly called, since 1953. That's the year he "retired" from his first profession as a civilian specialist with the Ordnance Corps of the Department of Defense.

Captain Jervey was born in Summerville, South Carolina, in 1893, the year after Tillman Hall was completed. And since his first days as a Clemson cadet in 1910, he nurtured a fierce loyalty and devotion to Clemson, and an unwavering awareness of what this institution means to the youth and economy of the state, region, and nation.

Captain Jervey graduated from Clemson in 1914 with a B.S. degree in mechanical and electrical engineering. When World War I came along, he served with the U.S. Army and was severely wounded in 1918 during the battle for France. He was awarded the Distinguished Service Cross for extraordinary heroism and the Italian Marito de Guerro.

He joined the Ordnance Corps in 1924 as assistant ordnance engineer and rose through the ranks to chief engineer, becoming one of the world's foremost authorities on incendiary and small ammunition.

During World War II, his dedicated service and contribution to the nation's war effort with the Ordnance Corps earned Captain Jervey the Exceptional Civilian Service emblem, presented during Pentagon ceremonies.

In 1953, he and Mrs. Jervey, the former Anne Dornin White, moved from Washington, D.C., to Clemson for what was to be a short-lived retirement. Captain Jervey was presented an honorary Doctor of Science degree from Clemson in 1953, and in May 1959, the Board of Trustees unanimously voted him vice president for development.

This appointment—which he held through December 1963—gave official status to a series of activities which Captain Jervey had performed beyond true measure, more or less unofficially, for nearly half a century.

He held such positions as president of the Washington, D.C., Clemson Alumni Club, vice president of the Alumni Association, and served as its national president for two terms. Captain Jervey was greatly instrumental in obtaining two grants totaling nearly $2 million from the Olin Foundation for construction and equipping of the ceramic and chemical engineering buildings.

From a statement upon the opening of the Jervey Center in 1973:

Captain Jervey has been, is, and always will be Clemson's premier Ambassador of Good Will whose advice and assistance was ever-ready at the call of the administration. He is a life member of the Clemson Board of Trustees.

Captain Jervey kept regular hours at his campus office, and was very active in church and civic affairs, holding such posts as a directorship with the Clemson Chamber of Commerce.

Clemson president Dr. Robert C. Edwards dedicated the Jervey Athletic Center on behalf of the university. He described Captain Jervey as a man whose "intense interest in and great loyalty to Clemson has never wavered for the slightest moment."

Edwards recalled that he had been closely associated with Jervey in their professional capacities at the university for 18 years, "His considerable talents and skills have always been at Clemson's service.

"No road has been too long for him to walk and no task has been too small for him to do, if, in the walking and in the doing, he could further the best interest of an institution which he has clearly loved and faithfully served," Edwards continued.

Above all, however, a greater Clemson University has long been the magnificent obsession of the man who gave his name to this new building. In these difficult and uncertain times for higher education, any institution would be proud and most fortunate to have a steadfast friend on its team like Frank Johnstone Jervey— Captain Jervey.

53 Rodney Williams

The chant started from one end of Frank Howard Field, and soon it filled the whole stadium. "Rod-ney! Rod-ney! Rod-ney!"

The scoreboard above the west end zone stands even got into the act.

"It sounded a lot better this time," Clemson quarterback Rodney Williams said after his Tigers beat rival South Carolina 29–10.

The year before, Williams was greeted with a similar chant at Williams-Brice Stadium in Columbia. Except on that night, it had a negative connotation to it. His last pass—which was intercepted and returned for a touchdown by safety Brad Edwards—lifted the Gamecocks to a 20–7 victory, which got the 77,000 fans in Columbia that night to chant, "Raaahhdnee! Raaahhdnee!"

A Columbia, South Carolina, native and a graduate of Irmo High School, that night and that chant specifically, haunted the Tigers' signal-caller for a whole year. But with 10:44 left in the 1988 tussle, Williams spun into the end zone to cap Clemson's final scoring drive of the afternoon.

It was fitting that Williams scored the game-clinching touchdown, and that he did it the way those who remembered watching him play know him for—running Danny Ford's triple-option offense to near perfection.

"It was just a regular option," Williams said. "We had been running it to both sides during the game, but we decided to run it to the weak side then.

"I came down and faked it to Tracy [Johnson]. The defensive tackle took Tracy and the defensive end took Terry [Allen], and the tackle did a great job blocking the outside backer and making a seam for me."

Williams had 43 of the Tigers' 225 rushing yards on that wet afternoon in Clemson. His seven-yard touchdown on his final carry in Death Valley put Clemson securely in front 29–7. Usually calm and reserved, which sometimes Ford wished he was not, Williams finally showed some emotion by pumping his fist to the crowd and then hugging Ford as he came over to the sideline.

"Scoring on my final play was a great thing to happen," Williams said.

Williams, who had won more games (32) at Clemson than any other Tigers' quarterback (now tied with Tajh Boyd), threw for 192 yards in his final game at Death Valley.

"Rodney played well, and he has excelled for us for a lot of different reasons," Ford said after the game. "He has had a great four years with us, and we're glad all of his seniors went out winners."

But few in the history of Death Valley had gone out the way Williams did. With a little more than 4:00 to play, Ford let Williams take the field to start the last drive of the game, and then after one play, he substituted him for back-up Chris Morocco.

As Williams jogged over to the sideline and was greeted with hugs and high-fives from his teammates and coaches, the 84,000 fans who were wearing orange in Death Valley gave him a standing ovation, and soon the chants of "Rod-ney! Rod-ney! Rod-ney!" filled the stadium one again.

"I definitely like to know that they know my name," Williams said. "But it means even more when they're yelling your name because they appreciate you."

54 Homer Jordan

He was short at 6', quiet, and equipped with a smile that seemingly never disappeared. Strange for a football player. But Homer Jordan had immense determination to play football in college and made an eternal impact on Clemson football by leading the Tigers to their only national championship in 1981.

It didn't come easy, at least not for Jordan. He wasn't recruited as a quarterback from Cedar Shoals High School in Athens, Georgia. He played defensive back and wide receiver but never quarterback until his senior year. Despite leading Cedar Shoals to an 11–1 record under the eyes of the University of Georgia, Jordan didn't receive many scholarship offers. The ones he did projected him as a defensive back or a wide receiver.

But Jordan didn't see it that way. He wanted to be a quarterback, and it was Clemson that promised him a chance to play the position—that became the determining factor to head for Tiger land. Jordan felt pressure from the start knowing that the only black quarterback at Clemson played the position for only half of a season in 1975. Oddly, his name was Willie Jordan, no relation to Homer.

"We knew Homer was a football player, but we didn't know if he was a quarterback," Danny Ford confessed. "He was under a lot of pressure that first year. When you're one of the first black quarterbacks at a school, you're going to hear things and get criticized and face a pretty gigantic burden."

He took on a similar burden his senior year at Cedar Shoals, the only time he played quarterback. A skinny kid, he wasn't outgoing and not one to revel in whatever success he had. After a game he would come directly home with no social engagements. But the kids from school always gathered around to greet him. In many ways he was a loner.

"I don't know how he made so many friends," his mother, Alice, said, "because li'l Homer doesn't say anything—even around home."

As a freshman he was back-up to Billy Lott before the 1980 season. He was listed as a defensive back on the Tigers' depth chart. But he kept pleading to try out at quarterback.

"I have quick feet and can throw when I have to," he argued.

When fall practice began, Jordan was hopeful. Three days before the season opener against Rice, Ford surprised the Clemson world by naming Jordan as the starter, and he stayed with him all season as Clemson finished 6–5.

It wasn't any easy year for anyone at Clemson or its fans. Rumors swept through the town about discontent among the players, and Ford received a great amount of unsolicited opinions from cocktail-party coaches. Much of it was about Jordan, and much of it contained racial overtones.

Ford never wavered. He supported Jordan. In his mind Homer would start the 1981 season.

"The fans around here don't know much about Homer," Ford defended. "Early on, he was quiet, very quiet—very, very shy. Didn't talk much. Homer controls what we are going to do. How he plays is how we play. The games that he's had a little trouble in are the ones we had a hard time winning. When your quarterback can play bad and you still win, then he's got to be pretty good. And we think Homer is pretty good."

In 1981, Jordan showed everyone that he was very good. He would sprint out or drop back, whatever the situation demanded. He was so good he was named All-ACC as a quarterback in taking Clemson to the Orange Bowl victory over Nebraska and the national championship.

All the doubts and the criticism about Jordan were drowned in Lake Hartwell. Overnight, Jordan was the town hero—a quiet one indeed, yet a hero nonetheless. His teammates loved him and ribbed him all the time as he stayed alone in his room listening to music and ironing his shirts. They also took turns about poking fun at his diet of chicken and peanut butter and jelly sandwiches. That got him the nickname "Bird." They also came to respect Jordan's play on the field.

"Homer's grown up so much this year," wide receiver Perry Tuttle praised. "He's the story of our success. It really started with the last four games in 1980. Before that he was never really sure of himself. When it was time to check off a called play at the line, Homer didn't know what to do. I would put my arm around him and say, 'Homer, don't worry. The coaches have confidence in you. Go with your instincts.'

"The thing about Homer is that he's quiet. But understand, when Homer talks, people listen. One time late in the first half of the Georgia game, it was 0–0, everybody was panicking. Going crazy. Homer walked into the huddle and yelled, 'Shut the hell up.' Oh, man. Everybody went 'Whaa!' Nobody ever heard Homer cuss before. And then everybody cracked up. I said, 'Honest? What, that's not you man.' Homer looked coolly at me. On the next play, he threw me the eight-yard touchdown pass."

That was the Jordan way.

55 Raymond Priester

Raymond Priester holds Clemson marks for career rushing, single-game rushing, most 100-yard games, and most carries. He also holds the marks for most 100-yard games in a season and consecutive 100-yard games.

Priester came to Clemson from a little town in the lower part of South Carolina called Allendale. He left there in 1993 as Allendale-Fairfax High School's all-time leading rusher with 5,673 yard and 71 touchdowns. He was a four-year starter and earned a spot on South Carolina's 1993 Shrine Bowl team.

Both Clemson and South Carolina wanted his services, but he chose Clemson because recruiting coordinator Rick Stockstill promised him a chance to play running back and USC was more interested in him playing linebacker.

Priester discovered it was not going to be as easy as he first thought. There was a lot of competition at tailback, and after fall camp he fell to third on the depth chart.

For a little while, he thought hard about transferring, but his mother, Rosella, told him without hesitation that he was staying put and he was going to work it out. "I told them he was going to stay right here and wait his turn," she said. "You don't play by yourself, you play as a team."

It turned out that the 6'1", 230-lb. running back did not have to wait long to get his turn. After a 1–2 start in the 1994 season, Clemson head coach Tommy West decided to shake things up. In practice he told Priester he was getting his shot. He started and rushed for 88 yards in the Tigers' 13–0 victory over Maryland.

Priester never left the starting lineup after that. His first 100-yard game came against Florida State in 1995, the first of three straight games in which he eclipsed the 100-yard plateau. He finished the 1995 season with five 100-yard games, but what happened on November 11, 1995, against Duke is still the best single-game rushing mark in Clemson history.

After rushing for 263 yards on 32 carries, Priester's offensive linemen wanted to carry him off Clemson's Frank Howard Field.

"I asked them not to do it," he said. "They're the ones who are basically responsible for it, so why should they carry me off?"

The 263 yards allowed Priester to top the 1,000-yard mark—the first running back at Clemson to do it since Terry Allen in 1988. The very next week against South Carolina, he shattered Terry Flagler's single-season mark, and he finished the year with 1,322 yards and six touchdowns.

As impressive as he was at running the football in 1995, the numbers he put up in 1996 were even better. Priester went over the 100-yard mark a record seven times, including four consecutive times to end the year. His four straight 100-yard games is also a single-season record.

"We take pride in Raymond's accomplishments," said one of his offensive linemen, Jim Bundren. "It's a unique situation, but when Raymond breaks a record, we really feel a part of it, and Raymond always gives us credit."

Priester closed out 1996 by rushing for 100 more yards five times in the last six games. The one time he didn't hit the mark was because the Tigers were comfortably ahead of Maryland in a 35–3 victory. West pulled him out after he gained 85 yards on 19 carries.

The next week he began the greatest four-game stretch for a running back in Clemson history. First he rushed for 122 yards in a 24–16 victory at No. 15 Virginia and then for 146 yards in a 40–17 rout of N.C. State. The following week against South Carolina, he broke off a 65-yard run—the longest of his career—and rushed for 137 yards on 18 carries. He capped off the year with 151 yards against LSU—still a Clemson bowl record—in the Peach Bowl on December 28.

The 556 yards he gained in the last four games allowed Priester to break his single-season record by 23 yards (1,345), while it also allowed him to pass Kenny Flowers as the all-time leading rusher at Clemson. He also became the first running back in Clemson history to rush for 1,000 yards in back-to-back seasons.

"Blocking for Raymond Priester adds to our motivation," lineman Glenn Roundtree said. "We take a lot of pride in the records he breaks because when Raymond is running the ball well, we win."

Never was that more evident than on October 25, 1997. Though Maryland and everyone else in the college football world knew Clemson's game plan on this particular afternoon—give the football to Priester—the Terrapins could not stop him.

Priester ran for 204 of the Tigers' 245 yards that afternoon, while tying a single-game record with 36 carries in the 20–9 victory. He also scored both of Clemson's touchdowns.

In the first quarter, he carried the ball seven consecutive times and gained 50 of the Tigers' 63 yards on the touchdown drive.

He finished off the Terps in the fourth quarter with nine straight carries (10 total) for 81 yards on a 94-yard touchdown drive.

"Ask any back in the nation how many times they want the ball, and they'll tell you as many times as they can," Priester said.

Nobody at Clemson has gotten the ball more than Priester. He finished his career with a school-record 805 carries and is still the school's all-time leading rusher with 3,996 yards. His 15 100-yard rushing performances are also a program best.

"I consider myself lucky," he said. "So many guys haven't had the chance to do what I've done. I'm blessed to have walked that road. I'm happy today. I'm happy tomorrow. I'm happy the next day. I wouldn't change a thing."

56 The Humor of Frank Howard

"We got a lot of Ph.D.s at Clemson. They're okay after four or five years. But they want to make a name for themselves by flunking football players. We straightened them out soon."

"Senator Strom Thurmond, a 1923 graduate of Clemson, wanted to go with me on some speaking trips when he was president of our alumni association. Trouble was he'd talked about a half an hour about Clemson and an hour and a half about Strom."

"I really ain't much of an after-dinner speaker, and I don't mind talking for it. I've often wondered where I'd be today if my first ambition in life had been realized. Then, my chief aim was to go to Auburn and be a chicken farmer."

"The alumni are ambitious. They want Knute Rockne for football coach, Casey Stengel to coach baseball, and Adolph Rupp for basketball."

"Other people may have called South Carolina coach Paul Dietzel 'Pepsodent Paul.' But I called him 'Colgate Paul' because that's the only team that he could beat when he was coaching at Army."

"Jimmy Carlen, the new coach at South Carolina already got two sponsors, Kentucky Fried Chicken and Schick razors. They're gonna call his TV show the Chicken-Schick Show.*"*

"My players are going to be making more money than a lot of those pro players in the long run. I got boys out there who are bank presidents, college professors, engineers, college presidents, and diplomats, and I even have four or five who are preachers."

"I've said a lot of things I shouldn't have said. I often wonder if all the talk does any good. It makes me look awful stupid sometimes. But it's too late for me to change now."

"I had a lifetime contract but the administration declared me dead."

"I retired for health reasons. The alumni got sick of me."

"The only good thing comes out of Columbia is I–26."

"Everybody kept asking me why can't we have a team like Oklahoma and Notre Dame? And, in 1961, we did. All three of us finished 5–5."

"The score is tied and we're winning."

"I don't want the best team to win. I just want us to win."

"The goal line is called the alumni line since if you don't cross it, you'll be fired by the alumni."

2011 ACC Champions

Twenty years of frustration was cured on December 3, 2011, in Charlotte as 20th-ranked Clemson scored 21 points in the third quarter to beat No. 5 Virginia Tech 38–10, winning its first ACC Championship in 20 years.

"We're a championship program, and tonight we added to a great tradition," Swinney said. "And I think this was our 18th [conference title] overall and 14th ACC Championship.

"It's our first time to win 10 games in 20 years. It's our first time to win an ACC Championship in 20 years, first time to go to the Orange Bowl in 30 years.... So it's just great to be a Tiger, and we're 10–3, and we're excited about representing the ACC in the Discover Orange Bowl."

With the game tied 10–10 at the break, Clemson forced the Hokies to a three-and-out in their first possession and then used a 10-play, 87-yard drive to regain a lead it would not relinquish the rest of the night. Clemson quarterback Tajh Boyd, who was named the Most Valuable Player of the game, threw his second of three touchdown passes with an eight-yard pass to tight end Dwayne Allen in the corner of the end zone to cap the drive.

That gave Clemson a 17–10 lead with 10:45 to play in the third quarter. Allen and Boyd hooked up for a 24-yard touchdown in the first quarter, as well. Boyd finished the night 20-of-29 for 240 yards and three scores. In the process, he set Clemson single-season records for total yards and passing yards.

It was a nice comeback for Boyd, who had struggled the previous two weeks.

"Somewhere here you've just got to dig deep inside yourself and work through things," the Clemson quarterback said. "Obviously, you do get a sense of complacency, and if you let it, if you let the outside world influence how you carry yourself and how you act, I mean, that's just one of the life lessons learned.

"I feel like that's one of the things that happened, and it happened for a reason, to let you know that all you can really do is believe in yourself and your family, which is my teammates. I mean, I'm just proud to be here."

Boyd got even prouder on the Tigers' next possession, as he hit Sammy Watkins in stride for a 53-yard touchdown pass that gave Clemson a 24–10 lead.

After another three-and-out forced by the Clemson defense, which held ACC Player of the Year David Wilson to 32 yards on 11 carries, the Tigers scored again, this time on a 29-yard touchdown run by Andre Ellington.

The Clemson running back finished with 125 yards on 20 carries. This was a week after the Hokies held Virginia to 30 yards rushing. Clemson finished with 217 yards.

"I'm proud of our running back, Andre Ellington," Swinney said. "He was a big-time player tonight on a big stage. He was one of the big keys in the game for us because we were able to run the football."

Boyd added his fourth touchdown responsibility of the night to cap the scoring with a one-yard plunge with 13:04 to play. From that point, the celebration was on.

The Perry Brothers—The "Fridge" and Michael Dean

Michael Dean Perry will never forget the first play of his college career. It was the season opener against Appalachian State in 1984.

He lined up alongside his older brother, William, who was already a two-time All-American player at middle guard for the Tigers and was part of Clemson's National Championship team of 1981.

"Playing next to William was exciting in and of itself," Michael Dean said. "We grew up playing alongside each other in middle school, junior high, and high school, and now I get the opportunity to play with him at the next level in a big-time college environment.

"It was a great feeling, and I enjoyed every minute of it."

Especially the first play of the game when William broke through the line, sacked the quarterback, stripped the football, and Michael Dean recovered it for a touchdown.

"It was so exciting. It was without a doubt the most memorable play of my career," the younger Perry said.

It did not take long for Michael Dean to be part of another great moment involving his brother. Nine weeks later, the Tigers hosted Virginia Tech in a game that featured the greatest matchup of defensive linemen in the history of Death Valley.

Besides the Perry brothers, the Hokies had 1984 Outland Trophy winner and future Pro Football Hall of Famer Bruce Smith.

"How many big-time players were in that game? I know William was in it and Bruce was in it, but who was the third one? I didn't have anything on those two guys at the time," Michael Dean said.

But the freshman had the better game.

"I remember all the hype and buildup surrounding it that week," said Michael Dean, who played at Clemson from 1984 to 1987. "But if I recall correctly, I believe I had a pretty good game that day. Now that I look back at it, that game might have been the day when I started coming into my own."

Michael Dean came into his own, alright. Though he is the little brother to William "The Refrigerator" Perry, Michael Dean was never one to live in the shadows of his brother. He made a name for himself and broke all of his brother's records.

"We don't really talk about the records when we get together," Michael Dean said. "We actually just sit around and catch up on what has been happening in our lives. Believe it or not, we rarely even talk about football."

Michael Dean is no longer all alone as the school's all-time sack leader with 28, but he still solely holds the record for tackles for loss, with 61.

During his time at Clemson, he was part of a defense that ranked among the best in the nation in 1986 and 1987, plus he

All-American William Perry was on Clemson's 1981 National Championship team.

All-American Michael Dean Perry is the younger of the Perry brothers and broke all of his big brother's Clemson team records.

helped guide the Tigers to two ACC Championships, while earning All-ACC and All-American honors both times.

Before C.J. Spiller took home the ACC's top honor in 2009 as the conference Player of the Year, Michael Dean was the last Clemson player to earn such an honor—an even more special feat considering he was a defensive tackle.

After Clemson, Michael Dean went on to play 10 seasons in the NFL after being drafted by the Cleveland Browns in the second round of the 1988 NFL Draft. While playing for Cleveland, Denver, and Kansas City, he earned All-Pro honors eight times—a record for a former Tiger—and played in six pro bowls over the course of his career.

Michael Dean has since been named to Clemson's All-Centennial team, a member of the ACC's 50-Year Anniversary Football Squad, and inducted into the Clemson Athletic Hall of Fame.

As for William, he finished his career with 60 tackles for loss and 27 sacks, while earning All-American status in 1982, 1983, and

1984. He was a consensus First Team All-American player in 1983 and a first-team selection in 1984. He is still the only Clemson player to be named All-American three times in his career.

William was a member of two ACC Championship teams (1981 and 1982) as well as the 1981 National Championship team. His Clemson teams posted a 37–6–2 record in his four years in Tigertown.

After Clemson, William was drafted No. 22 overall in the 1985 NFL Draft by the Chicago Bears. He made the All-Rookie team and was part of the Bears' Super Bowl title run that year, where he scored a touchdown in Super Bowl XX. He was known as "The Fridge."

At more than 300 lbs., he is still the biggest man to score a touchdown in a Super Bowl. William went on to play 10 years in the NFL for the Chicago Bears and the Philadelphia Eagles.

Looking back years later, Perry said that he "wished Walter Payton could have scored" in that Super Bowl.

Like Michael Dean, William is a member of the Clemson Hall of Fame, was named to Clemson's All-Centennial team, and was selected for the ACC's 50-Year Anniversary Football squad.

59 Bennie Cunningham

When he was at Blue Ridge High School in Seneca, South Carolina, Bennie Cunningham started out playing the clarinet as a member of the Bobcat band. Before school opened for the fall semester, he decided that although he liked music, he didn't like the work involved. Instead, he turned to football, a sport he always loved.

A few weeks into practice, however, Cunningham realized football wasn't all it was cracked up to be. He discovered he hated practice. He didn't like the fact he had to condition his body and lift weights, and learning the playbook was like having extra homework.

He discovered he was working harder in football than he ever did in the band, so the week before the first game he told the coaches he was quitting the team.

"I got fed up with football because I didn't realize how hard it was to play football," Cunningham said.

The coaches were puzzled by Cunningham's decision. Since the start of practice, he did nothing but succeed. They had already penciled him in as a starter, though he had never played the game before he came out for the squad.

But none of that mattered, as he still quit the team.

That afternoon, Cunningham went back home and did his homework and studied like everything was okay. Life was good. He was getting what he wanted out of it, or so he thought.

Later that evening when his dad came home and discovered his son had quit the team, it was time for a good heart-to-heart conversation.

"My father came to me upset and said, 'Listen, you quit the band because it was tough, and now you have quit the football team because it was tough. I don't care what you do in life, there are going to be times when things get tough. You can't quit every time something gets tough,'" Cunningham recalled.

"So that's when I decided to go back out for the team and prove to myself and everybody else that I can do this."

And did he ever prove it. After integration moved him to Seneca High School, Cunningham went on to become a three-time All-State player for the Bobcats, which led to Shrine Bowl honors and a football scholarship to Clemson.

During his time with the Tigers, Cunningham became the most decorated tight end in Clemson history and the ACC, for that matter. He became Clemson's first consensus All-American player in 1974 and then the Tigers' first two-time First Team All-American player the following year.

In 1974, the Tigers were 7–4 and had a 6–0 record at home with wins over Georgia, Georgia Tech, and South Carolina. In 1975, Cunningham was also chosen on many teams as a senior, despite a down season at Clemson. He was also a two-time First Team All-ACC pick and was selected to play in the Hula Bowl, Japan Bowl, and the East-West Shrine game after his senior year.

Clemson didn't have a lot of guys going to the pros. Still, the man who became the first African American to be a consensus first-team All-American in his junior year was shocked to hear the rumor that he had been picked by the Pittsburgh Steelers in the first round of the 1976 NFL Draft following his senior year. The last Clemson player drafted by the pros was Jay Washington two years earlier. Charlie Waters was drafted six years earlier.

Cunningham was sitting in his dorm room on April 8 when someone on his hall raced to his room to tell him the news.

"Someone came and told me, 'You got picked,'" Cunningham said. "I was in my dorm room. I hadn't even heard it on the radio. They didn't even contact you back then. I just found out by word of mouth."

Cunningham confessed he was more surprised than excited. Sure, he loved football, but he was ready to complete his degree in secondary education and possibly go into coaching.

"It was out of the blue," he said. "I wasn't going to try out for a team after my senior year because I just thought everything was over," he said. "I was going to finish school and be a teacher."

Cunningham eventually became the all-time receptions leader among tight ends for the Steelers with 202 catches and 20 career touchdowns.

A series of knee surgeries plagued Cunningham in his last few years with the Steelers.

"It was time to move on," he said.

In 1974, Bennie Cunningham became Clemson's first consensus All-American selection. (Photo courtesy of the Clemson University Sports Information Department)

After the 1985 season, Cunningham decided to call it a career after 10 years with the Steelers, where he amassed 2,879 yards, plus blocking for most of Franco Harris' 91-career rushing touchdowns. In 2007, when the Steelers celebrated their 75th anniversary, the Pittsburgh fans voted Cunningham on the all-time roster, the only tight end on the team.

Just because Cunningham's pro career was at an end didn't mean he wasn't still hard at work. By 1986, he had finished his master's degree in human resources from Clemson, his mother's advice ringing strong in his ear.

"I kept going back in during off-season to take courses," he said. "My mother told me I had to graduate, but it was a lot of commitment to come back after the season was through."

Cunningham continued to keep his focus on becoming a guide for children throughout their education. Football was a big part of his life, but he knew he needed to make a bigger difference in his community than he could on the gridiron.

After a few years of coaching at Hillcrest High School in Greenville, Cunningham found his current job as guidance counselor at West-Oak in 1993.

"I want to help children find something they really enjoy as a career," he said. "There's no question that I want to be remembered as a teacher."

60 Woody Dantzler

Was he a quarterback with a runner's feet or a tailback with a powerful arm? That's what Coach Tommy West had to determine when he recruited Woody Dantzler in 1998 from just 120 miles away at Wilkinson High School in Orangeburg, South Carolina. Bowden was cognizant of Dantzler's athleticism that generated 7,113 passing yards and 3,134 rushing ones that were off the charts.

The 5'11" sprinter was recruited by every major school but was shrouded by doubt. There were many critics who were doubtful of his passing ability. There were plenty others who felt he should play another position. But Dantzler had enough confidence in his ability to come to Clemson, play quarterback, and prove his critics wrong—which he certainly did.

Before he graduated, Dantzler was one of the most publicized athletes in Clemson history. His accomplishments are well documented, including his quest for a 2,000 yards passing/1,000 yards rushing season, the incredible number of records he established, the seemingly endless ESPN *SportsCenter* highlights he provided, and a fitting Heisman Trophy nomination.

Receivers coach Rick Stockstill, who recruited him, was a visionary. He saw the talent and believed it was there to develop into a star quarterback.

"You could visualize him doing what he's doing," was Stockstill's first observation. "I knew what type of person he was and knew how hard he could work to raise his game to that level."

In 1988 Dantzler was not a complete quarterback, not by any stretch. In fact, the offensive coaches designed a "Woody" package of plays that consisted of rushing plays to take full advantage of his exceptional running abilities. And Dantzler bought into it but kept working to improve.

It had been nearly 20 years since the Tigers had won a national championship when Tommy Bowden arrived from Tulane with an unbeaten 11–0 campaign as Clemson's new coach for the 1999 season. He liked what he was told about Dantzler.

"Even though he could play another position, we would be hurting ourselves if we move Woody," offensive coordinator Rich Rodriguez said. "He's a quarterback. A pure quarterback. He knows what's required of that position in our offense."

The turning point was the North Carolina game the fourth week of the season. On a quarterback keeper around the left corner, Dantzler shook off two tacklers and tiptoed down the sideline for a 56-yard touchdown that clinched a 31–20 victory after he had thrown a 49-yard touchdown pass the previous quarter. Dantzler became the quarterback that Saturday.

As the full-time starter his junior season, Dantzler had heads turning with electrifying runs and passing touchdowns with an ACC record 220 yards against Virginia. He also reeled off four consecutive games with 100 yards rushing and 300 yards of total offense, a first in college annals. Slowed by an ankle injury, he nevertheless finished with 1,028 yards rushing, which was an ACC record for a quarterback, as Clemson rolled to a 9–3 record.

What more to expect from Dantzler his final season? He continued to perform at a record level and generate a lifetime of memories for Clemson loyalists. The first was Clemson's biggest road win in 20 years when the Tigers, behind Dantzler's performance, upset

71.7 Winning Percentage This Decade

Clemson has a 71.7 winning percentage (38–15) for the second decade of this century, and that is the second-best mark in Tigers history. There are many more games to be played this decade, but only the decade of the 1980s is better.

In the 1980s, Clemson had a 76.7 winning percentage under head coach Danny Ford, the fifth-best winning percentage in the nation for that time period. Clemson won 65.8 percent of its games in the 1950s under head coach Frank Howard, 15th best in the nation during that decade.

Record by Decade

Decade	Record	Win %	Winning Season
1890s	11–6–0	64.7	3–0–1
1900s	40–21–7	64.0	7–1–2
1910s	42–35–6	54.2	5–3–2
1920s	41–47–5	46.8	5–5–0
1930s	51–37–7	57.4	5–3–2
1940s	51–38–5	55.9	4–5–1
1950s	64–32–5	65.8	7–2–1
1960s	50–48–2	51.0	5–2–3
1970s	56–54–3	50.9	4–6–0
1980s	87–25–4	76.7	9–0–1
1990s	69–47–1	59.4	6–3–1
2000s	79–47–0	62.7	10–0–0
2010s	38–15–0	71.7	4–1–0
Totals	**678–452–45**	**59.6**	**73–31–14**

ninth-ranked Georgia Tech 47–44. He ran for 164 yards and threw for 254 more and scored the game-winning touchdown in overtime on an 11-yard run.

A week later, he did even more. He topped his performance when he accumulated 517 yards of total offense, fifth best in ACC history, against N.C. State's 17th-ranked defense, as they won 45–37. The six touchdowns he accounted for was a school record. It left the Wolfpack coach Chuck Amato breathless.

"He put on a display out there that I don't know will ever be seen again in this stadium," Amato exuded. "They got 561 total yards, and he got 517 of them. He's their football team. He's their inspiration. I can't imagine there being a better player in America than Woodrow Dantzler."

Against Duke in the final game of the season, Dantzler became the first player in NCAA history to throw for 2,000 yards and run for 1,000 in a single season. There was nothing more for him to do. His two performances against Georgia Tech and N.C. State alone elevated Dantzler to a national stage with a Heisman Trophy nomination.

Dantzler kept a low profile through it all. That was his whole personality during his entire time at Clemson. "You can't get caught up in all the media attention," Dantzler said. "There's a great danger to that."

He won't say it or maybe not even think it, but one of Clemson's greatest players, Banks McFadden, did. "He'll go down as one of the best quarterbacks that Clemson has ever had and maybe one of the best athletes Clemson has ever had," volunteered McFadden, who is considered just that.

61 Da'Quan Bowers

When he saw the busses coming down the road on Highway 78 in Bamberg, South Carolina, Da'Quan Bowers could hardly contain himself. Like a little boy waving down the ice cream man on a hot summer day, Bowers darted into the middle of the busy highway to show the bus drivers where to park.

When the busses finally came to a stop, the 6'4", 280-lb. defensive end greeted each of the 70 or so teammates individually that made the three-hour bus ride from Clemson to Bamberg to be there for him when he laid his father, Dennis, to rest.

"It just means so much to me to see all of you here," Bowers told the team and coaches later in the church. "You guys all showed me how much you really care for me, my dad, and of course my family. This means the world to me. Thank you so much."

Later on that evening, Bowers promised to make this day up to his teammates. He was so touched that they were there for him in one of the worst moments of his life that he wanted to repay them by being the best teammate and leader he could be.

In 2010, no one in the country was better at both than Da'Quan Bowers. A former top prospect coming out of Bamberg in 2008, Bowers made offensive tackles and quarterbacks fear him. The Clemson defensive end registered 73 tackles, 15.5 sacks, and 26 tackles for loss.

His 15.5 sacks, which led the nation, set a record for a Clemson defensive end and ranked second all-time in Clemson history. His 26 tackles for loss also ranked second all-time, and it was the second-best mark in college football.

"When you look at what Da'Quan did, you can tell there was something different about the way he approached this year," Swinney said. "He made a promise to his dad, even before his dad passed away, that he would dedicate this season to getting better and proving he was the dominant player we all knew he was.

"When his dad died, he stayed committed to following his father's wishes and dedicated the season to him. I'm proud of the way Da'Quan has handled himself through all of this."

The most telling of that came after the Florida State game that year. Clemson was officially eliminated from the ACC Championship race after FSU kicker Dustin Hopkins nailed a 55-yard field goal as time expired in a 16–13 loss.

Though heartbroken that his team would not have a chance to defend its ACC Atlantic Division title, Bowers stood up in front of

Defensive end Da'Quan Bowers. (Photo courtesy of the Clemson University Sports Information Department)

his teammates and challenged them to continue to play hard, finish the season strong, and earn themselves a bowl invitation.

"I learned a long time ago with the tragedies I have had to go through not to ask why," Bowers said. "It's all in God's plan. He has a plan for us all, and he is trying to show us something."

His teammates listened. The next week, Clemson went out and beat Wake Forest 30–10 to become bowl-eligible for the 12th consecutive season. Bowers contributed by recording two sacks. At the time it was his ninth consecutive game with at least one sack—a Clemson record.

62 Dwayne Allen

Dwayne Allen is one of the best tight ends in Clemson history. His dedication and hard work enabled him to be named the nation's best tight end of the year in 2011.

"A lot of credit goes to the coaching staff we have here at Clemson," Allen remarked. "Coach Swinney does a great job preparing guys for the next level. In my decision to leave, Coach Swinney came to me and said, 'Dwayne, I think you are doing the right thing. I hate to see you go, but you are doing not only the right thing for you, but for your career.' That's the type of guy Coach Swinney is."

Allen's footprint is firmly imbedded in Clemson history, as well. Thanks to former players like C.J. Spiller, Thomas Austin, and Michael Palmer, to name a few, Allen saw what it meant to be a Clemson Tiger and why Clemson was family.

Just a redshirt freshman at the time, the 2009 seniors and especially Palmer showed Allen how much of a family the Clemson football program really is, to appreciate what your teammates mean to you and how to do things the right way.

"When a player matures at Clemson, he really understands what it means to be a Clemson Tiger," Allen said. "In my case, I was very fortunate to open up my eyes and mature enough to the point where I was able to see it before I decided to move on with my career.

"Being a Clemson Tiger, you want your team to be successful more than anything in the world. You want your fans to be happy more than anything in the world. I had more joy signing autographs and taking pictures with fans than I did scoring touchdowns

Tight end Dwayne Allen. (Photo courtesy of the Clemson University Sports Information Department)

or catching passes. That is the honest truth. Being a Clemson Tiger, it is all about giving back to Clemson and to the community of Clemson."

Allen gave back both on and off the field. On the field, he had 93 receptions for 1,079 yards and 12 touchdowns in his three-year career. His 93 receptions and 12 touchdowns tied the Clemson career records for the tight end with former Tiger and Pittsburgh Steeler John McMakin, who did the same from 1969 to 1971.

In 2011, Allen had the most prolific season by a tight end in Clemson history and one of the top five years in ACC history. He became the first Clemson tight end to catch 50 passes in one season for a record 598 yards while also catching a record eight touchdowns.

He was the first Clemson tight end to make an All-America team since Bennie Cunningham in 1975. Cunningham went on to win two Super Bowl titles with the Steelers in the late 1970s.

Off the field, Allen gave a lot back to the community, as he spoke to children at area elementary schools and did as many community service projects as he could during his four years at Clemson. In the classroom, he was one of the best students on the team.

"We are so proud of him," Swinney said. "What a tremendous example to all of us coaches on why we got into this profession. He is an example of why. That's my favorite part about coaching. To see a guy that develops into a man, to mature and learn a lot about life and is prepared. He is prepared for whatever comes his way."

63 Chris Gardocki

Chris Gardocki's accomplishments as a punter and place-kicker are unprecedented in Clemson and college football history. One publication ranked him as the top kicker in college football for the 1990s.

Only one player in NCAA history has been ranked in the top 10 in the nation in punting and field goals per game in two different seasons, and Chris Gardocki is that player. His abilities in both aspects of the game gave Clemson one of the top special teams in the nation from 1988 to 1990.

In 1989, as a sophomore, Gardocki ranked sixth in the nation in field goals and was 10th in punting with a 43.0 yard average. As a junior, he was fourth in both areas, averaging 1.73 field goals per game to go with a 44.48-yard punting average.

The native of Stone Mountain, Georgia, tied an ACC record for the longest field goal with a 57-yarder against Appalachian State in 1990 and saved his longest punt for his final punt in Death Valley, a 78-yarder in the 1990 South Carolina game. He concluded his career with 63 field goals and had a record 72 consecutive PATs. As a punter, he averaged 43.48 yards per boot for his career, including a 39.1 net average. A one-step punter, Gardocki had just one punt blocked his entire career in the ACC. The Tigers were 30–6 in Gardocki's career.

As a 19-year-old sophomore, Gardocki was one of eight college players selected by *Sports Illustrated*'s Paul Zimmerman as among the best pro football players for the year in 1995. It was quite a prediction. It certainly was a surprise to many, and no one more than Gardocki.

"I'm overwhelmed," he gushed. "My mom was real excited. For me, it's hard to believe. I've never even thought of being in

Georgia Killer

David Treadwell will always be remembered for beating Georgia inside the last 10 seconds in 1986 and 1987.

On September 20, 1986, Clemson defeated Georgia 31–28 as David Treadwell kicked a 46-yard field goal with no time left on the clock in Athens, Georgia. The next season on September 19, 1987, Treadwell booted a 21-yard field goal with two seconds left to beat Georgia 21–20 on national TV in Death Valley.

Treadwell was a consensus First Team All-American player in 1987. He won or tied games six times in his career inside the last three minutes of the fourth quarter. He was a place kicker with the Denver Broncos and the New York Giants in the NFL.

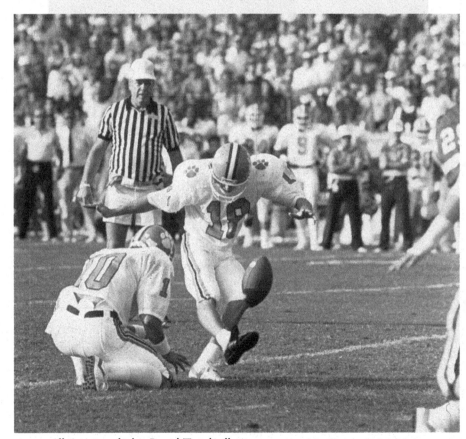

All-American kicker David Treadwell. (Photo courtesy of the Clemson University Sports Information Department)

something like that. Especially the 1995 All-Pro team. That's a long way down the road."

It had been a rocky road for Gardocki as a youngster. The first occurrence was when his parents divorced. A judge asked him, "Who do you want to live with?" "Forget it," Chris snapped. The judge placed him with his mother.

The other was when his father died later that year. He died on a Wednesday and the funeral was the very next day. Gardocki attended the services.

"I had gotten there on Monday but he was unconscious," Gardocki recalled. "It really hurt me that I didn't get there earlier when I could be with him or at least talk with him."

On Saturday, Gardocki was in uniform for a game against Maryland. He helped Clemson generate an 18–17 victory with a clutch field goal.

While most kickers are high strung, Gardocki was the opposite. He was laid back and quiet. He just shrugs his shoulders when asked about his demeanor.

"My mom is a really laid-back person who just sort of goes with the flow," he remarked. "I guess I got it from her."

It was because of his mom that he decided to forgo his final season of eligibility at Clemson.

"My family situation was part of the reason I decided to come out," Gardocki disclosed. "My mom worked really hard, and I'd really like to be able to set her up."

At the time, his mother was working two jobs and living with his sister in Stone Mountain, Georgia. During weekdays she was a doctor's assistant, and on the weekends she was checking patients in at the hospital emergency room.

With his Georgia upbringing, Gardocki was a big fan of the Bulldogs. They actually recruited him, but Clemson was where he decided to go.

"I just had the feeling that I wanted to go to Clemson," Gardocki said. "Coach Tommy West, who recruited me, was great. He didn't put any pressure on me to make a decision and was very straightforward with me."

When he left Clemson, he did so as a third-round pick of the Chicago Bears. He later played for the Baltimore Colts, Cleveland Browns, and the 2005 Super Bowl champion Pittsburgh Steelers.

64 ACC Trifecta 1986–88

Clemson won the ACC Championship three consecutive times from 1986 to 1988, which began a stretch that saw the Tigers compile four straight 10-win seasons from 1987 to 1990. In fact, starting with Clemson's 1986 ACC Championship team, the Tigers won at least eight games for six straight seasons—the best six-year stretch in the program's history. Clemson posted a 57–12–3 record during that period of time.

In 1986, the Tigers were 5–1–1 in ACC play. Heroic efforts by quarterback Rodney Williams and tight end Jim Riggs and a 20-yard David Treadwell field goal with 20 seconds left forced a 17–17 tie with Maryland, giving the Tigers the conference crown.

Both Clemson coach Danny Ford and Maryland coach Bobby Ross coached the game from the press box due to suspensions imposed by the ACC. The Tigers capped the season with a 27–12 victory over Stanford in the Gator Bowl. The Tigers scored all 27 points in the first half. Clemson finished 17th in the final Associated Press poll.

In 1987, the Tigers again won the ACC and finished the year with a 10–2 record. Clemson surprised the football world with a

35–10 win over Penn State in the Citrus Bowl. It was the largest margin of victory against a Joe Paterno squad in a bowl game.

Instead of depending on the running game, the Tigers took to the air and dominated the Nittany Lions. Clemson gained 499 yards. Williams was named the Player of the Game as he threw for 214 yards. Running back Terry Allen rushed for 105 yards and wide receiver Keith Jennings caught seven passes for 110 yards, giving Clemson a 200-yard passer, 100-yard rusher, and 100-yard receiver in the same game for the first time since 1969. Clemson was ranked No. 10 in the final UPI Poll.

In 1988, Clemson won the ACC and finished the season with a 10–2 record. The Tigers again defeated a perennial power in the Citrus Bowl. This time the Tigers owned an exciting 13–6 game over No. 10 Oklahoma.

Clemson became the first ACC team to defeat Oklahoma. The Tigers held the Oklahoma offense without a touchdown for just the second time in the decade of the 1980s.

Clemson was ranked No. 8 by the UPI, No. 9 by the Associated Press, and No. 10 in the *USA Today* Coaches' Poll when the final rankings came out.

1981: Clemson 29, South Carolina 13

Clemson entered the 1981 game with a perfect record and needed just one more win to close out its first perfect regular season since 1948. In that season, the Tigers had defeated South Carolina by a score of 13–7 at midseason (it was the Big Thursday era of the rivalry) thanks to a blocked punt by Phil Prince. With the line of scrimmage at the South Carolina 28 and Clemson trailing with less than 5:00 left, Prince blocked a punt. The ball was recovered at the 11 by Oscar Thompson, who ran it in for a touchdown with just 4:15 left in the game. Thirty-three years later, Clemson trailed South Carolina 7–0 in the first quarter. With the line of scrimmage at the Gamecocks 28, Chris Norman waited to receive the punt snap. Rod McSwain came in from the left and blocked the punt. Johnny Rembert, who later became a teammate of McSwain in the NFL, pounced on the ball in the end zone for a touchdown.

Two undefeated seasons and two blocked punts 22 years apart led to scores in the same end zone in the same stadium. And the line of scrimmage was the same at the same end of the field.

While that 1981 blocked punt took place in the first quarter and Clemson still trailed after the play (the Tigers missed the extra point), the momentum had definitely swung to Clemson's favor.

As noted columnist Furman Bisher of the *Atlanta Constitution* wrote, "The momentum had switched. The Tigers were back on top of their game, doing what they do best, playing defense, and it was a matter of time before they would ride over the Gamecocks like an orange scourge."

That orange scourge was in the form of running back Chuck McSwain, Rod McSwain's older brother. He was not to be outdone this day by his sibling as he had a career-high 151 yards rushing and two scores. Both scores came in the second half when he had 111 yards and two touchdowns. He was the big reason Clemson gained 254 yards on the ground and controlled the flow of the game.

Clemson needed McSwain's big second half because the Gamecocks actually cut Clemson's advantage to 15–13 on their first possession of the third quarter. Gordon Beckham, whose son with the same name is the current starting shortstop at Georgia, threw a 10-yard touchdown pass to Horace Smith with 10:28 left in the third quarter. It marked just the second time all year an opponent had scored more than one touchdown against the Tigers defense.

The next drive was classic Clemson. South Carolina stopped Perry Tuttle at the 14 on his kickoff return. But the Tigers then drove 86 yards in 18 plays. Chuck McSwain had 29 of those yards rushing, including the touchdown with 4:07 left, putting Clemson in front 22–13. Two possessions later, McSwain gained 52 yards on an 80-yard drive, again ending with a touchdown, this time from 23 yards.

South Carolina totaled just two first downs in the fourth quarter thanks to a defense led by Bill Smith, who had two sacks in the game. The Gamecocks ended the contest with just 205 yards of total offense and a 32 percent completion mark.

Tigers fans, who were certainly concerned that this South Carolina team was capable of ruining their "dream season," could now breathe again.

November 21, 1981, at Columbia, South Carolina

CLEMSON	6	9	7	7	29
SOUTH CAROLINA	7	0	6	0	13

USC	Wright 1 run (Fleetwood kick), 1st, 9:05
CU	Rembert recovered blocked punt (Pauling kick failed), 1st, 5:28
CU	Pauling 24 FG, 2nd, 12:10
CU	Jordan 11 run (pass failed), 2nd, 4:39
USC	Smith 10 pass from Beckham (run failed), 3rd, 10:28
CU	C. McSwain 1 run (Pauling kick), 3rd, 4:07
CU	C. McSwain 23 run (Pauling kick), 4th, 9:32
Attendance: 56,971	

66 2003: Clemson 63, South Carolina 17

Clemson ended the regular season on a three-game winning streak in decisive fashion as the Tigers took care of the Gamecocks 63–17 in Columbia. The 63 points were the most in the history of the series by either team. It also marked the most points scored since Clemson defeated Wake Forest 82–24 in the 1981 national championship season. The 46-point victory margin was the highest in the series since Clemson won 51–0 in 1900.

Clemson came out firing in the first quarter and never looked back. On the first play of the game, Leroy Hill and Khaleed Vaughn sacked Dondrial Pinkins. The play set the tone for a physical evening for the defense.

Clemson got the ball after a three-and-out to open the game and responded with the first touchdown. Derrick Hamilton caught a 36-yard touchdown pass from Charlie Whitehurst. For Hamilton, it marked the fifth consecutive game in which he caught at least one touchdown, setting a school record.

Following another three-and-out, Clemson again went to the air. This time, Whitehurst connected with Columbia native Airese Currie for a 28-yard touchdown. It was Currie's first touchdown catch since the Georgia Tech game on September 20 and second of his career in his hometown.

The Tigers extended their lead to 21–0 on their third offensive possession after Whitehurst again threw a touchdown pass. After an audible at the line, he found Ben Hall wide open over the middle for a 39-yard score, his first of the season. In the first quarter alone, Whitehurst was 7–7 for 149 yards and three touchdowns.

The Gamecocks responded with 10 points in the second quarter, but Clemson put the game out of reach in the first five minutes of the quarter. Chad Jasmin scored on a one-yard run to extend the lead 28–10. He then added his second touchdown minutes later from the same distance. The Tigers' 35 points at halftime were the most scored by Clemson against South Carolina in one half.

On South Carolina's first possession of the second half, Pinkins had a pass tipped and then intercepted by Leroy Hill. It was his third interception of the season. Jasmin scored again from one yard out to put the Tigers ahead 42–10.

South Carolina pulled to within 42–17 after a muffed punt by Hamilton at the Clemson 6. Brian Brownlee caught his second touchdown pass for the Gamecocks. Clemson came back quickly, and Whitehurst hooked up with Duane Coleman on a throw to the left sideline. Coleman scored easily from 27 yards out to give Clemson a 49–17 lead.

Clemson pushed the lead to 56–17 late in the third after Jasmin scored his fourth touchdown run of the game. He became the first Tiger since Boo Armstrong in 1918 to score four touchdowns against the Gamecocks. The play was set up by Jamaal Fudge's second interception of the game. Fudge appeared to be well on his way to scoring before tripping inside the 5-yard line.

The Tigers added a final touchdown when Chansi Stuckey gave everyone a glimpse of his potential. He scored on a 33-yard quarterback draw in which he dragged defenders into the end zone.

Whitehurst ended the game 18-of-26 for 302 yards and four touchdowns. He also rushed for 43 yards. He tied the Clemson single-season record with 21 touchdowns first established in 2001 by Woodrow Dantzler.

Offensively, the Tigers gained 542 total yards, a season high for 2003. Clemson had 240 rushing yards, also a season high. The Tigers averaged 8.1 yards per play over the course of the game.

Defensively, the Gamecocks were held below their season average with only 153 rushing yards. Part of the reason was the play of several Tigers defenders. Hill had four tackles for losses, the second time he had four in a game.

Fudge had two interceptions for Clemson on the night. It was the first time all season a Tigers defender had multiple thefts in a game. Travis Pugh, the other starting safety for Clemson, had six tackles, a pass breakup, and a blocked field goal.

November 22, 2003, at Columbia, South Carolina

CLEMSON	21	14	21	7	63
SOUTH CAROLINA	0	10	7	0	17

CU	Hamilton 36 pass from Whitehurst (Hunt kick), 1st, 11:–19
CU	Currie 28 pass from Whitehurst (Hunt kick), 1st, 8:24
CU	Hall 39 pass from Whitehurst (Hunt kick), 1st, 4:38
USC	Weaver 26 FG, 2nd, 12:56
USC	Brownlee 2 pass from Pinkins (Weaver kick), 2nd, 7:15
CU	Jasmin 1 run (Hunt kick), 2nd, 5:56
CU	Jasmin 1 run (Hunt kick), 2nd, 0:12
CU	Jasmin 1 run (Hunt kick), 3rd, 11:48
USC	Brownlee 3 pass from Swygert (Weaver kick), 3rd, 4:22
CU	D. Coleman 27 pass from Whitehurst (Hunt kick), 3rd, 2:42
CU	Jasmin 1 run (Hunt kick), 3rd, 0:08
CU	Stuckey 33 run (Anderson kick), 4th, 3:28

Attendance: 83,987

67 2004: Clemson 29, South Carolina 7

Clemson scored 14 early points and only allowed South Carolina to snap the ball in Tigers territory four times, as Clemson beat the Gamecocks for the seventh time in eight years by the score of 29–7. It was Clemson's 11th win in its last 12 games at Death Valley since 2003, as well.

The game got off to an exciting start for the Tigers when David Dunham hit Cory Boyd on the opening kickoff, jarring the ball loose from the Gamecocks return man. Steven Jackson recovered for Clemson on the 9-yard line.

After a Charlie Whitehurst pass to Cliff Harrell, Reggie Merriweather scored his first of three touchdowns on the day from three yards out, and Clemson had a 7–0 lead 52 seconds into the contest. It was the earliest Clemson had scored in a game since September 28, 1996, when Joe Woods caught a Nealon Greene pass and raced 80 yards on the game's first play from scrimmage in a 21–10 victory over Wake Forest.

The Tigers moved the ball 58 yards in nine plays, with the drive culminating in a seven-yard Merriweather scoring run. Seven of the nine plays on the drive gained five yards or more.

Neither team could sustain a drive for the remainder of the first quarter, and the Gamecocks finally struck 7:00 into the second quarter. On a third-and-14 play, South Carolina quarterback Syvelle Newton scrambled and threw deep to Boyd. The Gamecocks receiver made a diving catch and skidded across the goal line to cut the Clemson lead in half at 14–7.

Clemson went on one of its most impressive drives of the season to open the second half when it covered 80 yards in 14 plays and burned 7:14 off the clock. Merriweather carried seven times on the drive for 48 yards and scored his third touchdown of the day from 12 yards out.

On the next Gamecocks possession, Gaines Adams tipped a Mike Rathe pass and Cory Groover intercepted the ball for the Tigers. It was the fourth interception of the season by a Clemson defensive lineman. After a seven-yard return, Clemson had the ball deep in Gamecocks territory at the 12.

After forcing another punt, the Tigers offense went on its final scoring drive of 2004. Merriweather carried five times, and Whitehurst hit Curtis Baham for 23 yards for a key third-down conversion on a drive that ended with Jad Dean converting his third field goal of the day, this time from 20 yards out.

Merriweather led the ground attack by carrying 28 times for 125 yards. Whitehurst completed 15-of-28 passes for 151 yards, and Chansi Stuckey caught seven passes for 74 yards. Tramaine Billie led the Tigers defense with nine tackles and a sack, while Tye Hill had four pass breakups.

November 20, 2004, at Clemson, South Carolina

CLEMSON	14	0	12	3	29
SOUTH CAROLINA	0	7	0	0	7

CU	Merriweather 3 run (Dean kick), 1st, 14:08
CU	Merriweather 7 run (Dean kick), 1st, 5:17
USC	C. Boyd 54 pass from Newton (J. Brown kick), 2nd, 8:01
CU	Merriweather 12 run (Dean kick failed), 3rd, 7:46
CU	Dean 21 FG, 3rd, 2:34
CU	Dean 24 FG, 3rd, 0:40
CU	Dean 20 FG, 4th, 9:16

Attendance: 82,372

68 2007: Clemson 23, South Carolina 21

Mark Buchholz kicked a 35-yard field goal as time expired to lift No. 21 Clemson to a 23–21 win over arch-rival South Carolina at Williams-Brice Stadium on November 27, 2007. It was the Tigers' first "buzzer-beater" since the 1986 season. The victory also gave Clemson its ninth win in the last 11 years in the series and ninth win in its last 10 trips to Columbia.

The Tigers outgained South Carolina 443–364 in total yardage thanks to 33 more offensive plays (85–52). Clemson had 214 rushing yards and 229 yards through the air. The Tigers also had 26 first downs and held the ball for 38:27.

James Davis and C.J. Spiller combined for 210 rushing yards on 37 carries, including 122 yards by Davis and 88 yards by Spiller. Cory Boyd led the Gamecocks with 74 rushing yards on 19 carries.

Cullen Harper was 28-of-38 for 229 yards and one touchdown pass. His favorite target was Aaron Kelly, who had nine receptions for 134 yards, including four catches for 70 yards on the game-winning drive. Nelson Faerber added four catches for 20 yards and a score.

Chris Chancellor intercepted Blake Mitchell on the first play of the game. Then Davis' 29-yard carry moved the ball into Gamecocks territory. But the Tigers had to settle for Buchholz's 48-yard field goal.

On South Carolina's ensuing drive, Faerber blocked Ryan Succop's punt. La'Donte Harris scooped up the ball and raced 10 yards for a score.

The Gamecocks responded with a 74-yard scoring drive to narrow Clemson's lead to 10–7. On second-and-19, Boyd caught a pass out to the backfield and sprinted 39 yards to the Tigers 21. Three plays later on third-and-8, Mitchell lofted a pass to Kenny McKinley for a 19-yard touchdown.

After the two teams traded punts, Clemson went on a 10-play, 88-yard drive to up its lead to 17–7. Davis and Spiller each had rushes of 19 yards, while Davis went over the 3,000-yard career rushing mark on the drive. Harper capped the drive with a four-yard touchdown pass to Faerber.

Early in the third quarter, the Tigers squandered another scoring chance. Harris rushed up the middle untouched and blocked another Succop punt as Paul Macko recovered the ball at the Gamecocks 22. Then on a second-and-goal from the 2, Emanuel Cook intercepted Harper in the end zone and returned the ball to the Gamecocks 34.

Four plays and 66 yards later, Mitchell hit McKinley over the middle for a 40-yard touchdown pass, narrowing Clemson's lead to 17–14.

The Tigers answered with a 13-play, 69-yard drive to up their lead to 20–14. Kelly's 20-yard reception moved the ball near midfield. A six-yard pass interference penalty on third-and-14 extended the drive that ended in Buchholz's 28-yard field goal.

South Carolina later drove 72 yards in the fourth quarter to take a 21–20 lead. McKinley's 35-yard catch and run gave the Gamecocks first-and-goal. Two plays later, Mitchell found Dion Lecorn in the end zone and a four-yard score.

The Tigers were forced to punt on their next drive, as Maners' 55-yard boot and McKinley's seven-yard return set up South Carolina at its own 12. After Boyd rushed 16 yards on the first play of the ensuing drive, Boyd's number was called again on the next three plays. But the Tigers defense was up to the test, as it stopped the senior running back on third-and-4, forcing a punt with 2:09 left.

Clemson took over at its own 22 and moved near midfield when Kelly caught a 26-yard pass over the middle. It was Kelly's 81st reception of the year, setting a school record.

After a seven-yard sack and one-yard loss on the next two plays, the Tigers faced third-and-18. But Harper calmly completed a 14-yard pass to Kelly on third down and a 12-yard pass to Kelly on fourth down. Then Kelly's 18-yard catch moved Clemson into field-goal range. After Harper's spike and kneel-down in the middle of the field, Buchholz kicked the game-winning 35-yard field goal as time expired.

November 24, 2007, at Columbia, South Carolina

CLEMSON	10	7	3	3	23
SOUTH CAROLINA	7	0	7	7	21
CU Buchholz 48 FG, 1st, 9:13					
CU Harris 10 blocked punt return (Buchholz kick), 1st, 6:01					
USC McKinley 19 pass from Mitchell (Succop kick), 1st, 2:52					
CU Faeber 4 pass from Harper (Buchholz), 2nd, 5:52					
USC McKinley 40 pass from Mitchell (Succop kick), 3rd, 8:35					
CU Buchholz 28 FG, 3rd, 2:25					
USC Lecorn 4 pass from Mitchell (Succop kick), 4th, 9:00					
CU Buchholz 35 FG, 4th, 0:00					
Attendance: 82,410					

69 1992 Virginia Game

October 10, 1992
Scott Stadium, Virginia
Clemson 29, UVA 28
October 10, 1992, was a landmark date in Clemson history. Clemson overcame a 28-point deficit in defeating No. 10 Virginia 29–28. It was just the third win over a top 10 team on the road in Clemson history.

Going into the game both Clemson and Virginia ranked in the nation's top 15 rushing offense and defense. The Tigers ranked fifth in the nation in rushing offense and the first in the ACC, while Virginia was second in the conference and sixth in the nation.

There was a battle on the other side of the ball, as well, with Virginia ranking 11th in the nation and first in the ACC in rushing defense, while Clemson was 16th in the nation and third in the conference.

Despite the rushing statistics, Virginia scored four times in the first half, all on touchdown passes from quarterback Bobby Goodman. Tyrone Davis scored the first two touchdown passes—a 33-yard pass and a 37-yard toss—to make it 14–0 in the second quarter.

Patrick Jeffers scored on a 20-yard pass with 8:40 left in the first half, and then Jeff Tomlin scored on a four-yard pass after the Cavaliers drove 45 yards in just five plays. Goodman threw four TD passes, all in the first half.

The Tigers' only score of the half came with 1:53 remaining when quarterback Louis Solomon, who replaced the injured (hip) Richard Moncrief, took the ball for a 64-yard scoring rush.

Clemson started the second half with two rushing touchdowns from Rudy Harris and Rodney Blunt to cut Virginia's lead to 28–20 heading into the final period.

With just 5:31 left in the contest, Harris, who had 12 carries for 96 yards and two touchdowns in the game, bulled his way for the score from 27 yards out. A two-point conversion failed, but the lead was now cut to 28–26.

A Darnell Stephens interception gave Clemson possession at the Virginia 35 with 3:53 left in the game. A 45-yard pass from Solomon to Larry Ryans put the ball at the Virginia 9-yard line. Three plays later Nelson Welch completed the comeback with a 32-yard field goal for a 29–28 Tigers win.

The comeback was the greatest in Clemson football history in terms of gaining victory after trailing by the largest deficit at any time in a game. In fact, it was just three points away from tying the national record for the greatest comeback in college football history. Maryland came back from 31 points down to win 42–40 at Miami in 1984.

Ironically, the previous Clemson record for the greatest point deficit overcome to gain victory also took place against Virginia. In

1966, Clemson trailed the Cavaliers 35–18. The Tigers came back to win that game 40–35.

The Tigers gained 402 yards on the ground, the second straight 400-yard game, a first in Clemson history. Two Tigers went over the 100-yard mark, Blunt and Solomon, and they nearly had a third as Rudy Harris gained 96. Terry Kirby had 132 yards rushing in the game but suffered a shoulder injury on a hit by Robert O'Neil in the third period. The other UVA players had just four yards rushing between them.

CLEMSON	0	7	13	9	29
VIRGINIA	7	21	0	0	28

VA	Davis pass from Goodman (Husted kick), 1st, 6:26
VA	Davis 37 pass from Goodman (Husted kick), 2nd, 12:05
VA	Jeffers 20 pass from Goodman (Husted kick), 2nd, 8:40
VA	Tomlin 4 pass from Goodman (Husted kick), 2nd, 3:54
CU	Solomon 64 run (Welch kick), 2nd, 1:53
CU	Harris 1 run (Welch kick), 3rd, 6:52
CU	Blunt 53 run (kick failed), 3rd, 1:16
CU	Harris 27 run (2pt run failed), 4th, 5:31
CU	Welch 32 FG, 4th, 0:52
Attendance: 45,400	

1959 Sugar Bowl

January 1, 1959
New Orleans, Louisiana
Clemson 0, LSU 7

By 1958 the ACC was becoming established as a strong football conference, and Clemson was emerging as one of its stronger teams. That season, the Tigers won the title with an 8–2 record. It was the fourth straight year in which Clemson won at least seven games. During that period, the Tigers produced a 29–9–2 record. Although they were recognized as a powerful force within the conference, they still hadn't quite earned the national recognition that goes with the success they had achieved the past four years. Still, Sugar Bowl officials were impressed enough with Clemson to give them a bid to the 1959 Sugar Bowl.

Now it was the New Orleans press that was not pleased with the committee's selection. No sooner had Clemson accepted the invitation than the critics roared their disapproval. Although the game had been a sellout as far back as November 4, anti-Clemson sentiment was high. The self-proclaimed experts had good reason to be pleased with the selection of local favorite LSU. The Bayou Tigers were rated the nation's No. 1 team. In addition, they were also a colorful team. Led by All-American running back Billy Cannon, they were favorites of the press because of their lightning-crack defensive unit, nicknamed the "Chinese Bandits." The practice of Coach Paul Dietzel maintaining three full teams (besides the "Chinese Bandits" there was the "Go Team" and the "White Team") also brought them attention.

What troubled the critics was Clemson's record. Certainly, judging LSU's record wasn't difficult; the team won all 10 games that it played that season. But it was an inspired Clemson team that would hold LSU scoreless in the opening quarter.

Although Clemson didn't have the range of talent that LSU had from employing 33 players for each game, the Tigers were loaded with strong runners. Howard made use of eight players, and they each gained 130 yards or more. Doug Cline led the rushers with 438 yards and was supported by Rudy Hayes, Mike Dukes, Bill Mathis, Harold Olson, George Usry, Charlie Horne, and Bobby Morgan. Howard also had two good quarterbacks, Harvey White and Lowndes Shingler, both of whom had missed several games during the season due to injuries. Clemson was strong up front as well, being led by All-American candidate tackle Lou Cordileone.

Of course it bothered Howard any time Clemson was placed in the position of underdogs, but he was used to it, as well. In Clemson's other bowl appearances, they held the same role.

In a speech to the Biloxi Chamber of Commerce, Howard rolled out his homespun psychological attack. Not only did he loosen up the guests with laughter; more importantly, he loosened up some of his players who were in the audience.

"This coaching business will get you if you let it. More letters come in from alumni and even small boys and girls telling me what I have to do about Cannon and the Chinese Bandits. If I didn't have a coaching job, I'd be between the shafts of a plow. But with all its trials, coaching beats plowing. I've always found you meet a lot of dumb guys in the newspaper and radio business, and tonight's no exception."

Howard's psychological ploy didn't go unnoticed by LSU coach Paul Dietzel. In fact, he became unhappy with what he described as a psychological edge being enjoyed by Clemson.

"If Frank Howard had planned it, he couldn't have had it any better," Dietzel said.

The morale on the LSU team was high. They had 33 regulars, which made for 33 happy players. Their extensive use in each game captured the imagination of the press. The "White Team" or first team was used both offensively and defensively. The "Go Team" was strictly an offensive unit, and the celebrated "Chinese Bandits" operated only on defense.

It was a cool 44 degrees when LSU kicked off. Despite all the pregame banter of a mismatch, a crowd of 82,000 turned out, with the majority of the fans rooting for LSU. Clemson couldn't do anything after receiving the kickoff, and neither could LSU in its first offensive series. Near the end of the period, the Bayou Tigers had reached the Clemson 25-yard line when time ran out.

On the first play of the second quarter, Tigers end Ray Masneri pounced on an LSU fumble on the 23-yard line to end the threat. Yet, during the remainder of the period, Clemson couldn't get its offense on track. The furthest it ever advanced was to its own 44.

LSU had two good opportunities to score and failed both times. Midway through the period, LSU had reached the Clemson 20-yard line. On fourth down, it lined up for a fake field-goal attempt. However, quarterback Warren Rabb's pass, intended for Cannon in the end zone, was too long.

The first time Clemson had the ball in the second half, it appeared as if the Tigers would score. However, Usry fumbled on second down, and LSU recovered on its own 28-yard line. As the third-quarter clock was winding down, LSU got a break. Mathis was standing back to punt on Clemson's 10-yard line. Center Paul Snyder got off a bad snap that hit Cline, who was in the backfield to block, on the leg. The ball rolled to the 11-yard line where LSU recovered.

After Cannon got only two yards on two carries, he was set to run again. Instead, he threw a halfback option pass to end Mickey Mangham for a nine-yard touchdown. Cannon proceeded to kick the extra point that gave LSU a 7–0 lead. Nobody realized at the time that it would be the only touchdown in the hard-fought contest.

Clemson came close to scoring the last time it had the ball during the game. The Tigers began a drive at the end of the third period from their own 17 that had reached the LSU 24-yard line. About five minutes remained when the Tigers attempted a screen pass that failed. The play was well designed, but Usry dropped the pass and Clemson's hopes with it.

If Usry had held on to White's short pass on the LSU 24-yard line, the outcome might have been different. Usry had blockers in front of him to produce a big gain.

"Clemson is the best football team we met this year," Cannon said after the game. "They really hit. I don't know his name but No. 74 [Lou Cordileone] gave us fits. Anytime I looked up, he was on my back."

Never has a Clemson team gained so much respect from a loss. "I wish we could line up and play LSU again—today," team captain Bill Thomas exclaimed. "A lot of people felt SMU should have played LSU. We didn't get much respect, but we came to play."

CLEMSON	0	0	0	0	0
LSU	0	0	7	0	7
LSU Mangham 9 pass from Cannon (Cannon kick)					
Attendance: 82,000					

1959 Bluebonnet Bowl

December 19, 1959

Houston, Texas

Clemson 23, TCU 7

Clemson closed its 1959 season with an 8–2 record, disposing of Furman in Greenville 56–3 to win its second consecutive ACC title. But nervousness filled the air on the Clemson campus due to the fact that the Tigers had not received a bid to a major bowl. It was something they had been accustomed to in recent years. Appearing in a postseason bowl game would make this the third time in four years, and hopes were high because their record indicated they deserved an invitation. Not only were they the ACC champions, but they had finished 11th in the final national poll.

While the football team returned to Clemson, Coach Frank Howard remained in Greenville, hoping to celebrate a bowl bid with members of his staff, the press, the Clemson officials, and guests in the banquet room of a local hotel. Although there had been other celebrations during the season after big wins over North Carolina 20–18 on Opening Day, South Carolina 27–0 in the final Big Thursday game, and Wake Forest, a 33–31 victory that clinched the second consecutive ACC crown, this one was special. For one thing, Howard considered this year's team possibly the best one he had ever coached. Then, too, Clemson was anxious to snap a streak of three straight bowl losses.

Clemson had lost to Georgia Tech 16–6 in the third game of the season. After winning four games in succession, it stumbled against Maryland 28–25. It was a veteran team with many of the players having played in the last two bowl games—the Orange in 1957 and the Sugar in 1959. Analyzing the bowl situation, Clemson officials determined that the only two bowls that remained unfilled were the Liberty Bowl in Philadelphia and the Bluebonnet Bowl, launching its first year, in Houston.

In the midst of all the speculation that was going on, Howard was called to the telephone. He got up from his chair and went into another room. The minutes seemed like hours. Then Howard sent word that he wanted his assistant coaches to meet him in his room. The suspense continued. Later, when Bob Bradley, Clemson's sports publicist, entered the banquet room, he was immediately asked whom Howard was talking to.

"Don't know," Bradley answered. "The head man's still in the room on the phone. We should know any time now."

Howard returned with his coaches. He had a twinkle in his eyes as he approached the head table and banged on a glass with a spoon.

"Ladies and gentlemen," he began. "I just finished talking to some people on the telephone about a bowl game and have accepted an invitation to play TCU in the Bluebonnet Bowl in Houston, Texas, December 19th. We didn't get no guarantee. That guarantee stuff is all paper talk. Ain't none of them bowl games going to give you a guarantee, but we'll do all right. We're going to be given about 10,000 tickets to sell at $5.50 apiece. They have probably as fine a football stadium out there at Rice as there is in the country. It holds about 72,000, so let's try to fill it."

Although Clemson's bowl record was 3–3, it had played exciting football with but one exception: when it had been beaten 14–0 by Miami in the 1952 Gator Bowl. Other than that, all of Clemson's games had been decided by seven points or less. Once again, just as it had been in all their bowl dates, the Tigers were established underdogs. This time the oddsmakers made TCU, who also was 8–2 and ranked eighth nationally, an eight-point pick.

TCU was big and rugged. It had a pair of solid performers in All-American tackles Don Floyd and Bob Lilly (who went on to star with the Dallas Cowboys), guard Roy Lee Rambo, and running back Jack Spikes, and it was the top defensive team in the Southwest Conference. Clemson had a pair of standout tackles in Lou Cordileone and Harold Olson and had offensive punch in quarterback Harvey White, fullback Doug Cline, who topped the Tigers in rushing for the second straight time with 449 yards, and halfback Billy Mathis, who led the ACC in scoring with 70 points.

The crowd was not that big. Only 55,000 turned out on a damp, humid day with the temperature at 57 degrees at game time. Clemson moved downfield after the opening kickoff, reaching the TCU 41-yard line before Cline fumbled away the ball. However, when the period came to a close, the Tigers had reached the TCU 9-yard line.

They got as far as the 4-yard line, where they had to settle for a 22-yard field goal by Lon Armstrong and a 3–0 lead early in the second quarter. Midway through the period, TCU scored when speedy halfback Harry Moreland slipped out of the backfield and caught a 19-yard touchdown pass. The half ended with TCU in front 7–3.

There wasn't any excitement the entire third quarter. Neither team threatened; both were determined to keep the ball on the ground. The period went by quickly with Clemson and TCU only having the ball twice. In the final period, however, Clemson exploded. White brought the crowd to its feet with a 68-yard touchdown pass to Gary Barnes. Armstrong converted, and Clemson went in front 10–7.

The next time Clemson got the ball, it scored again. This time Lowndes Shingler hit Tommy King down the middle with a 23-yard touchdown pass. Shingler missed the extra point, and Clemson led 16–7. When they gained possession again, the Tigers scored for a third straight time. They drove 63 yards in seven plays, with Shingler accounting for 46 of them on a 35-yard run and an 11-yard pass. Ron Scrudato went the final yard for the touchdown, and Armstrong added the conversion to push Clemson to a 23–7 lead. The Tigers had scored 20 points in seven minutes to seal the victory. Their final total of 23 points was the most scored against TCU in 56 games.

Clemson's first touchdown, the 68-yard pass to Barnes, turned out to be a prudent second guess by Howard. The veteran coach admitted that he had called another pass play but yielded to his younger assistant coach Charlie Waller's call instead. Howard refused to describe the pattern that got Barnes open.

"Shucks," he said. "I want to use that pass again next year. Just say he goes down and cuts out."

Co-captain Paul Snyder, who played an outstanding game at center, tightly clutched the game ball. The senior center wasn't about to give it up to anybody. He had reason not to.

"I didn't get one during the season, and I told them I was going to keep this one," Snyder said.

CLEMSON	0	3	0	20	23
TCU	0	7	0	0	7
CU	Armstrong 22 FG				
TCU	Moreland 19 pass from Reding (Dobson kick)				
CU	Barnes 68 pass from White (Armstrong kick)				
CU	King 23 pass from Shingler (Kick failed)				
CU	Scrudato 1 run (Armstrong kick)				
Attendance: 55,000					

72 Panthers Meet the Tigers

The NFL Carolina Panthers won their first game in team history, not in Charlotte but at Clemson's Memorial Stadium. After some eight years of politicking, owner Jerry Richardson finally brought professional football to Charlotte as the National Football League's 29th member in 1995. The team had a nickname but didn't have a stadium. A venue that somewhat resembled an NFL stadium was at Clemson 140 miles away, which at the time had a capacity of 76,000.

In reality, Clemson wasn't Richardson Sports Group's first choice. They looked directly south to Columbia, South Carolina, which was closer by 93 miles, and a more appealing attraction for Charlotte-area fans. When negotiations stalled with University of South Carolina, it didn't take long for the group to zero in on Clemson. They were in a time warp and had to act fast.

From the beginning it was a natural union. Richardson played his football at Wofford and made it to the NFL as a wide receiver with the Baltimore Colts. His clutch fourth-quarter touchdown pass from Johnny Unitas clinched Baltimore's 31–16 victory over the New York Giants in the 1959 NFL Championship Game.

Jerry's son, Mark, who was general manager of the Richardson group, was a linebacker on Clemson's 1981 NCAA championship team. It didn't take long for father and son to reach a quick agreement with Clemson officials. It was a win-win for Clemson and the Panthers. And what's better than Panthers playing in the Tigers' lair?

It should have been that all along for a number of viable reasons:

- Stadium capacity. Clemson had some 9,000 more seats than USC.
- Luxury boxes. Clemson had 100 while USC proposed building only 18 of them.
- The 1995 schedule. Clemson had two weekends available each month while USC had none available in October.
- Ticket surcharges. Clemson charged $1 and USC $3 to pay for bonds that financed its stadium constructions.

"This is definitely the biggest thing to hit Clemson," proclaimed Gary Ransdale, head of the city's NFL Task Force. "Heck, there are only about 25 cities that had ever handled something like this. The services of a major urban area are usually needed to pull this off, and we're doing it with a town of 12,000."

What Ransdale was referring to was the income rewards for the school and the community. The university would earn $2.3 million to $3.2 million along with a $100,000 academic scholarship funded by the Panthers. Town merchants could realize an increase of 30 percent for their weekend opportunities.

"We think the NFL and college football are compatible," the elder Richardson pointed out. "There are people who watched Perry Tuttle play football here and William Perry and Michael

Dean Perry and Kevin Mack. Now the players they enjoyed watching here at Clemson can enjoy watching these same players play at the professional level."

The Panthers finished their inaugural season with a 7–9 record that included a four-game winning streak. Not bad for a team that played all their games on the road.

There were a number of season highlights that established the Panthers as not an ordinary expansion team.

- They won an expansion record consecutive wins (4) in defeating the San Francisco 49ers, marking the first time an expansion team defeated the defending world champions.
- Panthers ended their inaugural season with a 7–9 record, more than doubling the previous best-mark of three wins.
- Their seventh-ranked defense had the best record of any non-playoff team in the league over the last 11 games, posting a 7–4 record over that period.
- The team notched an expansion-best home record.

73 1977 Gator Bowl

December 30, 1977
Jacksonville, Florida
Clemson 3, PITT 34

The invitation to play Pittsburgh in the 1977 Gator Bowl marked a milestone in Clemson's football history. It was the first appearance of the Tigers in a bowl game in 17 years, and it also signaled the restoration of Clemson's football prowess on the national level. During the transitional period after the 1959 Bluebonnet Bowl, the legendary Frank Howard had retired in 1970 and two of his successors, Hootie Ingram and Red Parker, were forced to resign after failing to rebuild a winning football program.

Yet in his first season as Clemson's new coach, Charley Pell did just that. The Tigers completed an 8–2–1 campaign and a second-place finish in the ACC. Pell, who had been an assistant on Parker's staff the year before, brought in a new coaching staff that dramatically improved the Tigers. Nobody had figured the Tigers would roar back so loudly after winning only five games during the consecutive losing seasons.

"I felt that we'd be good sometime during the year because of all the hard work that our players and coaches had put in," Pell said. "But at the start of the season, I didn't know when we'd be good or how good we would be."

Clemson opened its regular season with a tough 21–14 loss to Maryland. After that the Tigers won seven games in a row, beating Georgia 7–6, Georgia Tech 31–14, Virginia Tech 31–13, Virginia 31–0, Duke 17–11, North Carolina State 7–3, and Wake Forest 26–0. In the final three weeks, they tied North Carolina 13–13, lost again in a tough game against Notre Dame 21–17, and beat South Carolina 31–27.

The star of the revved up Clemson offense was quarterback Steve Fuller, a junior who blossomed under Pell's coaching. Named ACC Player of the Year, Fuller completed 106-of-205 passes for 1,655 yards and eight touchdowns. The passes he threw were the most by a Clemson quarterback since Tommy Kendrick attempted 267 in 1970, which remains the school's record. Still, the 1,655 yards that Fuller gained with his passes set a new Clemson mark of achievement. Fuller looked forward to the excitement of playing as he anticipated the first bowl game of his career.

"We've got to play crazy," Fuller said. "We can't afford to get out there and feel them out. We'll be wild out there. It'll be a crazy football game."

The game was being looked upon as a duel between two fine quarterbacks—Fuller and Pittsburgh senior Matt Cavanaugh. Cavanaugh received some mention as an All-American. He had more bowl experience, too, having played in the 1977 Sugar Bowl when Pittsburgh was voted the nation's No. 1 team after trouncing Georgia 27–3.

Yet there was no discounting the presence of Cavanaugh. Like Fuller, he was the key to his team's offense. Among other things, his being a drop-back passer caused Clemson to change its defense strategy. Clemson's star linebacker Randy Scott appeared ready for the challenge.

"He doesn't drop back as deep as a lot of quarterbacks, and that means we won't be able to pressure him as much from the corners," Scott pointed out.

Cornerback Rex Varn was aware that the Tigers defensive backfield was facing in Cavanaugh the best quarterback they had seen all year.

"They have got by far the best passing game we will face," Varn said. "Their receivers run pro routes, and they all go to the ball well."

On paper, the teams appeared evenly matched. The Panthers gave up 11.9 points a game, and the Tigers 11.7. Both had 8–2–1 records, and each lost to Notre Dame. Pittsburgh was ranked No. 10 in the writers' poll and Clemson No. 11. Another oddity was that Pell and Pittsburgh's coach, Jackie Sherrill, both played football at Alabama under Coach Bear Bryant, and both were in their first seasons as head coaches. Sherrill felt that possibly this year his team might be better than last season, even though All-American running back Tony Dorsett had graduated.

"We do more things with the football," Sherrill explained. "Last year what we did most of the time was hand the ball to Dorsett. Defensively, we are more aggressive than last year. The difference in the game this week will be one or two plays. Depending on how some of the other games come out, the winner could end up being ranked between fifth and eighth. And don't forget, Clemson played Notre Dame better than we did."

A new attendance record was established as 72,289 fans, 41 more than the crowd at the 1969 game, paid their way despite the threat of showers. They didn't have to wait long to see the first touchdown. The first time Pittsburgh got the ball after a Clemson punt, Cavanaugh hooked up with Elliot Walker for a 39-yard touchdown pass. With 1:07 left, Pittsburgh scored again on a 24-yard field goal by Mark Schubert. Fuller tried to bring Clemson back, but his pass was intercepted on the Pittsburgh 18-yard line just as the period was coming to an end.

The Panthers used the interception as a springboard for another touchdown in the opening minutes of the second quarter. This time Cavanaugh hit Walker with a 10-yard touchdown pass to complete an 82-yard drive. Clemson finally got points on the scoreboard following the kickoff. Obed Ariri booted a 49-yard field goal to bring the Tigers to within two touchdowns at 17–3. The half ended 10 minutes later without any further scoring and with Pittsburgh clearly in charge.

Cavanaugh continued to find success with his passes in the third quarter. He threw his third touchdown pass of the game, this time hitting Gordon Jones for 10 yards. Pittsburgh's lead increased to 24–3 and held until the end of the period.

The Tigers needed to score big in the fourth period to pull out of impending defeat. They couldn't do it. Instead, Schubert kicked a 21-yard field goal, and Cavanaugh combined with Walker for a 25-yard touchdown pass to overwhelm Clemson 34–3.

"From this point on we're going to be an experienced bowl team," Pell said. "I'm smarter today that I was yesterday. I learned a whole lot from losing, like pass defense for one thing. We played too cautious, and that's my fault. I need to apologize to the team. I didn't prepare them for this game. We have the opportunity to be a fine football team next year. We came a million miles from last January. This has been a Cinderella ballclub. It's done what no one said it could do."

CLEMSON	0	3	0	0	3
PITT	10	7	7	10	34

UP	E. Walker 39 pass from Cavanaugh (Schubert kick)
UP	Schubert 24 FG
UP	E. Walker 10 pass from Cavanaugh (Schubert kick)
CU	Ariri 49 FG
UP	Jones 10 pass from Cavanaugh (Schubert kick)
UP	Schubert 21 FG
UP	E. Walker 25 pass from Cavanaugh (Trout kick)

Attendance: 72,289

74 Josh Cody

Although a lot of changes have taken place in college athletics since Josh Cody paced the sideline as head football and basketball coach in the late 1920s and early 1930s, some principles he stressed should never change.

After leaving Clemson after the 1930 season with a 29–11–1 record, Cody coached at Vanderbilt, Florida, and Temple, which was his final stop in coaching and administration. At one time or another, he coached both the football and basketball teams at these schools.

Cody played football at Vanderbilt. He remains the only Commodore to earn All-American honors three times (1915, '16, '19). The 1920 Vanderbilt graduate was selected as an All-Time All-American by the Football Writers Association. The Commodores

Josh Cody.
(Photo courtesy of the
Clemson University Sports
Information Department)

had a 23–9–3 record, as he was a devastating lineman on both sides of the ball under legendary head coach Dan McGugin.

On occasion, he played in the backfield and was both a great passer and drop-kicker. He once converted on a 45-yard drop-kick against Michigan.

As one teammate recalled, "He would tell the running backs on which side of him to go, and you could depend on him to take out two men as needed. He was the best football player I've ever seen."

Cody also played basketball, baseball, and was on the track team at Vanderbilt, earning 13 varsity letters in all. And if that wasn't enough, he was a lieutenant in World War I in 1917 and 1918.

Another teammate who witnessed his greatness once said, "He was a farm boy and he had no polish, but he was very honest and sincere. He didn't have a scholarship—we had none in those days—but he had a real job. He cleaned the gym every day, cleaned up the locker rooms and the showers, and tended to the coal furnace after practice."

There was also much documentation of his roughness. Teammates remembered that he did not like to wear pads, so he cut up an old quilt and sewed it into the shoulders of his jersey.

Upon graduation, Cody started his coaching career at Mercer in 1920 as coach of all sports and athletic director. In 1923, Cody came back to Vanderbilt as head basketball and baseball coach and as an assistant in other sports. In 1926–27, the Commodores finished 20–4 and won the Southern Conference basketball title under his tutelage.

In his first year as head football coach at Clemson (1927), he led the Tigers to a 5–3–1 record, then guided Clemson to back-to-back 8–3 seasons in 1928 and 1929.

Cody was a popular man among the Clemson student body. He was nicknamed "Big Man" because of his large stature. According to one account when he was seen on campus and the name "Big Man" was yelled, he would turn and wave and smile the largest grin. He loved and respected the students at Clemson, and they loved him.

This probably was best exemplified when it was rumored he was leaving after three years at Clemson. To show their appreciation for his fine record (including a then 3–0 mark against South Carolina), the students, faculty, and staff acted quickly and took up a collection to buy him a brand new black Buick, and presented him with a new car in front of the steps at Tillman Hall on May 6, 1929. He would stay for one more year after this kind of gesture. In 1930, the Tigers finished with an 8–2 mark in his final football season at Clemson, the first time in history the Tigers had won at least eight games in three consecutive years.

Cody is the only coach in Tigers history who has been around more than two years who never lost a football game to South

Carolina. He also defeated Furman three straight seasons, had a 13–0–1 home record, and had a 72 percent winning mark overall, fourth best in Clemson history. He also coached Clemson's first All-American, center O.K. Pressley. Cody also coached basketball at Clemson for five years and led the Tigers to a 16–9 slate in 1930. During the 1928–30 seasons, he guided Clemson to a 22–4 mark at home on the hardwood.

Upon leaving Clemson, Cody returned to Vanderbilt as an assistant football coach and head basketball coach. He was the head football coach and the athletic director at Florida from 1936 to 1939.

In 1940, Cody was a line coach at Temple and was appointed head basketball coach in 1942. He held that post until he became athletic director in 1952. During his tenure as basketball coach, Cody racked up 124 victories and guided the Owls to the NCAA Tournament in 1944, the first NCAA Tournament appearance in the history of the program. That team reached the Elite Eight of the tournament.

In 1955, he coached the football team at Temple after the original coach resigned on the eve of the season. The Owls were winless that year (0–8), but Cody never complained and instead stressed, "They were improving and trying hard."

During his time at Temple, Cody had an African American playing on the basketball team. When asked before the NCAA Tournament what he would do if segregation became an issue and his team could not stay in the same hotel or eat at the same restaurant, he simply replied, "We will not play in that city. We go together as a team or not play at all."

Such was Cody—he loved his players and respected them, and they did the same.

"I've always tried to treat a player the way I'd expect my son to be treated," was another of his guiding principles.

Another rule he lived by was, "It's important to realize how much influence a coach can have on his youngsters," he once said.

Cody retired to a farm in New Jersey. He died of a heart attack on June 17, 1961, in Mount Laurel, New Jersey, at the age of 69. He was inducted into the College Football Hall of Fame as a player in 1970 and the Tennessee Sports Hall of Fame in 1999.

Cody enjoyed a wide reputation as athlete, coach, administrator, and gentleman. Although many things have changed in the last 80 or so years since Cody was at Clemson, some things that he stressed, including the importance of character and respect for others, will never change.

75 E.J. Stewart

Edward James (E.J.) Stewart served as head coach at Clemson in 1921 and 1922. He also made stops at other notable schools during his career.

Stewart played football and baseball at Scio College and played football, basketball, baseball, and ran track at Western Reserve University. He was the first athlete there to win letters in all four sports in the same school year. Upon his graduation, he played, organized, and served as head coach of the Massillon, Ohio, professional football team.

He began coaching college athletics at Mount Union College in Alliance, Ohio, and in 1907 papers rated his team as the strongest in Ohio. The basketball team that he coached was without a doubt the best in the state.

In 1908–09, Stewart left Mt. Union College and was named head basketball coach at Purdue University. After four consecutive losing seasons, the first-year coach directed Purdue to an 8–4 season and a second-place finish in the Big 10 Conference.

In addition to coaching Clemson's football team, E.J. Stewart also coached the baseball and track teams. (Photo courtesy of the Clemson University Sports Information Department)

He coached at Oregon State in 1911 and won the Pacific Coast Championship in basketball his first season. He built the football, basketball, baseball, and track programs, and the Oregon State Aggies ranked athletically with the best of the Pacific Coast.

Stewart left Oregon State and was hired as the head football and basketball coach at the University of Nebraska. At Nebraska, he led the Cornhuskers football team to a combined record of 11–4 in 1916–17. They also won the Missouri Valley Conference title both seasons. He gave up the position when he left for World War I. He also served as basketball coach for three seasons, compiling a 29–23 record. After leaving the service, he entered the automobile business as president and treasurer of Stewart Motor Co. Because of the economic conditions at the time, he decided to go back into coaching, and this time he took a job at Clemson.

In the spring of 1922, Steward coached the baseball and track teams while conducting spring football practice. In the fall, Stewart's football team went 1–6–2 but improved to a 5–4 mark in 1922. It was in the 1922 season that Clemson had its first homecoming game, a 21–0 loss to Centre on September 30. He coached the track teams in 1922 and 1923. He was also the head basketball coach in 1922 and 1923 and had a 19–19 record for both years. In 1923, the team had an 11–6 mark.

He was also signed to coach a third year at Clemson, but a larger school, the University of Texas, came calling, and he went on to coach there for four seasons.

At Texas, he coached the team to an 8–0–1 mark in 1923 and a 5–3–1 record in 1924. In 1925 they had a 6–2–1 record, and in his final season the team compiled a 5–4–0 mark. The 1923 and the 1925 teams finished second in the Southwest Conference.

After his stint at Texas, he went to the University of Texas El Paso for two seasons, 1927 and 1928. In 1927, they had a 2–2–2 record and in 1928, the team finished with a 3–4–1 mark. Stewart was tragically killed in a hunting accident in Texas on November 19, 1929.

Stewart is believed to be one of the first coaches to use communication from the press box or top of the stands to the field while the game was in progress. Eastern coaches, such as those at Harvard, thought that they had come up with the idea in the late teens and early '20s. The idea of using a telephone during a football game was evolved by Stewart during his regime at Oregon Agricultural College (Oregon State). He first tried it during the Oregon–Oregon State game in 1913 and used the telephone play repeatedly in subsequent important contests on the Oregon State schedule.

After he went to Nebraska to assume the head coaching position, he reverted to his telephone scheme during the Nebraska-Syracuse game on Thanksgiving Day 1917. Seated on the top of a covered stand at the north side of the Nebraska field, a vantage point that enabled him to get a better view of every play and player than if he were on the sideline, Stewart used a telephone in passing information to his aides on the Cornhuskers' bench. It is not known if he used this technique at Clemson or not, but programs around the country on all levels of football uses this scheme today.

76 Charley Pell

Charley Pell arrived at Clemson in 1976 and discovered a Tigers team that had finished 3–6–2 in the aftermath of a 2–9 season the year before, which contributed to a disgruntled alumni base. It wasn't a pleasant undertaking, to say the least. Pell arrived with a solid background that began with Bear Bryant indoctrination at Alabama.

Despite playing only a year of high school football, Pell made the squad. He made an early impression on the legendary coach and was a member of the 1961 national championship team. Upon graduation in 1964, Bryant called Pell into his office.

"What are you going to do next?" Bryant asked.

"I don't have any plans," Pell answered.

"I'll tell you what you're going to do. You're going to stay here and work for me," Bryant ordered.

"Yes sir," Pell replied without hesitation.

After a year, Pell left and went as an assistant to Charlie Bradshaw at Kentucky, which lasted four years. When Bradshaw resigned after the 1969 season, Pell felt it was time to leave. An opening developed at Jacksonville (Alabama) State and Pell called Jimmy Smothers, the sports editor of the *Gadsden Times* for help. He complied and called Houston Cole, the school's president, and recommended Pell for the job.

Pell was only 28 years old when he set foot in Jacksonville. In only his second season there, Pell produced an unbeaten 10–0 team and defeated Florida A&M in the Orange Blossom Classic. He left Jacksonville in 1974 and joined the staff as an assistant at Virginia Tech where the head coach, Jimmy Sharpe, was an ex-Alabama assistant.

In 1976, Pell made it to Clemson as a defensive coordinator for Coach Red Parker. When the Tigers suffered a second straight losing season, athletics director Bill McLellan ordered Parker to fire a number of his assistants. When Parker refused, McLellan immediately fired him and offered the vacant job to Pell.

If Pell was happy, he didn't show it. Parker accused him of "stabbing him in the back." McLellan said it never happened and quickly proceeded to clear the air.

"Red was a good recruiter, but Charley could take his and beat yours or take yours and beat his," McLellan said. "I called Bear Bryant, and he couldn't say enough good things about Charley."

It assured McLellan that he made the right decision in picking Pell. Before he gave him the job, he asked Pell if he would stay on staff if he hired Auburn's Pat Dye.

"Hell no," Pell replied tersely. "I can do the job as well as Pat Dye."

And he did. After an opening 1977 loss to Maryland, Clemson produced a major upset by defeating No. 17 Georgia 7–6 in Athens on the way to an 8–3–1 season and a berth in the Gator Bowl. It was the first top 20 season since 1959, and Clemson fans were happy again.

In 1978, Clemson went 11–1. The only loss was to Georgia 12–0 as the Tigers won their first ACC championship since 1967. They beat Ohio State 17–15 in the Gator Bowl and finished ranked No. 6 in the country, but Pell wasn't around to celebrate. A few days before the Tigers left for Jacksonville, Pell made a visit to Florida where he was introduced as the Gators' new head coach, which created chaos.

"He told me 30 minutes before he left that he was going," McLellan revealed. "Next thing I know he made the decision. He called me from the Anderson airport before he flew out with the Florida president."

It left a bad taste in Pell's mouth. He said he was contacted, and informed McLellan that Florida was interviewing him, Arkansas' Lou Holtz, Texas' Darryl Royal, and Mississippi's Steve Sloan.

Bobby Robinson, who was now Clemson's athletic director, looked at Pell's departure succinctly. "Red Parker got the players here, but Charley showed us how to win," he remarked. "I look at it as he gave us two great years and put us on the track to great things."

1952 Gator Bowl

January 1, 1952
Jacksonville, Florida
Clemson 0, Miami 14

By December, an ominous cloud hung over the Clemson campus. It placed a shadow on another winning season, one that the Tigers completed with a 7–3 record. Their success had earned them another bowl bid, this time to the Gator Bowl, in which Clemson would face Miami in a rematch of their thrilling Orange Bowl meeting in 1951. In late November, Clemson had polled conference members for permission to play in the Gator Bowl and received a negative answer. Nevertheless, they decided to accept the Gator Bowl offer, which was a direct violation of the conference's rule. Since Maryland had accepted a bid to play Tennessee in the Sugar Bowl, the Southern Conference found itself embroiled in a volatile situation.

Meanwhile, Howard had to concentrate on getting his squad ready to meet the University of Miami for a second straight time. There was no love lost between the two schools, either. Howard gave his squad four days off for the Christmas holidays and told them to come back lean and mean. He warned them that Miami would be ready for them since they were still smarting from the previous year's defeat.

The Tigers really came alive in the final four games of the season. Up until that juncture, they appeared mediocre with a 3–2 record. Then they roared past Wake Forest 21–6, Boston College 21–2, Furman 34–14, and Auburn 34–0. It was this strong finish that attracted the Gator Bowl officials to Clemson. Howard accomplished wonders after graduation removed the four mainstays of his 1950 backfield—Ray Mathews, Fred Cone, Jackie Calvert, and Dick Hendley.

In the four ending victories, Clemson had scored 110 points while surrendering only 22. Most of the offense was supplied by tailback Billy Hair and end Glenn Smith, both of whom were named to the All-Southern team. Hair's passing produced 1,004 yards, and his running accounted for 698 more. Smith caught seven touchdown passes and led the Tigers in scoring with 42 points.

Howard was still rankled when he arrived in Jacksonville five days before the game. He poked sarcasm at the censure that had been inflicted on Clemson by the conference.

"They say we are bad," Howard snapped. "Well, if going to bowls makes you bad, I'd like to rot a little bit. Other conference teams can't play us because we're going to a bowl, but they can play Tennessee and Georgia Tech and Miami. They're going to bowls, too.

"But I'm more concerned with the game we're getting ready to play. I think we're going to have a fine game. Miami has a pretty good team, better than last year, and I don't know whether we can beat them or not. I don't know whether they can beat us. It's a toss-up."

Clemson was appearing in its third bowl game in four years. They were a successful bowl participant, too, having won all three games. While the crowd wasn't anywhere as large as the one that turned out for the previous year's Orange Bowl, it was nevertheless a record Gator Bowl throng of 37,208 that was made comfortable by a sunny afternoon.

It didn't take long for the fans to become excited. Hair brought the crowd to its feet on the kickoff by racing 72 yards to Miami's 26 before he was pulled down. The Tigers were in excellent position to drive for a touchdown, but they only gained six yards on four plays and had to give up the ball.

With 3:00 left in the first period, Miami drove 82 yards for a touchdown. Harry Mallios took a pitchout on the 11-yard line and raced to the corner of the end zone. Elmer Tremont accounted for the extra point, and Miami led 7–0.

In the second period, the Hurricanes scored again. They got the opportunity when they blocked Hair's punt on the Clemson 33-yard line. This time Mallios cracked over the 2-yard line, and Tremont converted again to send Miami into a 14–0 halftime lead.

While the opening half was fairly evenly contested, the Tigers appeared fired up in the third period. Yet, they couldn't score. They held the edge in the final period and again came up empty. Despite holding Miami without a first down the entire second half, Clemson still lost the first bowl game in its history 14–0. The team simply made too many mistakes offensively.

CLEMSON	0	0	0	0	0
MIAMI	7	7	0	0	14
UM Mallios 11 run (Tremont kick)					
UM Mallios 2 run (Tremont kick)					
Attendance: 37,208					

78 Bruce McClure

It was his mother's dying wish, one that Bruce McClure has never forgotten. A senior guard, McClure was anxiously looking forward to playing against TCU on an October day in 1965. It was the first time that Clemson was playing against Southwestern Conference School. The Horned Frogs, who were coming off a Sun Bowl appearance, presented a tough challenge for the Tigers who had split their first four games.

McClure, who was recruited by assistant Coach Whitey Jordan from Myers Park High School in Charlotte, was confronted with another challenge, one that weighed heavily in his heart. A day before the Saturday encounter, McClure learned that his mother had died. McClure, who had a close relationship with his mom, was grief stricken. Although she was frail from illness, she managed to gather enough strength to attend the games at Memorial Stadium.

But on that Friday morning in his dormitory room, he received a message that Coach Frank Howard wanted to see him as quickly as he could. He wondered why. His first thought was that he had done something wrong and was going to be disciplined, maybe not get to play the next day. Howard greeted him with a hand shake and asked him to sit down. "Boy, your momma is dead," Howard told him.

McClure just sat there, his hands on his face. Howard left the room, and left McClure alone with his thoughts. When he returned some five minutes later, McClure gave him his answer.

"I told him that I would play," McClure remarked. "But first I was going to Charlotte tonight to spend time with my family."

The first thing McClure did after leaving Howard's office was to find his brother who was a freshman at Clemson. His mind was still with his family.

"I was the oldest brother and I have to take care of my family," he remembered. "I knew I had to get home to Charlotte with my brother. It was the longest drive I had ever made in my life. I drove back to Clemson with a family friend early Saturday morning and got back around 2:00 AM and went straight to my dorm room. I couldn't sleep for maybe two hours. I kept thinking that Mom always told me, whether she lived or died, that I had my own life to live. 'You'll get into trouble if you stay in Charlotte. Just finish school and fulfill your commitments under any circumstances.'

"I was still in shock even though she had been sick with leukemia but I thought there was more time. She had been coming to the games. At the time, they were coming out with new innovations and treatments and we were very encouraged. However, during surgery she had a brain hemorrhage and died."

It was a somber pregame meal the next morning. The coaches led by Howard all talked to McClure. In the dressing room it was more of the same with trainers Fred Hoover and Herman McGee. The players let McClure have time to himself. Howard felt it would be better if McClure didn't start.

In the press box, McClure's name was not included on the depth chart. It wasn't a slight. Bob Bradley, the sports information director, explained it simply: "We didn't put his name on the chart because we didn't figure he would play given the circumstances."

McClure sat on the bench the entire first quarter. It was just after the second period began before Howard sent him on the field. At the halftime break, Howard talked to McClure. He wanted to be sure that McClure wanted to continue. It was Senior Day, and McClure answered yes.

The game was a tough struggle. Clemson was holding a slim 3–0 lead as the game was winding down. All that was left for quarterback Tommy Ray to do was to run out the clock. He did so on a quarterback sneak to the cheers of the crowd. Ray was under a crowd of TCU defenders. When he finally got up, he looked for McClure who played a strong game under an emotional strain. He handed him the game ball.

"Take this," he ordered. "We won this one for you." McClure was thrilled.

"It would have been Mom's wish that I played," he smiled. "She wanted me to live up to my commitments. That's the only thing that enabled me to do it."

79 Bubba Brown

Marlon "Bubba" Brown is the all-time leading tackler in Clemson history. When you review the legendary list of linebackers who have played for Clemson, that is quite a statement. He is finally got his due with his induction into the Clemson Hall of Fame.

It has taken a while for Brown to get his due simply because of the great teammates Brown had in his era (1976–79). But a look at the statistics shows us that Brown was the team's top tackler, a ferocious hitter, and an enthusiastic player.

Two games stand out in his career. In 1978 Clemson traveled to Raleigh for an ACC showdown with N.C. State. N.C. State was promoting their Brown, running back Ted, for the Heisman Trophy. He had riddled Clemson for four touchdowns and 227 yards rushing three seasons earlier.

Although the national media did not portray the game as a "Battle of the Browns" (Clemson also had running back Lester Brown), Bubba took the confrontation as a personal challenge. By the end of the game, Bubba had 17 tackles and held Ted Brown to less than 100 yards rushing and out of the end zone. When *Sports Illustrated* was released the next week, it was Bubba who caught the national headlines as Defensive Player of the Week.

Clemson finished the 1978 season with a 10–1 record and was chosen to play Ohio State in the Gator Bowl on national television. Clemson won the historic game 17–15. Again, the pregame headlines were all about Danny Ford's first game as head coach and his meeting with future Hall of Fame mentor Woody Hayes. Brown personally stymied the Ohio State rushing game with 22 tackles, still the second highest single-game total in Clemson history.

Brown truly earned his induction into Clemson's Hall of Fame. He was a late signee in 1976 and wasn't heavily recruited out of high school. Nevertheless, Clemson offered him a scholarship. Coach Charley Pell saw the potential of the Loudon, Tennessee, youngster who needed work to succeed. He lacked endurance, which Pell attributed to his weight and had Brown lose 25 pounds to reach 205.

Coach Charley Pell saw the raw potential in Bubba Brown and gave him a football scholarship to Clemson. (Photo courtesy of the Clemson University Sports Information Department)

Brown didn't play much his first year, but Pell saw improvement in his sophomore season. He finished second in tackles with 120 even though he shared playing time with Ronnie Smith.

"Bubba did a great job for us the entire season," Pell mentioned. "He was real strong in our improvement on defense. He worked as hard and anyone day in and day out. He understands that he has to make up for his lack of size at 5'11" with desire and intensity. The extra perseverance is what made him such a good football player."

When the 1978 season began, most of the attention centered around Randy Scott. The senior linebacker had an excellent season with 72 tackles and two interceptions. But Brown dominated the statistical sheet and led the team in tackles and first hits.

Looking back, Pell expressed admiration for Brown's contributions during his four-year career.

"He came in as a young linebacker but grew up in a hurry," Pell said. "He got right into the thick of things and was real quick to pick up the way we play defense."

Marlon "Bubba" Brown made his mark.

80 2013 Georgia Win

August 31, 2013
Clemson, South Carolina
Clemson 38, Georgia 35
Clemson was ranked No. 8 in the nation and became the first non-SEC team in college football history to defeat top 10 SEC opponents in consecutive games with its 38–35 win over No. 5 Georgia at Memorial Stadium.

Clemson had defeated No. 7 Louisiana State 25–24 in the Chick-fil-A Bowl to end the 2012 season, thus setting up its shot to make history against Georgia.

But that had little to do with what transpired on the field, according to Clemson head coach Dabo Swinney. "We have all the respect in the world for the SEC, but it's not about a league, it's about a program, bottom line," Swinney said. "We love being in the ACC and we're very proud of all that stuff, but we're worried about Clemson. And these guys don't feel like they take a back seat to anyone."

A back-and-forth affair throughout, the Tigers opened up a double-digit lead in the fourth quarter on Stanton Seckinger's nine-yard touchdown catch from Tajh Boyd and hung on to defeat the Bulldogs in the first season-opening meeting of the top 10 teams in Clemson history.

Seckinger's decisive score was fitting in that his jersey is No. 81 and it came on the night Danny Ford, the legendary head coach who led Clemson to its only national title in 1981, was inducted into the Ring of Honor. It also came against the team that was arguably the Tigers' fiercest rival during Ford's tenure.

"This was a special night for Clemson," Swinney said. "I'm happy for Coach Ford to finally be inducted into the Ring of Honor. It was awesome to see all our former players back tonight. That is Clemson. This was an awesome night."

After the offense traded three-and-outs to open the game, Clemson marched 76 yards and found the end zone on a four-yard run by Boyd for a 7–0 lead.

Georgia needed 12 seconds to tie the score, however, as Todd Gurley took a pitch on the next snap from scrimmage and raced 75 yards to pay dirt.

Not to be outdone, Clemson needed 12 seconds after the ensuing kickoff return to jump back on top, as Boyd found Sammy

Watkins on the Tigers' next play from scrimmage, and Watkins outran the Georgia defense for a 77-yard touchdown.

However, Georgia got rushing touchdowns by Keith Marshall and Quayvon Hicks to take a 21–14 lead, and when Clemson's next drive fizzled, the Tigers badly needed someone to make a play on defense.

Vic Beasley rose to the occasion.

On third-and-5 from the Georgia 19, the junior defensive end came off the end like he was shot out of a cannon and took down Aaron Murray from behind for the first of four Tigers sacks on the night.

"Our defense needed a spark from somebody, somebody to make a big play, and I believe I was the one to make the big play that sparked us," Beasley said.

On the Bulldogs' next drive, it was defensive end Corey Crawford who came up with the big play for the Clemson defense. After Georgia netted one yard on its first two plays, Crawford broke through the line and stripped Murray of the football. Linebacker Spencer Shuey fell on the fumble at the Bulldogs' 16-yard line, and the Tigers had the momentum-shifter they needed.

Five plays later, Boyd scored on a two-yard touchdown run to tie the score 21–21.

Clemson's defense came up with another big play before halftime, as defensive coordinator Brent Venables dialed up a zone blitz and Crawford, who dropped into coverage, picked off Murray for the first interception of his career to keep the score tied at halftime.

"It was a zone blitz, and I was just doing what I'm coached to do by Coach [Marion] Hobby and Coach Venables...cutting off the dig [route]," Crawford stated.

After another strong stand by the Tigers defense to open the second half, Clemson promptly regained the lead on a 31-yard touchdown pass on a wheel route from Boyd to running back Zac Brooks.

46 Straight Polls

Clemson has a streak of 46 straight polls with a top 25 ranking in at least one poll, including every week during the 2012 season and every week in 2013. It is the second-longest streak in Tigers history.

It is the longest streak that Clemson has been ranked in at least one poll since the October 23, 1989 to October 24, 1992 period, when the Tigers were ranked in 50 consecutive AP polls. Alabama, Clemson, Louisiana State, Oklahoma, Oregon, South Carolina, and Stanford are the only schools in the nation with an active streak of being ranked in at least 45 polls.

Active AP Streaks

Rk School	Weeks	Years
1. Alabama	98	2008–13
2. Louisiana State	81	2009–13
3. Oregon	77	2009–13
4. Oklahoma	65	2010–13
5. South Carolina	64	2010–13
6. Stanford	64	2010–13
7. Clemson	**46**	**2011–13**
8. Florida State	36	2011–13
9. Ohio State	33	2012–13
10. Texas A&M	27	2012–13

Georgia tied the score at 28–28 when Gutley rumbled in from 12 yards, but Clemson regained the lead on its next possession on a 24-yard field goal by Chandler Catanzaro.

Georgia had a first-and-goal from the 5-yard line on its ensuing possession and was primed to take back the lead, but the Clemson defense hunkered down and held the Bulldogs out of the end zone on three straight runs.

Georgia lined up to kick a chip-shot field goal that would have tied the score, but the snap was high and the Bulldogs' holder was forced to fall on the ball, which turned it over on downs and preserved Clemson's 31–28 lead.

"That was huge," Crawford said. "That was another turning point in the game because it looked like they were going to gain momentum."

The Tigers extended their lead to double-digits, the only double-digit lead of the game, on the ensuing possession, as Seckinger hauled in his second career touchdown, a nine-yard catch on third-and-goal.

The sideline official initially ruled that Seckinger stepped out of bounds at the 2, but replay clearly showed he had tight-roped the sideline without stepping out of bounds.

"That was the biggest catch of the game right there," said Boyd, who led the Tigers to their first win over Georgia since 1990, snapping the Bulldogs' five-game winning streak in the series.

Boyd was one of four Tigers who received ACC Player of the Week honors, Clemson's most in a week since 2006. Boyd (offensive back), Ryan Norton (co-offensive lineman), Watkins (receiver), and Shue (linebacker) all earned ACC accolades.

CLEMSON	14	7	10	7	38
GEORGIA	14	7	7	7	35

CU   Boyd 4 run (Catanzaro kick), 1st, 9:29
UGA Gurley 75 run (Beless kick), 1st, 9:17
CU   S. Watkins 77 pass from Boyd (Catanzaro kick), 1st, 8:58
UGA Marshall 4 run (Beless kick), 1st, 4:12
UGA Hicks 1 run (Beless kick), 2nd, 13:00
CU   Boyd 2 run (Catanzaro kick), 2nd, 3:51
CU   Brooks 31 pass from Boyd (Catanzaro kick), 3rd, 10:58
UGA Gurley 12 run (Beless kick), 3rd, 7:41
CU   Catanzaro 24 FG, 3rd, 4:46
CU   Seckinger 9 pass from Boyd (Catanzaro kick), 4th, 7:40
UGA Murray 1 run (Beless kick), 4th, 1:19

Attendance: 84,350

81 2000 USC Win

A sold-out crowd erupted in Death Valley as Aaron Hunt's 25-yard field goal provided Clemson with a thrilling 16–14 comeback victory over archrival the South Carolina Gamecocks. Starting from their own 32, the Tigers trailed by one point with 59 seconds remaining. Rod Gardner caught a 49-yard pass from Woodrow Dantzler with just 10 seconds left to setup Hunt for the winning field goal. Clemson's 19 seniors became just the third class since 1940 to post four consecutive victories over the Gamecocks.

Dantzler played his first complete game since the Maryland contest. He finished with 265 yards of total offense—185 passing and 80 rushing. Gardner was once again Dantzler's favorite target. For the second consecutive year, Gardner sealed the Gamecock's fate. In 1999, his 29-yard touchdown reception clinched a Clemson bowl bid. Gardner's four-catch, 107-yard effort gave him the Clemson record with nine 100-yard games in his career.

Clemson scored its only touchdown of the game on its first possession. Travis Zachery ran the ball seven times for 23 yards during a 17-play, 77-yard drive that Zachery finished with a one-yard scoring run. South Carolina answered quickly when Derek Watson broke a 61-yard touchdown run just over two minutes later.

Aaron Hunt connected on a field goal with three seconds remaining. The freshman gave Clemson a 10–7 advantage going into halftime.

The third period was scoreless. Alex Ardley provided two highlights for Clemson with a pair of interceptions. The

Gamecocks drove to the Clemson 32 when Arldely recorded his second interception of the period. More than 10 minutes elapsed on the clock before Clemson earned a first down in the second half. Neither team scored in the third quarter.

Hunt's longest field goal of the day came on a 31-yard connection with 14:05 remaining in the final period. South Carolina then began a 9:00 drive that put the Gamecocks at the Clemson 5-yard line. Trailing by six, South Carolina went for the touchdown on fourth down. Clemson took over after Darrel Crutchfield broke up an end zone pass intended for Jermale Kelly.

On South Carolina's next possession, Petty threw two consecutive first-down passes that put South Carolina in the Clemson red zone. Pass interference was called on the Tigers, and the Gamecocks received a first-and-goal at the 2-yard line. Watson then fumbled when he collided with Keith Adams. The ball went into the end zone where it was recovered by tight end Thomas Hill. Jason Corse's extra point put South Carolina in front by a point.

Brian Mance brought the ensuing kickoff from the 4-yard line to the 32. Following an incomplete pass and a sack, Dantzler threw a pass to Gardner, who was streaking down the right sideline. Falling backward, Gardner made the catch at the South Carolina eight. The Tigers sprinted to the line, and Dantzler spiked the ball with seven seconds remaining. Hunt's 25-yarder gave Clemson its ninth victory of the year, solidifying the most successful Tigers regular season since 1991.

Reggie Herring's defense turned into a solid effort, only allowing the pair of touchdowns. Alex Ardley and Keith Adams earned ACC Player of the Week recognition. Chad Carson had a team-high 18 tackles. Adams and Robert Carswell followed closely with 16 and 11 tackles, respectively.

November 18, 2000, at Clemson, South Carolina

CLEMSON	7	3	0	6	16
SOUTH CAROLINA	7	0	0	7	14

CU	Zachery 1 run (Hunt kick) 1st, 4:25
USC	Watson 61 run (Corse kick), 1st, 2:16
CU	Hunt 22 FG, 2nd, 0:03
CU	Hunt 31 FG, 4th, 14:05
USC	Hill fumble recovery (Corse kick), 4th, 0:59
CU	Hunt 25 FG, 4th, 0:03

1995 USC Game

A 21-point outburst in the fourth quarter helped Clemson to a 38–17 win in front of 74,990 fans at South Carolina's Williams-Brice Stadium. It marked the fourth straight Tigers win in Columbia and capped off a perfect 5–0 road season for the Tigers, just the second perfect road season for the Tigers since 1948.

South Carolina started the scoring in the first quarter with a seven-yard touchdown pass from Steve Taneyhill to Monty Means at the 10:08 mark. The scoring drive came on the Gamecocks' opening possession and covered 90 yards on 11 plays.

The Tigers answered the score with a first-quarter score of their own. Emory Smith bulled his way over from the 1-yard line on fourth down at the 3:29 mark of the first quarter. The drive was set up by a 22-yard punt return from Antwuan Wyatt that gave the Tigers possession at the USC 26-yard line.

The Tigers defense came up big in the second quarter when they stuffed Stanley Pritchett on four straight carries inside the

3-yard line. South Carolina, however, got the ball back with 1:09 to go in the half and was able to strike with a Reid Morton field goal and a 10–7 halftime advantage.

After a Jeff Sauve field goal, a Pritchett touchdown, and a Clemson fumble in its own territory, the Gamecocks looked to be in control. But South Carolina couldn't capitalize, and the momentum began to shift in Clemson's favor.

Raymond Priester, who had suffered a hamstring injury in the first half when he had just seven yards rushing in four attempts, re-entered the game and provided a spark for the Tigers. Wyatt turned a five-yard Nealon Greene pass into a touchdown by eluding most of the Gamecocks secondary and darting 56 yards for a touchdown. The touchdown was the first of four straight TDs for the Clemson offense.

Priester scored from six yards out on the Tigers' next possession, giving them their first lead of the day at 24–17. Priester set the Clemson single-season rushing record on the drive and ended the day with 1,286 yards rushing.

Greene carried in the next touchdown for Clemson from the 2-yard line, capping off a 46-yard drive that gave the Tigers a commanding 31–17 lead halfway through the fourth quarter.

Leomont Evans set up the last touchdown with a 24-yard return of an interception of Steve Taneyhill's last collegiate pass. After a 15-yard unsportsmanlike conduct call on the Gamecocks, Smith rambled 54 yards to the USC 7. Smith would end the scoring of the day four plays later with his second touchdown.

Anthony Simmons led the Tigers defense with 19 tackles and 1.5 sacks. Andye McCrorey chipped in with nine stops for the defense that gave up only 90 yards rushing on the day.

November 18, 1995, at Columbia, South Carolina

CLEMSON	7	0	10	21	38
SOUTH CAROLINA	7	3	7	0	17

USC   Means 7 pass from Taneyhill (Morton kick) 1st, 10:08
CU   Smith 1 rush (Sauve kick) 1st, 3:29
USC   Morton 27 FG, 2nd , 0:00
CU   Sauve 35 FG, 3rd, 19:57
USC   Pritchett 3 pass from Taneyhill (Morton kick), 3rd, 7:46
CU   Wyatt 56 passes from Greene (Sauve kick), 3rd, 3:29
CU   Priester 6 rush (Sauve kick), 4th, 11:34
CU   Greene 2 rush (Sauve kick), 4th, 8:40
CU   Smith 1 rush (Sauve kick), 4th, 0:37
Attendance: 74,990

1997 USC Game

Clemson exploded for 44 unanswered points to turn a 14–3 deficit into a commanding 47–14 lead early in the fourth quarter as the Tigers cruised to a 47–21 victory over arch-rival South Carolina in Columbia. Senior Nealon Greene completed 12-of-15 passes for 157 yards and three touchdowns, and Tony Horne became the first player in Clemson history to score touchdowns on a punt return and a reception in the same game. The win marked the seventh consecutive victory by the road team in the series and the 47 points were the most by a Clemson team against South Carolina since 1900.

Raymond Priester put to rest questions about the health of his ankle on the Tigers' opening drive. Clemson's career rushing leader carried for 13 yards on the 12-play, 64-yard drive that ended with a 20-yard field goal by David Richardson. Priester had missed most of the three previous games with an ankle injury.

South Carolina bounced back with a 14-point explosion on touchdown runs of 54 and 35 yards by Tory Hambrick on consecutive possessions. The scores gave the Gamecocks a 14–13 lead at the end of the first quarter.

After a 32-yard Richardson field goal cut the Carolina lead to 14–6, South Carolina appeared to be driving for a third score late in the second quarter, when a single play seemed to turn around the entire game. Troy Hambrick tossed a bad pitch on a reverse and freshman safety Chad Speck fell on it at the Clemson 26 with 1:48 remaining in the first half. The Gamecocks would not cross into Clemson territory again until the Tigers were up 47–14.

Greene rushed for 23 yards on two carries and was 4-for-4 passing for 41 yards in guiding the Tigers offense to the end zone in only 1:15. The touchdown drive cut the halftime deficit to 14–13 and marked the first six straight possessions in which Clemson scored touchdowns.

Antuan Edwards, who was moved from safety to cornerback in week seven, and Tony Horne turned the third quarter into their personal showcase. Edwards intercepted South Carolina quarterback Victor Penn on the third play of the second half to give Clemson possession at the Gamecock 44. Six plays later, Greene found Tony Horne in the end zone for a 15-yard touchdown. The two-point conversion failed, but the Tigers had taken the lead for good at 19–14.

South Carolina was forced to punt on its next possession. Horne allowed the punt to take a high hop before fielding it on the run, then he eluded several would-be tacklers and raced 39 yards for his second touchdown of the night. Edwards intercepted another Penn pass on USC's next possession and raced 42 yards for a touchdown of his own to up the score 33–14.

South Carolina punted on its next possession, giving Clemson possession at its own 37 and allowing the offense a chance to flex its muscle. Priester carried five times for 19 yards, and Greene connected with tight end Lamont Hall on a middle screen for 23 yards. Greene then connected on a wide receiver screen to Mal Lawyer for 15 yards and a touchdown to increase the Tigers' lead to 40–14.

South Carolina punted into the end zone on its next possession and Clemson's ball-control offense took over. Priester carried twice for a total of 31 yards. Freshman Javis Austin then carried the ball for the next five plays, including the 19-yard scoring run that finished the Tigers' scoring for the night with 10:00 remaining.

South Carolina answered with its own 80-yard drive, but it proved to be too little, too late as Clemson won for the fifth straight time in Columbia.

Edwards was named the ACC Defensive Player of the Week for his seven-tackle performance. Senior middle guard Raymond White added nine tackles, and senior Tony Plantin chipped in seven, including three for losses.

November 22, 1997, at Columbia, South Carolina

CLEMSON	3	10	27	7	47
SOUTH CAROLINA	14	0	0	7	21

CU   Richardson 20 FG, 1st, 8:45
USC   T. Hambrick 54 run (Florio kick), 1st 6:46
USC   T. Hambrick 35 run (Florio kick), 1st, 2:42
CU   Richardson 32 FG, 2nd, 11:07
CU   Wofford 7 pass N. Greene (Richardson kick), 2nd, 0:33
CU   Horne 15 pass from N. Greene (pass failed), 3rd, 11:19
CU   Horne 39 punt return (Richardson kick), 3rd, 8:51
CU   Edwards 42 interception return (Richardson kick), 3rd, 6:52
CU   Lawyer 15 pass from N. Greene (Richardson kick), 3rd, 0:41
CU   Austin 19 run (Richardson kick), 4th, 10:00
USC   Mortiz 9 run (Florio kick), 4th, 6:32

84 Charlie Whitehurst

Charlie Whitehurst is known simply as the guy who bested South Carolina four times, the only quarterback on either side in the 111-year history of the rivalry to go 4–0 against his archrival.

"I kind of downplayed it early," he said. "It's a team honor. I guess my name gets put on it." Whitehurst beat the Gamecocks in all kinds of ways, so he deserves to have his name on it.

In 2002, his first game against USC, he rallied the Tigers from a 20–13 deficit after Dondrial Pinkins gave the Gamecocks the lead with a four-yard run at 3:04 to play in the third quarter.

From that point on, the game belonged to Whitehurst. A freshman at the time, he calmly led Clemson down the field, converting on two third-down plays—first passing 21 yards to Airese Currie on third-and-8 from the USC 32 and then scoring on an 11-yard scramble on third-and-10.

On the touchdown, Corey Jenkins chased Whitehurst out of the pocket on a safety blitz, but Whitehurst spun to the left, going toward the sideline, and then outran the USC defensive to the end zone with 13:52 to play.

When Clemson got the ball again, the freshman continued to make big plays as he led the Tigers on the game-winning drive. First Whitehurst hit Derrick Hamilton for 32 yards then tight end Bobby Williamson for six more before completing a 30-yard pass to Jackie Robinson that moved the football to the USC 1-yard line.

Moments later, running back Bernard Rambert took a pitch from Whitehurst and ran around the right side to score from two yards out for a 27–20 lead.

The Gamecocks tried to answer the Tigers' two scores as they drove to the Clemson 30 on their next possession, but Eric Sampson knocked down kicker Josh Brown's fourth-and-5 pass on a fake field goal to give the ball back to the Clemson offense. From there, the Tigers pounded the ball with running back Yusef Kelly and ran out the final 6:25 to win the game. Kelly carried seven times for 48 yards on the final drive.

Whitehurst also proved he was going to be a problem for the Gamecocks for another three years, as he completed 27-of-38 passes for 287 yards. If they had not figured it out by then, they figured it out the next year in Columbia.

The 2003 game is simply known as "63–17" by Clemson fans, but it should be noted that it was perhaps Whitehurst's finest hour as the Tigers' quarterback. He completed 18-of-26 passes for 302 yards and four touchdowns, while also rushing for 43 more yards.

He established new records against the Gamecocks for passing yards, touchdown passes, and total offense in the victory.

The 63 points were the most scored by either team in the rivalry, and that mark still stands today. It also was a statement game for the entire Clemson team, who after the game said they were playing to make sure Tommy Bowden stayed on as head coach.

Rumors had swirled after losing to Wake Forest that Bowden would be gone, but the Tigers beat No. 3 Florida State—their first win again the Seminoles since 1989—then drilled Duke before humiliating South Carolina in front of its home crowd.

The 2004 game was unfortunately outshined by the fourth-quarter brawl that embarrassed both schools and the state, but on the field, Whitehurst again owned the Gamecocks. Though his numbers weren't as dominant as the year before, the now-junior still completed 15-of-28 passes for 151 yards as the Tigers routed USC again 29–7.

Charlie Whitehurst is the only Clemson quarterback to best South Carolina four times. (Photo courtesy of the Clemson University Sports Information Department)

Clemson outgained the Gamecocks 313-to-197 in total yards and were 8-of-17 on third down, while USC was 4-of-16. The Tigers scored a minute into the game after recovering a fumble on the opening kickoff and cruised from there.

They rushed for 162 yards on 48 carries and controlled the clock with a time of possession of 36:23. Running back Reggie Merriweather led Clemson with 125 yards and three touchdowns.

The Tigers knew it was not going to be easy to beat South Carolina in 2005, but like always their leader found a way to get it done, even if he did need 35 yards to pick up a first down. Whitehurst got Clemson out of the long-distance situation and drove his team down the field in the final moments to beat South Carolina 13–9 in Columbia on a James Davis touchdown run with 5:58 remaining.

Following clipping and holding penalties on back-to-back plays, the Tigers found themselves buried at their own 22-yard line and needing to get to the USC 43 for a first down. But Whitehurst completed three passes in a row, the last a 28-yard strike to Curtis Baham on third-and-12 from the 35.

The pass moved the ball to the South Carolina 27. Davis then rolled off a 23-yard run to the 4-yard line, and then he rushed two yards before scoring the game-winner on the next play.

"At the end, put the game in Charlie Whitehurst's hand, and he came through," Bowden said.

After Davis' score, the Tigers intercepted USC quarterback Blake Mitchell twice. The last came when defensive end Charles Bennett picked off a Mitchell pass that was deflected by defensive tackle Rashaad Jackson.

South Carolina had one more chance to get the ball back, but once again, fittingly enough it was Whitehurst who dashed the Gamecocks' hopes. On third-and-1 from midfield, he called his own number on a quarterback draw and picked up 10 yards to seal the win.

As he got up, Whitehurst got to one knee and used his index finger on his right hand to signal first down, sending the 10,000 or so Clemson fans at Williams-Brice Stadium into celebration mode.

"It's the sweetest feeling I have ever known in sports," Whitehurst said.

Whitehurst finished his career against the Gamecocks by completing 77-of-118 passes for 912 yards. He completed 65.4 percent of his passes and, more importantly, he was 4–0 against the Tigers' archrival.

85 Andre Ellington

He was a little guy, 5'9" coming out of Berkeley High School in Moncks Corner, South Carolina. But Andre Ellington played like someone who was much bigger with a resume that contained 1,822 yards and 24 touchdowns as a senior. That didn't go unnoticed either because Florida, Georgia, Kentucky, South Carolina, Maryland, and North Carolina were after him before he escaped to Clemson. That's how highly thought of he was.

Coach Dabo Swinney heard all about it during spring practice in 2009. Swinney walked into an offensive meeting and heard the talk. The first thing he heard when he got through the door was all about Ellington who was a redshirt freshman the year before. He was recruited by Clemson as the eventual replacement of star running back C.J. Spiller who would be graduating in 2010.

Ellington wasn't even on the Clemson depth chart at the beginning of spring practice but began making a big impression as a shifty redshirt freshman tailback. One couldn't help noticing him.

"He's caught everybody's eye, and I had to remind them at their meeting that we still had C.J. Spiller and Jacoby Ford, and all that stuff about the Andre Ellington play sounds good but we'll stay with what we have," Swinney ordered. "Ellington is a dynamite little player, and I think the fans will see that as we develop him through the year."

Ellington wasn't the least bit upset when he was told about red-shirting in 2008. He realized that his chances of playing as a frosh were slim with Spiller and Ford out front.

"Redshirting me right now works out best for me," Ellington admitted. "It's a chance to learn the offense line. I'll learn more and get more experience."

Midway during the 2009 season, Ellington broke out in a game against Florida State. He only touched the ball six times but generated 54 yards and a touchdown. Besides the fans, Ellington's performance even impressed Spiller.

"He's my guy," C.J. exclaimed. "I went to Andre and told him my legs were feeling a little weak and that I was going to need him. When Andre came out there, he had fresh legs and you saw it on his runs. The guy responded."

Ellington contributed 491 yards as a freshman, which was enough to become a starter the next season. He ran as a tandem with Jamie Harper. However, week after week, Ellington began to establish himself as a featured back. By the third game, he was just that. A 140-yard performance against Auburn was a convincer. It even merited a call from Spiller who was now a rookie with the Buffalo Bills.

"Andre has been very productive," running backs coach Andre Powell said. "He has proven to be one of our best players on offense. When you get a guy like that, you have to give him the ball."

However, it didn't quite happen. In Clemson's ninth game of the season he was injured and lost for the remainder of the schedule. He was heading for a 1,000-yard campaign but was caught short at 636.

The injury was foreign to Ellington. He had never been seriously hurt playing football before. The rehab during the off-season was also new to him. But he worked hard and was determined to have a big junior year.

"My goal is to play a whole season," Ellington remarked. "I would like to get in the 1,500-yard range."

He had a shot at it, too. Despite the nagging injury that Ellington admitted was bothering him, he was putting up some big numbers the first half of the campaign. There were long runs and 100-yard games and a 200-yard effort, so 1,500 yards was doable.

"I think everyone saw that Ellington's explosiveness is back," offensive coordinator Chad Morris said. Sweeney did. "I think he's poised to have a great second half."

It wasn't mean to be. He missed his next two games with an ankle injury, along with a hamstring and was hobbled after that in finally being shut down at the 1,178-yard mark.

Although he never played a full healthy season, Ellington started his senior season as the ACC's rushing leader with 2,255 yards and 25 touchdowns. But the injury but continued to limit him to 1,081 yards in finishing his career with 3,436 yards, fourth on Clemson's all-time list, and a 5.5 yards per carry average.

86 Hootie Ingram

Hootie Ingram knew about legends, and not only because he was raised in Tuscaloosa, Alabama. Ingram played for the Crimson Tide and its legendary coach—Bear Bryant—who is still revered today. But Ingram never knew about replacing a legend until he became the coach who replaced Frank Howard.

Clemson reached out to Ingram late in the 1959 season. He was an assistant coach in Arkansas under Frank Broyles. At the time, the Razorbacks were playing in the Sugar Bowl when Ingram was reached. He accepted Clemson's offer several days before the game and left New Orleans immediately afterward the next day to be introduced as the new Clemson coach.

Howard did the introduction at a hastily arranged press conference. He referred to Ingram as a 36-year-old defensive genius, "a man who has what we want in a winning tradition." At the same time, Howard, who was the athletic director since his retirement, cleared the air about any involvement in coaching.

"I don't need to run his business—he'll be the coach," Howard bellowed assuredly.

In Ingram, Clemson signed a coach who knew the south, not only X's and O's, but in the important area of recruiting. On the recruiting trail he had met several Clemson coaches over the years, which gave him a good background for what Clemson was all about.

"There are a lot of different ways to win in football, but there is only one way and that's good hard work," he remarked at his opening press conference. "I can tell you we'll have plenty of that."

Ingram's first concern was recruiting. He knew enough about Clemson's travails from conversations with the Tigers coaches along the trail. He also knew about the Clemson compound and what was lacking.

"Clemson was very competitive under Coach Howard, but I do think in the latter years, the recruiting was off," Ingram observed. "It's not necessarily because the coaches were doing a bad job, but Clemson was behind on facilities. Other programs had better facilities.

"Clemson had great fans. There were always great fans at Clemson. IPTAY, however, was an organization that banded people together more than most universities. That put Clemson a little ahead in that area."

Ingram also knew that Clemson had football tradition but fell on hard times during the 1960s. He attributed that not only to the facilities but inferior player talent.

"The coaching facilities and player facilities at Fike Field House were awful," Ingram pointed out. "It was a pretty rough situation. The assistant coaches had some offices upstairs. They didn't have any offices for the head coach. They had a closet in the back that had a meeting room beside it. We just made the best of it."

Ingram also realized that Clemson didn't have an image its students and fans could relate to and spoke about it with Clemson president Dr. Edwards. Ingram was excited about what Dr. Edwards told him—that the school had some credit with the Henderson Advertising Agency in Greenville and if you're interested in any of their time.

"I said, 'Shoot, yeah,'" Ingram said. "I got in my car and drove over there without an appointment."

Ingram's meeting at the Henderson Advertising Agency was the beginning of the Tiger Paw logo. It was also the beginning of upgrading the recruiting program. Ingram was focused.

"The state of South Carolina had maybe 12 quality prospects," Ingram said. "We had to go out and get players right off the bat. We figured we had to get most of them."

Ingram coached only three years at Clemson before he left with a 12–21 record. But it wasn't his won-lost record that mattered. He left knowing that he indeed built the recruiting system and improved the facilities for the football team—and those are the standards by which he is measured.

87 Red Parker

When his Tigers ran out of their dressing room and down onto the field for the first time on September 8, 1973, against The Citadel, Red Parker remembered the atmosphere was pretty stale that day.

In fact, as the former Clemson head coach recalled, there was no energy at all in the stadium. And due to that, his Tigers played stale as they squeaked out a 14–12 victory.

"When I went to Clemson, attendance was way down," said Parker, who coached at Clemson from 1973 to 1976. "It was just a period of time when the enthusiasm was not the way it is now. It was kind of a difficult time out on that football field before the game and during the game. It was not something that was fun."

That following Monday morning, Parker went to athletic director Bill McLellan and said they needed to do something to get the spirit and enthusiasm back in Death Valley. McLellan agreed.

"He said, 'What do you want to do?' And I said, 'I want to run down the hill.' Bill at that point said, 'We can't run down the hill because the reason we quit is because we spent thousands and thousands of dollars on a new dressing room on the west end of the stadium.' Which was true, they did. They did spend a lot of money on these dressing rooms, which they had to have. It was an absolute must. So I went back to my office and I got to thinking.

"I thought about a lot of things I had heard about Clemson before I went there. One of the things that struck me as being a goldmine of potential was the Tigers running down the hill in the east end zone. I saw that as a spirit up-lifter.

"Coach Howard had done it for years, and I felt like it did all that he wanted it to do. He accomplished a great deal with that,

Coach Red Parker brought back the tradition of players entering the stadium by running down the hill. (Photo courtesy of the Clemson University Sports Information Department)

and keep in mind running down the hill was Coach Howard's deal."

Clemson had stopped running down the hill in 1970 following Howard's final year as head coach. There were several reasons why, but the main reason had to do with the new dressing rooms being located in the west end zone.

"When I came to Clemson, I was astounded that running down the hill was dropped," Parker said. "It really, really disappointed me. After the first home game, I went to McLellan, and I said, 'Bill, there is not enough sprit and enough energy and enthusiasm in the stadium. There is just not enough to have what you have to have to play major college football. That is just the way it is.'"

During that period of thought was when "the most exciting 25 seconds in college football" was reintroduced to Tigers fans. However, it wasn't done the way they remembered it.

"When I first started coming to Clemson games in 1964, they did not run down the hill like they do now," Clemson senior associate sports information director Sam Blackman said. "When Coach Howard was here, they dressed inside old Fike Field House and would leave to go to the stadium from there. They would walk down Williamson Road. I can still see those helmets bouncing up and down now as they were coming down the street. You could see the tip of the orange helmets over the fence.

"Coach Howard had them enter the stadium through a fence that they used to sit at the top of the hill and they would come down the hill and into the stadium. They did it as convenience more than anything else.

"My father and I always went to watch that," Blackman continued. "There wasn't much fanfare then as there is now. Maybe a couple hundred people, if that many. But keep in mind, they came down the hill in those days prior to warm-ups. A lot of the fans were still tailgating at that time and had yet to enter the stadium."

Learning how Howard's team ran down the hill, and why they did it, helped Parker get creative. Knowing he had to use the west end zone locker rooms, Parker though of a plan that has been used by every Clemson coach since.

What Parker created is one of the best motivating events in sports, and one of the best recruiting tools in college football.

Clemson's next home game in 1973 did not occur until October 6. The Tigers were coming off back-to-back road losses to Georgia and Georgia Tech, and Parker was anxious to see how the crowd would respond as Clemson ran down the hill prior to its battle with Texas A&M.

"I decided at that point it would be worthwhile for me to figure out a way to run down the hill because you always have a little bit of dead time before the game," he said. "I thought it would be a worthwhile opportunity to seize this and move on with it. We always used two busses to go to the motel where we stayed for the pregame meal, and then we bussed into the stadium and dressed for the game. Well, after we got on the field and warmed up, we came back in the dressing room and did everything we needed to do.

"At that point, instead of going out onto the field for the game, we had the players get on the buses. We then drove them around the stadium to the other end of the field, got them off the buses, and came down the hill together. That made a big difference in our stadium. It got people excited."

And it still does today. Nobody in college football has such a unique entrance as Clemson.

"In my opinion, running down the hill is one of the greatest motivators in all of college football," Parker said. "In fact, when I was at Clemson, we believed if we could get the prospects there on a Saturday afternoon when the Tigers ran down the hill, we had a chance to recruit them. And we brought in a lot of them."

88 Daniel Rodriguez

The arduous months of telephone calls, paperwork, and appeals would have discouraged the average person but certainly not wide receiver Daniel Rodriguez. After a hazardous tour of duty in Iraq and another in Afghanistan, where he just missed being killed, it was more like a walk in the park to get NCAA and ACC approval for his request of immediate athletic eligibility at Clemson in 2012 and an eventual walk-on for the football team.

Rodriguez wasn't your ordinary G.I. Joe. Not at all. He was a four-year veteran who attended Clemson on the G.I. Bill. But he was more than that. He was a multi-decorated war hero. Rodriguez was wounded in the fierce Battle of Kamdesh in the Nuristan Providence of the far northeast corner of Afghanistan near the Pakistan border.

On the morning of October 3, 2009, he awakened to discover that 300 Taliban insurgents had surrounded his small outpost, of 60 Americans, eventually killing eight and injuring 22 others, including Rodriguez, in one of the most violent battles of the war. Rodriguez not only earned a Purple Heart but a Bronze Star for his heroism.

Shortly before the battle, he had promised his friend, PFC Kevin Thompson, that if he left Afghanistan alive he would go after his dream of playing college football. When the battle began, Thompson was killed almost instantly while Rodriguez suffered wounds in his neck, shoulder, and leg.

"But I got my quota," he recalled. "I vividly remember thinking this is it. My intent was to kill as many of them before they killed me. I kept a round in my pocket just in case. I was going to take my own life. But it wasn't my day to go."

289

Rodriguez dragged Thompson's body back to the barracks, ignoring his own wounds. Being outnumbered 5-to-1, what were the chances of survival? But the remaining members of the unit hung tough and fought off the Taliban until help arrived, three days later.

"I feel reluctance anytime I'm called a hero," Rodriguez disclosed. "People thank me for my heroism, but I believe the ones who gave their last breath to this country are the heroes."

Six months later, Rodriguez returned to his home in Stafford, Virginia. He had done his duty for his country, but he was disillusioned with nowhere to turn.

"I was basically drunk for the first two months I was home," he revealed. "When kids think that it's a major problem that they couldn't log on to Facebook, it makes you angry."

It wasn't until he remembered the promise he made to Thompson about playing football that Rodriguez found his focus. He committed himself into getting back into shape, pushed on by his pledge as well as a bunch of friends who ridiculed him.

"They all told me that I was too old to play college football and that I wasn't even 200 pounds and that I would get demolished," Rodriguez laughed.

But one friend, Stephen Batt, had a cousin with filmmaking experience and that he could help. Rodriguez agreed.

"I told Daniel that if you trust me to shoot and edit a short film, rather than as a standard recruiting video, it'll have a better chance of catching the notices of coaches," pointed out the cousin, Ryan Russell Smith.

The filmmaker was creative. He mixed artistic footage of Rodriguez training and catching passes with footage of him in combat. The film also explained why Rodriguez had been away so long from football.

Rodriguez took it from there. He got in touch with Jake Tapper of ABC News who was writing a book about the Battle of Kamdesh and had interviewed Rodriguez. Tapper linked it to his Twitter feed, which helped the film go viral and included Rodriguez's phone number, email, and home address.

It worked. Shortly after, Rodriguez was getting messages from strangers and, more importantly, college coaches. The most prominent ones were Virginia Tech, Virginia, and Clemson. He even got one from Dan Rather.

"I never thought I'd get this much attention," Rodriguez exclaimed. "I emailed Dan Rather back saying, 'Sure. I'll do a video shoot.'"

But it was the one from Dabo Swinney that made the biggest impression. He offered Rodriguez a spot as a preferred walk-on and he would work to gain an NCAA waiver for him because he was one credit short of his associate degree.

"I was mesmerized by his video," claimed Swinney, who was a walk-on at Alabama. "I'm watching and thinking, *Holy cow, he's amazing.*"

Rodriguez continues to make an impact as a role model for fellow veterans and post-traumatic stress disorder suffers.

"I hope my story can help veterans with PTSD and kids who aren't doing well in high school," Rodriguez said. "It's not too late to get back to what you love, and you can overcome PTSD. It just takes a lot of will to get it accomplished."

1957 Orange Bowl

January 1, 1957
Miami, Florida
Clemson 21, Colorado 27

Clemson won its first ACC title in 1956 by going 4–0–1 and was asked to play in the Orange Bowl. Overall, the Tigers finished the season with a 7–1–2 record. The only loss they suffered turned out to be a very embarrassing 21–0 loss to the University of Miami that went on to close its season with an 8–1–1 record.

The Tigers' opponent, Colorado University, wasn't a household name either when it came to postseason bowl games. It had appeared only once before, against Rice, in the 1938 Cotton Bowl, and the team's 1956 record wasn't very impressive. It finished with a 7–2–1 mark underscored by the fact that the university wasn't even the champion of the Big Seven Conference. Oklahoma had won the crown but was ineligible to return for a second straight time by conference rules.

Unfortunately for Clemson, on the day the team left for Miami, a normal three-hour trip turned out to be a seven-hour nightmare. The plane chartered for the trip never arrived at the Greenville airport. It wasn't until hours later that Pan American resolved the quandary by dispatching one of its clippers to rescue the stranded Clemson players, who had been waiting for four hours.

It didn't take long to remind Coach Frank Howard that he was back in Miami. No sooner had he arrived in the terminal than a local reporter asked him if his team was anxious to play a good game because of the 21–0 beating they had taken on November 16. It rankled the mild-mannered Howard a bit.

"Ain't they ever going to forget that?" he snapped. "We lost only one game, but we made the mistake of losing it here."

Both Clemson and Colorado relied almost totally on their running game. Passing was practically non-existent in the thinking of both Howard and his adversary, Coach Dallas Ward of Colorado. However, there were extenuating circumstances. In the last five games of the season, Clemson hadn't thrown a single pass. However, it wasn't until Howard arrived in Miami that he revealed that his quarterback, Charlie Bussey, had injured his hand and couldn't throw.

Joel Wells was the main reason Howard preferred to run. The senior was the key to Clemson's Split-T offense and set an ACC rushing record with 803 yards. The reason Colorado relied on its running game was John "The Beast" Bayuk, the spinning fullback out of its single-wing attack. Bayuk was a powerful, 220-lb. piano-legged runner and complete opposite of the speedy Wells.

As usual, Howard tried to stir interest in the game. Five days before the game he spoke before an audience of some 3,500 people at a Chamber of Commerce–sponsored luncheon in the Bayfront Park Auditorium

The first-quarter action turned out to be scoreless with little offense, and each had to punt away the ball all three times they had it.

However, Colorado fans began to cheer in the second period. Early in the quarter, Bayuk scored from two yards out to culminate a 75-yard drive that gave the Buffaloes a 6–0 lead. A short while later, Bob Stransky intercepted Bussey's pass on the Clemson 47-yard line, and Boyd Dowler followed a block by Bayuk around end to score from the 6-yard line and send Colorado into a 14–0 lead.

They weren't finished. A partially blocked punt gave the Buffaloes possession of the ball on the Clemson 26. In just one play, Howard Cook raced into the end zone for Colorado's third touchdown. The conversion attempt was no good and Colorado, seemingly on the way to a rout, led 20–0 at halftime.

It was a different looking Clemson team that came out for the third quarter. The Tigers took the second-half kickoff and drove

69 yards with Wells scoring from the 3-yard line. The next time Clemson got the ball, Wells brought the crowd to its feet. He broke through a hole over right tackle and scampered 58 yards for a touchdown. The game had a new look.

The Tigers still had the momentum when the fourth period began. They recovered a Colorado fumble on the 11-yard line. Three plays later, Bob Spooner went over from the 1-yard line to tie the game. Bussey kicked his third extra point to give Clemson its first lead of the game 21–20. It was an exciting comeback.

But then a strange thing happened. Bussey tried an onside kick, and guard John Wooten recovered for the Buffaloes on the Colorado 47. It took Colorado only eight plays to regain the lead when Bayuk scored from the 1-yard line. The extra point gave Colorado a 27–21 edge. Clemson's final hopes for a victory ended when Bussey's pass was intercepted on the Colorado 17 late in the game.

Howard's impassioned halftime plea had almost turned around the game.

"It told them I was going to resign," Howard revealed. "That was it. I told them I was going to hand in my resignation if they didn't play better in the second half."

Bussey took the blame for the loss. He had called the onside kick without consulting with the coaches.

CLEMSON	0	0	14	7	21
COLORADO	0	20	0	7	27

UC   Bayuk 2 run (Indorf kick)
UC   Dowler 6 run (Cook kick)
UC   Cook 26 run(Kick failed)
CU   Wells 3 run (Bussey kick)
CU   Wells 58 run (Bussey Kick)
CU   Spooner 1 run (Bussey kick)
UC   Bayuk 1 run (Indorf kick)

Attendance: 72,552

90 Dwight Clark

Dwight Clark's statistical chart didn't exactly shatter any Clemson records. His career total of 33 receptions didn't win him any accolades, but what he learned in his four years of Clemson football was a solid background that qualified him for the NFL and one of the most historic catches in the history of the San Francisco 49ers and the league.

He got in on the ground floor of Clemson's rise to prominence in the nation's football elite, being a member of the Tigers' first bowl team in 18 years—the 1977 Gator Bowl—and a year later when Clemson returned to Jacksonville and defeated Ohio State and its famed coach, Woody Hayes. Three years later, the national championship came to Clemson.

Clark arrived at Clemson as a quarterback. His roommate was Steve Fuller, who is still the total offensive leader of the Tigers. After trying out as a safety his freshman year, Clark switched to receiver his sophomore year, and his climb up the ladder is still talked about today.

The one memorable catch came in 1978 when Clemson defeated Maryland 28–24 at College Park. The reception covered 62 yards and tied the game at 21–21. Billed as one of the best games ever in the Atlantic Coast Conference, the win gave Clemson the league title and brought 7,000 fans out to Greenville-Spartanburg Airport for the team's triumphant arrival back home.

Clark's first major contact with San Francisco of the NFL came when Bill Walsh, the 49ers head coach, came to Clemson to look at Fuller. Walsh told Fuller that he was thinking about also drafting Clark.

When the draft came along, Kansas City made Fuller a first-round pick. San Francisco took Clark in the 10th round. Another member of that Clemson team was also a first-round choice. Jerry Butler was the fifth player chosen nationally, Fuller was No. 23, and Clark—would you believe—was No. 249. Clark joined Archie Reese—another Tigers alum—who was drafted in the fifth round the year before by the 49ers. Another Clemson standout, Jim Stuckey, was selected by San Francisco the next year in the first round. The three have five Super Bowl rings between them.

Clark played eight years with the 49ers, retiring as an active player after the 1987 season. He's one of the team's all-time leading receivers, having seven consecutive years with 50 or more receptions and 700 or more reception yards. Maybe his Clemson and San Francisco success was due to his roommates. Besides Fuller at Clemson, Clark roomed with Joe Montana with the 49ers.

Clark's banner year was 1982 when he was named All-NFC, Pro Bowl (also 1981), All-Pro NFL receiving champion, and *Sports Illustrated's* Player of the Year. He was also the recipient of the Len Eshmont Award, given for courageous and inspirational play. Clark had 100 or more yards receiving in 16 regular season and four postseason games. Forty-eight of his 506 receptions went for touchdowns.

But "The Catch" came in 1981 against Dallas (from Montana, of course), which made history and lifted the 49ers into Super Bowl XVI. The six-yard catch came with a minute to play and gave the 49ers a 28–27 lead. However, the game's verdict wasn't sealed.

Dallas, with two time-outs left and Danny White at the helm, was on the verge of moving within field-goal range, which would make for a 30–28 Dallas win if successful. However, Lawrence Pillers sacked White, forcing a fumble that Stuckey retrieved at midfield with only 30 seconds remaining.

Looking back, Clark said he benefitted from the tough regime he experienced in college, catching dozens of passes before practice, learning the skill to block on running plays, and working on fitness during the off-season. That's what Walsh noted the day he went to Clemson.

"I was lucky that day when Walsh was on campus," Clark reflected. "I was lucky he liked tall receivers. I was lucky I had a coach, Tom Moore, who took the time to teach me how to block. Undoubtedly, it got me ready when Bill Walsh came that day and I got that tryout. I was ready for it."

Walsh actually didn't know much about Clark before seeing him at the tryout. He was tipped about Clark during the 49ers' 1978 season and scheduled a January day to scout both Fuller and Clark.

"Pro football scouting systems aren't always perfect, and Dwight was a perfect example of that," Walsh confessed. "We were in need of a quarterback, and I arranged to have Fuller throw and Clark catch for him.

"Well, for all our needs, I was more impressed with Dwight than I was with Fuller. I liked his size, speed, hands, attitude, everything about him."

Maybe Clark didn't set any records at Clemson, but the handsome 6'3" receiver was one of the most popular persons on campus. He was such a heartthrob that his photo file in the athletic department was constantly raided by female students.

One, Shawn Weatherly, wasn't one of them. She didn't have to be. She was Miss South Carolina and later crowned Miss USA and Miss Universe. The pair began a four-year relationship when Clark was a junior and married four years later when Clark was established with the 49ers.

After his playing days, Clark remained with the 49ers organization. He was a respected personnel figure, rising in importance to general manager in 1988. He later served as general manager of the Cleveland Browns.

91 1979 Peach Bowl

December 31, 1979
Atlanta, Georgia
Clemson 18, Baylor 24

Clemson made its third consecutive bowl appearance in 1979 after an 8–3 season. The year included a 19–10 win over Gator Bowl–bound North Carolina and a dramatic, come-from-behind 16–10 victory at Notre Dame. The 1979 season was also Danny Ford's first full campaign as head coach.

The Tigers got on the board first with an eight-play, 66-yard drive highlighted by Billy Lott's 27-yard pass to Lester Brown. Brown scored two plays later on a one-yard drive over the middle, and Obed Ariri's point after made the score 7–0 midway through the first quarter.

Baylor took the lead on two second-quarter touchdown passes from Mike Brannon to Bo Taylor and Robert Holt. Robert Bledsoe converted after both scores and the Southwest Conference representatives led 14–7 at intermission.

Clemson took the second-half kickoff, and a combination of runs by Lott, Brown, and Tracy Perry took the Tigers to the Baylor 22. The drive stalled, and Ariri's 40-yard field goal narrowed the margin to 14–10.

Quarterback Mickey Elam led Baylor on a 64-yard field goal drive after the kickoff, and he later threw a seven-yard touchdown pass to Raymond Cockrell to push the Bears' lead to 24–10.

Mike Singletary (future All-Pro with the Chicago Bears) led the Baylor defense with 20 tackles. He was a major reason Clemson gained a season low 67 yards rushing in 51 attempts.

Andy Headen began Clemson's furious comeback with a blocked punt that was recovered by James Robinson at the Baylor 1-yard line. Chuck McSwain scored with 20 seconds left in the game, and Lott passed to Jeff McCall for the two-point conversion. Headen recovered the ensuing onside kick, and Lott completed a 30-yard pass to Perry Tuttle to move the Tigers to the Baylor 33. An interception killed the winning touchdown drive, however, and Baylor ran out the remaining seconds for the win.

CLEMSON	7	0	3	8	18
BAYLOR	0	14	10	0	24

CU   L. Brown 1 run (Ariri kick), 1st, 6:04
BAY   Taylor 3 pass from Brannon (Bledsoe kick), 2nd, 14:55
BAY   Holt 24 pass from Brannon (Bledsoe kick), 2nd, 12:20
CU   Ariri 40 FG, 3rd, 10:36
BAY   Bledsoe 29 FG, 3rd, 8:17
BAY   Cockrell 7 pass from Elam (Bledsoe kick), 3rd, 3:43
CU   McSwain 1 run (McCall pass from Lott), 4th, 0:20

Attendance: 57,731

2013 FSU Loss

October 19, 2013
Clemson, South Carolina
Clemson 14, Florida State 51
The turnover battle had been a big part of the formula for success in Clemson's 6–0 start to the season. It was just a key ingredient in a recipe for disaster against No. 5 Florida State.

In the first clash of top five teams in Death Valley history, No. 3 Clemson turned over the ball three times in the first half—more than it had in a game all season—and never recovered, as it fell to Florida State 51–14. The loss snapped Clemson's 11-game winning streak, all by double-digits, against ACC teams.

"That's something we haven't done," offensive coordinator Chad Morris said. "We haven't turned the ball over. In a game of this magnitude, if they would have turned the ball over to us, it would have been just like that with us. You don't take two top teams like that and give anyone anything, and we basically handed them some freebies."

Clemson had won five straight home games in the series with the Seminoles and had turned the ball over just six times in those contests. By contrast, it committed four turnovers and the Seminoles scored 24 points off those miscues. Florida State also scored the most points by an opposing team in Memorial Stadium history.

The turnover woes began for the Tigers on the game's first play from scrimmage, as Stanton Seckinger fumbled after a reception.

Florida State recovered the fumble at the Clemson 34 and three plays later found the end zone on a 22-yard pass from Jameis Winston to Kelvin Benjamin for a 7–0 lead just 82 seconds into the game.

After the Seminoles upped their lead to 10–0 with a field goal, Clemson coughed up the football again. Mario Edwards Jr. picked up Tajh Boyd's fumble and rumbled 37 yards for a touchdown to give Florida State a 17–0 lead with 3:07 left in the first quarter.

"When you spot a team that good 17 points, it's a huge uphill challenge," head coach Dabo Swinney said. "We never could swing the momentum back in our favor, and turnovers were a huge part of that."

Clemson stemmed the tide briefly by putting together an 11-play, 65-yard drive to score its first points of the game on a two-yard slant pass from Boyd to Sammy Watkins, who made a juggling grab in the end zone.

The Money Is Good

Clemson just might be the best place for being an assistant coach. Just ask Chad Morris, the Tigers' creative offensive coordinator. Now in his fourth season at Clemson. Morris is the country's highest paid Bowl Champion Series assistant at $1,309,605.

Before he came to Clemson, Morris coached a high-powered offense at Tulsa. He took a 5–7 team in 2009 and turned it around to 10–3 in 2010, averaging 41.4 points a game.

But the Seminoles added a long touchdown from Winston to Rashad Greene in the second quarter and a field goal just before halftime as they took a 27–7 lead into the locker room.

Boyd had been intercepted deep in Florida State territory late in the second quarter for a third first-half turnover for the Tigers.

The Seminoles scored on the opening drive of the second half to make it 34–7 on a 17-yard pass from Winston to Greene.

Clemson committed its fourth turnover of the night when Boyd was picked off by Ronald Darby midway thought the fourth quarter. For the game, Boyd finished 17-of-37 passing for 156 yards and a touchdown against two interceptions.

"I didn't perform the way I was capable," Boyd admitted. "As a leader, it's my job to go out and lead and perform, and I didn't do that tonight. There were some moments that I would like to have back, but you have to keep on working."

Winston scored on a four-yard run a few minutes later to make the score 41–7 with 4:04 left in the third quarter.

Florida State added another touchdown early in the fourth quarter on a two-yard run by Devonta Freeman, and it tacked on a field goal with 4:41 remaining in the fourth quarter.

Cole Stoudt engineered a 16-play, 71-yard march for the Tigers and finished it off himself with a two-yard plunge on fourth down with 13 seconds left in the game to provide the final margin.

Clemson's offense managed just 326 total yards, while Florida State amassed 565 total yards.

"Having those types of mistakes against a great team...you won't win," Watkins said. "Those two turnovers really hurt us, but it's more than just those turnovers. We as an offense never got started, never got clicking, and as an offense, we hurt ourselves. We have a lot of things as an offense to go over and fix."

CLEMSON	7	0	0	7	14
FSU	17	10	14	10	51

FSU	Benjamin 22 pass from Watson (Aguayo kick), 1st 13:38
FSU	Aguayo 28 FG, 1st, 4:18
FSU	Edwards 37 fumble return (Aguayo kick), 1st
CU	S. Watkins 3 pass from Boyd (Catanzaro kick), 1st, 0:51
FSU	Greene 72 pass from Winston (Aguayo kick), 2nd, 7:08
FSU	Aguayo 24 FG, 2nd, 0:03
FSU	Greene 17 pass from Winston (Aguayo kick), 3rd, 13:33
FSU	Winston 4 run (Aguayo kick), 3rd, 4:04
FSU	Freeman 2 run (Aguayo kick), 4th, 12:17
FSU	Aguayo 20 FG, 4th, 4:41
CU	Stoudt 2 run (Catanzaro kick), 4th, 0:13
Attendance: 84,277	

93 2013 USC Game

Clemson had its chances, but six turnovers proved too much to overcome in No. 9 South Carolina's 31–17 win at Williams-Brice Stadium.

The No. 4 Tigers held their own in a number of statistical categories, as they rallied from a 10-point deficit in the first half to tie the score 17–17 late in the third quarter.

But after South Carolina went back up by a touchdown in the fourth quarter, Clemson turned the ball over four more times to end its hopes of a rally.

"The story of the game was the turnovers," Coach Dabo Swinney said.

Clemson actually outgained the Gamecocks 352–318 in total yards in 21 less plays, but South Carolina did not turn the ball over, while it turned the Tigers' six turnovers into 21 points.

"We just lost the turnover margin," Tajh Boyd said. "If you want to look at the score and ask what's really wrong with it, just look at the turnover margin. That will tell you everything you need to know."

The Tigers dug themselves into an early hole with two first-quarter turnovers that their rivals turned into 14 points.

Clemson marched 46 yards in seven plays and moved the chains three times on its opening drive, but a bit of early trickery went awry when Sammy Watkins' pass was picked off near the goal line by Brison Williams. Boyd threw a lateral out to Watkins, who set himself and threw downfield to Adam Humphries. But Williams was waiting to snatch the ball out of the air.

"We wanted to be aggressive early and didn't have a problem on the play call, but they were better than us on the play," Swinney admitted.

South Carolina responded with a methodical 17-play, 80-yard drive that culminated in a three-yard touchdown run by Connor Shaw for a 7–0 lead.

Clemson wasted little time going right back down the field as Boyd hit Watkins for a 57-yard pass on the second play of the ensuing drive. Boyd plunged in from eight yards out two plays later to tie the score 7–7.

Clemson's defense came up with a quick three-and-out to force a punt, but another miscue gave the ball right back, as Martavis Bryant collided with Humphries, who was attempting a fair catch, and the Gamecocks recovered at the Tigers' 39.

"We didn't help ourselves on offense and we had too many turnovers on special teams," Watkins said. "When that happens against a great team, you're going to lose the game."

South Carolina converted on the mistake five plays later, as Shaw hit Shaq Roland for a nine-yard touchdown that gave the Gamecocks a 14–7 lead six seconds into the second quarter.

After a Tigers punt, the Gamecocks put together another long drive, 65 yards in 13 plays, but the Clemson defense held them to a field goal.

The Tigers pulled back within one score as time expired in the first half, as Chandler Catanzaro made a 38-yard field goal.

In addition to the two first-half turnovers, another reason for Clemson's deficit was its inability to get off the field defensively. South Carolina converted 8-of-11 third-down attempts in the first half, many of them in third-and-long situations, and that led to the Gamecocks possessing the ball for 19:42 in the first half.

Clemson's defense opened the second half with two stops in its own territory, and after the second one, the Tigers offense took

Tigers Hold Big Edge

Despite losing to South Carolina for the fifth straight year in 2013, Clemson still holds a decisive 65–42–4 edge in the rivalry. In fact, the Tigers also holds the longest winning streak of seven games during 1934–40. The average score of victories in the series also favors Clemson 19–3 points to South Carolina 13–9.

advantage. Clemson went with a power ground game, running the ball eight times as part of a 15-play, 88-yard march that ended in a four-yard Roderick McDowell touchdown run to tie the score 17–17 with 3:01 left in the third quarter.

McDowell, who finished with a game-high 111 rushing yards, took a wide handoff and lost ground initially but stiff-armed a defender at the 11, turned upfield, and hurled the ball into the end zone.

The Gamecocks came right back with a 75-yard drive and reached the end zone on a two-yard run by Mike Davis to take a 24–17 lead with 11:47 left in the game. Davis, one of the SEC's premier running backs, only had 22 yards on 15 carries with a long rush of just four yards.

Clemson looked to march for a tying touchdown, getting as far as the South Carolina 30 thanks in large part to a 22-yard run on third down by McDowell. But Boyd scrambled on a second-down play and fumbled the ball.

The Clemson defense forced a punt when it needed to, but Humphries fumbled the ball on the return and South Carolina took over on Clemson's 34. Three plays later, Pharoh Cooper threw a 26-yard touchdown pass to Brandon Wilds to make the score 31–17 with 3:44 left and seal the victory.

"This is a very painful loss," Swinney said. "I thought our guys fought hard."

November 30, 2013, at Columbia, South Carolina

CLEMSON	7	3	7	0	17
SOUTH CAROLINA	7	10	0	14	31

USC   Shaw 3 run (Fry kick), 1st, 4:23
CU   Boyd 8 run (Catanzaro kick), 1st, 2:45
USC   Roland 9 pass from Shaw (Fry kick), 2nd, 14:54
USC   Fry 21 FG, 2nd, 8:25
CU   Catanzaro 38 FG, 2nd, 0:00
CU   McDowell 4 run (Catanzaro kick), 3rd, 3:01
USC   Davis 2 run (Fry kick), 4th, 11:47
USC   Wilds 26 pass from P. Cooper (Fry kick), 4th, 3:44
Attendance: 84,174

2009 USC Game

South Carolina rushed for 223 yards, including 114 by Kenny Miles, in its 34–14 win over No. 15 Clemson at Williams-Brice Stadium on November 28. It was just the second Gamecocks win in Columbia in the last 11 meetings in the capital city.

C.J. Spiller opened the game with an 88-yard kickoff return for a score, the seventh of his career to set an FBS record. But the Gamecocks outscored Clemson 17–0 the rest of the first half.

In the second half, South Carolina extended its lead to 24–7 on Stephen Garcia's 14-yard touchdown pass to Tori Gurley. After the teams traded field goals, Kyle Parker connected with Michael Palmer for a 22-yard touchdown pass to narrow the Gamecocks' lead to 27–17. But Weslye Saunders' one-yard touchdown catch on fourth down late in the contest sealed the victory.

The Gamecocks had a 38–31 advantage in average starting field position, including starting their drives at the Tigers' 35 or better. Meanwhile, Clemson did not start a single drive outside its own 40. South Carolina also held the ball for 36:31 minutes and scored a touchdown on all four of its red-zone possessions.

Palmer totaled eight receptions for 106 yards, both game highs, while Jacoby Ford had five catches for 49 yards.

November 28, 2009, at Columbia, South Carolina

CLEMSON	7	0	0	10	17
SOUTH CAROLINA	14	3	7	10	34

CU   Spiller 88 kickoff return (Jackson kick), 1st, 14:41
USC Maddox 1 run (Lanning kick), 1st, 5:21
USC Saunders 9 pass from Garcia (Lanning kick), 1st, 2:01
USC Lanning 47 FG, 4th, 11:23
CU   Jackson 45 GG, 4th, 11:23
USC Lanning 38 FG, 4th, 5:22
CU   Palmer 22 pass from Parker (Jackson kick), 4th, 3:46
USC Saunders 1 pass from Garcia (Lanning kick0, 4th, 2:40

Attendance: 80,574

95 Kalon Davis

A football player who wears a kimono. The same one who loves soccer more than football. That's a quick take on Kalon Davis, a 6'5" guard who is possibly the only American-born college football player in the country who speaks Japanese.

"I've been fascinated by the Japanese culture for a long time," Davis revealed.

So much so that the native of Chester, South Carolina, is a modern language major with an emphasis on Japanese. What's more he spent a month in Japan during the summer of 2014 reporting to football practice to intensify his studies of Japanese culture. His main interest was to discover what he called his "ki," the Japanese term for the circulation of energy within the body, mind, and spirit.

That's something quite out of the ordinary for your average football player. But it has paid off for Davis, one of the biggest players on the squad. In 2013 Davis was a key player, seeing action in every game and being a starter on five occasions. Clemson coaches were pleased to see his improvement and expected him to see even more action his senior season.

"We felt all along that Kalon could be a great player," Coach Dabo Swinney said. "He's big, strong, has excellent feet, and he's very smart. In 2012 we felt he might be a starter, but he didn't take hold of it. But this past year he has been one of our pleasant surprises. He got the chance, and he performed consistently. I'm proud of Kalon because he has become important to me and he's having fun."

He certainly is, balancing mixing his fun with playing football.

"I'm not the full-on joker in class, but I like to crack one-liners," Davis confided. "And if I can get you to laugh, then generally by that time you already know what you're getting with me.

"Sometimes it's better to be loose and have fun out there than to have the mindset of, 'I'm going to be the nastiest guy here.' That ends up with you focusing on maybe being over-aggressive with some blocks and taking bad steps and stuff. I think back in the day I was too busy worrying about being that mean guy. Now I'm just having fun with it."

Through it all, he still doesn't hide his love for soccer, which he played as a kid.

"I've played soccer all my life," Davis pointed out. "Soccer was really my first love as far as sports. I still play during the off-season."

"I never tell people in my classes that I play football. Half of them probably guess. Playing football is probably my last thing. I don't want them to know me as a football player. I want you to know who I am."

He's also a video game enthusiast. And a gentle giant who rescued his dog, Rikku, from an animal shelter.

"I hang out with my friends, I have a puppy, and I like to play games," Davis said. "Usually they all intertwine. I'll invite people over and they hang out with my puppy and we all play games together."

Davis has left quite an impression on his teammates, especially on fellow guard Tyler Shatley, who came to Clemson as a fullback.

"Every once in awhile we'll get him to speak some Japanese for us," Shatley said. "I saw him one day and he came into the locker room with a kimono on. Sometimes the alarm on his phone would go off and it's a little Japanese ring tone so we give him a hard time about that.

"We're all different. It's just that the things he's interested in not a whole lot of people are interested in. Heck, when he plays soccer, he's not even the goalie. He's out there in the middle of the field."

It wasn't all sushi tasting for Davis in Japan. Joey Baston made certain of that. The Clemson strength coach handed Davis a workout schedule to follow—and he did.

Maybe Davis will call out an offensive play at the line of scrimmage in Japanese at a key moment of a big game to confuse the opponent. Now that would be fun.

96 Buck George

The one definitive description that defines Buck George is that he could run like the wind. During his playing days at Clemson, the speedy running back was known as the "Rock Hill Rocket" and "The Vanishing American." The last one was quite symbolic. George was a Native American of the Catawba Indian Nation. He broke the color line in South Carolina when he walked on the field his first year at Clemson.

George grew up in Rock Hill with his birth name of Evans. His speed in high school impressed Frank Howard who recruited him with the nickname "Buck." And he didn't disappoint. He played from 1951 to 1954, was the Tigers' captain his senior year, and set records that lasted for more than 50 years.

He was the first back to run for more than 200 yards (204) in a game against Presbyterian. His 90-yard touchdown run against Furman his freshman season remains the longest one in Clemson history and also ranks as one of the longest plays.

"Buck George was a terrific wingback for Frank Howard's teams of the early 1950s," pointed out Tim Bourret, Clemson's sports information director. "He was very fast and he used that talent to have a record-setting career. I know Clemson fans who go back to the 1950s still remember his 90-yard run against Furman."

Significantly, George was drafted by the Washington Redskins in 1955, but a knee injury kept him out of the NFL. However, it didn't slow him down in making a better life for the Catawba Indians, which he did for more than 40 years. He was instrumental in the tribe, acquiring state and federal recognition. George was a key figure in negotiations with government leaders in securing the Catawba Nation Indians the right to vote and become U.S. citizens. Even today in South Carolina, the Catawba is the only fully recognized Indian tribe.

"Buck George in his whole life was an advocate for Native Americans," former Catawba Chief Gilbert Blue said. "I will miss him as a friend, and the Catawba people will miss him."

Bill Harris, the current head of the Catawba nation, added to Blue's sentiments.

"George spent decades trying to improve the lives of the Catawba people," Harris said. "He stayed involved in the affairs of his people his entire adult life."

George died in his early eighties on December 22, 2013, in Rock Hill.

97 Tommy Bowden

On December 2, 1998, Tommy Bowden was named the head football coach at a school he called "his dream job."

Ever since the day he first visited Clemson's Death Valley as a young assistant coach at Duke University, Bowden pointed to Clemson as one of the 10 schools he would love to be a head coach at one day. He got that opportunity when Clemson parted ways with Tommy West following a turbulent 3–8 season in 1998.

Bowden, who was 18–4 at Tulane from 1997 to 1998, was known for his high-flying offense at the time, which led to the Green Waves' 11–0 record for 1998 and a top 10 national ranking.

He stated his biggest goal at Clemson was to improve the school's perception on the field, in the classroom, and the facilities. For the most part, Bowden did all of those things.

"Tommy has done some marvelous things for our program, and we have had some good success," former athletic director Terry Don Phillips said.

In his 9½ years at Clemson, Bowden's team won 61.5 percent of the time. His 72 wins rank third all-time in Clemson history behind Frank Howard and Danny Ford, while his 9½ seasons at the school rank as the third-longest tenure for a Clemson coach.

Bowden also won 13 games against top 25 teams, the third best mark in school history, including three of Clemson's top six road victories of all time—wins at No. 9 Georgia Tech (2001), No. 11 Miami (2004), and No. 9 Florida State (2006).

All nine of Bowden's pervious teams were bowl eligible, as he took the Tigers to two Peach Bowls and at least one appearance in the Gator Bowl, Chick-fil-A Bowl, Champs Sports Bowl, Tangerine Bowl, Music City Bowl, and Humanitarian Bowl.

The eight bowl appearances are the most by any Clemson coach. He was 7–2 against rival South Carolina.

Twice Bowden was named ACC Coach of the Year (1999, 2003), joining Howard, Charley Pell, and Ford as the only two-time recipients of that award in Tigers' history.

But it wasn't just wins and losses that defined what Bowden accomplished in his time at Clemson. Off the field, his players rarely got into trouble, and Clemson graduated nearly 80 percent of its seniors in his nine years.

"There is not a better man," said Vic Koenning, who served as Bowden's defensive coordinator for three years. "I don't think there is a classier guy. I don't think he could have worked harder and done more for the school and for these kids. I just can't say enough about him and what he did here."

Clemson's graduation success rate of 94 percent in 2005 was fourth-best among the 119 Division I-A programs. In 2003, Clemson was 11th in the nation in graduation success rate amongst these programs, including second among public institutions.

"Our off-the-field issues and academic issues and the many, many other things he has represented this university in, he did in a very positive fashion," Phillips said.

But there was one thing Bowden could not bring Clemson. And though he tried as hard as he could, he never got to the next level and won the ACC title.

And that in a nutshell describes Bowden's legacy at Clemson. Though he did a lot of good things, he never won a championship, and that ultimately led to his resignation after the Tigers started the 2008 season with a 3–3 overall record, including a 1–2 mark in the ACC.

Of all the numbers Bowden accumulated during his career at Clemson, the good and the bad ones, the most telling one of them all, and the one that defined him the most, was the nine losses as a ranked team to an unrated team.

"Until you win a championship it is always, 'Why did you lose it?' 'How do you lose to a team you should have beaten?' That's always going to be the case until you win a championship," Bowden said.

"Through Coach Swinney's leadership and the assistant coaches, I can't say enough good things about the joy they did. They railed and fought back and gave great effort," Phillips said. "I think as history goes along, and as Coach Swinney told the team in there, and I would copy off his words, this team is going to be remembered in history.

"This was a team that was written off and our kids gave great effort and you can't say enough of how proud we are and I can't say enough how proud I am of Coach Swinney. He is a man of character. I have had a chance to observe him for six years, and certainly I have observed him in one of the more difficult places that you can place a coach in."

If there was any doubting what Sweeney could do as a head coach, it ended with a beatdown he handed the favored Gamecocks.

98 Ken Hatfield

Ken Hatfield arrived on the Clemson campus as the Tigers' new head coach in 1990 under a dark cloud that he never knew existed. It had nothing to do with football because he was a successful coach at Arkansas where he produced an exemplary 55–17–1 record over the course of six seasons.

He was a coach with a reputation of building a successful program without breaking any NCAA rules, and he did so in taking the Razorbacks to a bowl all six years. While most of the Southwest Conference was being investigated for alleged crimes, the Hogs won big and stayed clean.

"He ran his program with honesty and integrity," TCU coach Jim Whacker praised. "Clemson couldn't have picked a better guy for the job. Ken Hatfield is the epitome of what the coaching profession should be."

The first thing that Hatfield needed to do was to clear the air of some preconceived notions. There were more than he expected. He was perceived as a bible-toting preacher, one who would change the Clemson rallying cry from "Tiger Rag" to "Peace in the (Death) Valley."

There were concerns that his wishbone offense would replace the option and he would run the football even more than before. Then, too, there were concerns among the players that Hatfield was bringing with him a stack of rules that would limit their freedom.

"What the media and other people say about you may not be the real you," Hatfield said. "The thing we tried to do was put individuals at ease on the preconceived notions that preceded you. It just takes time to be around and feel comfortable with one another."

It wasn't easy. Resentment existed among the Clemson fan base over the firing of Danny Ford. The popular Ford was looked upon as a legend who went 96–29–4 in 11 years and got Clemson its first national championship in 1981. The fans were demonstrative in their support of Ford. They held vigils on the lawn of President Max Lennon's home protesting Ford's ouster. Even the players were on the verge of revolting and threatened not to play unless Ford was reinstated or a successor was named from the staff. "Max must go," was the prevailing cry around town.

"I thought Clemson was a university that could do things in the right way and pull together," Hatfield observed. "I didn't know."

Hatfield didn't need much help his first season. He became the first Clemson coach to win 10 games in his first season, and his .833 winning percentage was the best for a first-year coach since 1900 when John Heisman went 6–0 as the Tigers finished ninth in the AP poll.

The transition was not problem-free but turned out smoother than most anyone could have expected, especially considering the explosive beginning. There was still some grumbling.

"There are certain things, as time goes by, that get easier," Hatfield philosophized.

His second season was just that. Clemson went 9–2–1 and won the ACC title. Yet, there remained some skepticism surrounding Hatfield. It intensified the following season when Clemson finished 5–6, its first losing season since 1976. That rankled Hatfield.

"It was the only year in my coaching career that I'd had a team that didn't play its best football at the end of the season," Hatfield reflected. "That lack of focus cost us a bowl game, and the players remembered that."

They did remember, and in 1993 they responded with a 9–3 performance that included a 14–13 victory over Kentucky in the Peach Bowl. But Hatfield didn't savor the comeback season for very long.

As fast as Hatfield won, he quickly left. He had requested an extension on his contract that had two years remaining but was denied. His four-year career was short but productive. He went 32–13–1 and led Clemson to an ACC championship and three bowl games.

"I'd like to thank the Clemson players of 1993 who played together as a team as well as any I have ever coached," Hatfield said when he left.

99 Tommy West

Tommy West's five-year resume as a head coach includes four bowl appearances, 12 road wins, and four wins over AP top 25 teams. The 1998 Peach Bowl was Clemson's third straight year in a bowl game, something only 16 other programs can claim. This was the first time since the 1985–91 era that Clemson had been to a bowl game three straight years, and he is just the second Clemson coach in history to take the Tigers to three consecutive bowl games.

His first four seasons saw the Tigers make a late-season run. In 1994, with the youngest offense in Clemson history, one that stared seven freshmen at times, the Tigers won three of their last four games, including a victory at 12th-ranked North Carolina.

The run of success at the end of the 1995 season had the Tigers in the top 25 of every poll. Clemson won its last five regular season games, including four wins by at least 17 points. West's Tigers were picked fifth in the ACC preseason poll that year, but thanks to the third best offense in Clemson history and a defense that ranked 10th in the nation in scoring, Clemson finished third in the ACC standings with a 6–2 record, its best league finish since the Tigers won the ACC title in 1991.

The 1995 campaign was one in which Clemson excelled in every area. The Tigers ranked fourth in the country in rushing, yet also led the ACC in yards per pass attempt. Defensively, Clemson rated in the top 20 in the nation in rushing defense, passing efficiency defense, and turnover margin. In terms of special teams, Clemson was the only school in the nation to have an individual rank in the top 25 in punting, place kicking, punt returns, and kickoff returns.

The 1996 season saw Clemson win five of its last six regular season games, including a victory at 15th-ranked Virginia, just the third road win over a ranked team in the decade of the 1990s. For the second straight year Clemson won the ACC rushing title and reached a top 25 ranking. Again, Clemson won 75 percent of its ACC games, this time finishing tied for second in the league standings with North Carolina. The Tigers were extended a bid to the Peach Bowl to face LSU.

The Tigers won four of their last five regular season games, including a 47–21 victory over South Carolina in the season finale that clinched a bowl bid. It was the most points scored by Clemson against South Carolina since 1900.

The season featured a record-setting passing attack led by Nealon Greene, who set season records for pass completions, passing yards, and completion percentage. The defense followed suit, led by first-team AP All-American Anthony Simmons, who led the conference in tackles and tackles for loss. Clemson's defense ranked in the top 20 in the nation in rushing defense, total defense, and scoring defense, and ranked third in the ACC in pass defense.

West's 1998 Clemson team continued the tradition of top defenses in Tigertown. Clemson ranked 12th in the nation in rushing defense and 25th in total defense. The squad finished second in the ACC to Florida State in both areas and led the league in sacks per game. Offensively, the young team made great strides over the season, averaging more than 15 points per game the last four contests. The team threw for more than 2,000 yards—just the second Clemson team in history to do that.

West ended his tenure at Clemson with a 28–19 victory over archrival South Carolina, the third time in four years he had beaten Clemson's chief rival. At the conclusion of the game, West, his wife, Lindsay, and son, Turner, were carried off the field by Clemson players, a testimony to their respect for Coach West.

West took over the head coaching position on November 29, 1993. Less than a month later he already had a bowl victory on his ledger, a 14–13 triumph over Kentucky in the Peach Bowl, Clemson's sixth bowl win in an eight-year period. With his debut in the Peach Bowl, West became the sixth coach in NCAA history to make his debut with a program in a bowl game. However, he was just the second coach in history to make his debut in a bowl game without previously coaching his new team as an assistant coach earlier in the season.

West was a mainstay of a Clemson coaching staff that led the Tigers to a 69–20–4 record and six Associated Press top 20 finishes between 1982–89. During West's first tour of duty with the Tigers as an outside linebacker coach, Clemson played in five bowl games (winning four) and claimed four ACC Championships, included three in a row from 1986 to 1988.

Clemson had a 44–10–1 record against ACC competition during West's era on the Tigers staff, an 81 percent winning mark. Additionally, five of those Clemson teams ranked in the top 15 in the nation in rushing defense and scoring defense, and three ranked in the top 12 in the nation in total defense.

Clemson's 1989 defense ranked fifth in the nation in total defense, rushing defense, and scoring defense, and West's outside linebackers had a lot to do with that success. His top four outside linebackers that year all played in the NFL in 1994. The list of former West players in the NFL includes Levon Kirkland and Wayne Simmons, both of whom played in the Super Bowl in recent years.

West began his coaching career as a graduate assistant at Tennessee (his alma mater) in 1977. He coached one year of high school football at White County High in Sparta, Tennessee, in 1978, then he became an assistant at Mississippi in 1979. For the 1980 and 1981 seasons, he served as an assistant coach at Appalachian State.

After his career in Clemson (1982–89), West became the running backs coach at Tennessee. During the 1990 season, Tennessee won the Southeastern Conference and captured the Sugar Bowl with a win over Virginia. The Volunteers scored a school record 442 points that year and averaged more than 410 yards a game in total offense, 205.7 rushing and 205.4 passing. He served as co-defensive coordinator at South Carolina in 1991 and 1992.

In 1993 West took over at UT–Chattanooga team that had won just two games in 1992. He doubled that total in 1993 and guided the Mocs to one of the landmark wins in school history, a 33–31 win over No. 1-ranked Marshall. He concluded the regular season with a 45–42 victory over Furman. Ironically, his first regular season game as Clemson coach was a victory over Furman.

100 Big Thursday

The seeds of bitterness that became the roots of the age-old Clemson–South Carolina rivalry existed even before the turn of the twentieth century. Benjamin T. "Pitchfork Ben" Tillman, a farmer from Edgefield, began the campaign for legislation several years earlier that established the agricultural college separate and apart from the main institution in Columbia. South Carolina was the first state institution and has always been recognized at the state university. Located in the capital, which is also the state's largest city, hasn't hurt its status, either. Clemson, then, had always been snubbed as the poor, country cousins. South Carolina fans never let Tigers followers forget that Clemson began as an agricultural school.

In 1896, Clemson's first year of football, South Carolina had already been playing football for five years. On November 12, 1896, Clemson and South Carolina met on the gridiron for the very first time as part of State Fair Week in Columbia. Although it rained at various intervals during the day, a crowd of close to 2,000 people paid a 25¢ admission charge to view the first of what became a long series of games that over the years were popularly referred to as Big Thursday. Not surprisingly, South Carolina won the first game 12–6. *The State* newspaper called it, "A Superb Game."

During the next four years, little Clemson defeated South Carolina every time. The 1901 game, unfortunately, was canceled due to a dispute with Fair officials about gate receipts. The disagreement was short-lived. Clemson and South Carolina returned to the battlefield in 1902 with both sides feeling all the pent-up frustrations that had resulted from the previous year's cancelation. Although Clemson's team had been known as the "Tigers" since they first began playing football, the year marked the first time the nickname "Gamecocks" was applied to South Carolina after several futile years in which the Columbia school searched for an appropriate name. Clemson was heavily favored. However, South Carolina managed to upset the Tigers 12–6.

Because of the seriousness of the 1902 incident, the Clemson–South Carolina series was then suspended for six years before being resumed in 1909.

From 1909 and on for the next six meetings, the Tigers emerged victorious five of the six times. The losses understandably rankled South Carolina. So in 1915 the Gamecocks employed ringers and handily won their first three games that season. An investigation uncovered the ruse before the Clemson game, and the unauthorized players were banned from participating against Clemson or any other team. The game produced the first tie in the series at 0–0. Then starting in 1916, Clemson won four consecutive times. This was the first time this had happened since the 1897–1900 period.

Coach Josh Cody in 1927–30 guided Clemson again through a streak of winning four consecutive games. Clemson established a winning edge over South Carolina at this time. Coach Jess Neely extended it even further. He led Clemson to seven consecutive victories from 1934 through 1940, the longest winning streak of the series. Unfortunately, in 1941 South Carolina edged Clemson 18–14 to snap the Tigers' winning skein.

This was the year Frank Howard began his long reign as Clemson's legendary coach, and the South Carolina fans were so grateful for the victory that they presented Coach Rex Enright with a Chrysler automobile and a silver service tea set. Clemson fans remembered that the Tigers missed a first down by a foot, which could have led to the possible winning touchdown near the end of the game. Howard, especially, didn't appreciate losing to his archrival his first year as coach, and he responded sharply, "The only difference between an automobile and a coffin is about twelve inches of dirt."

Big Thursday for a long time was a legal holiday in Richland County where the game was played. The entire state also observed the day because of the zealousness of football fans throughout South Carolina. It was a day in which loyalties were reaffirmed, and you can be sure there were no neutral feelings from the Atlantic Ocean to Hogback Mountain.

One of the more memorable Big Thursday incidents took place in 1946. The game created a great deal of interest because South

Carolina's popular coach, Rex Enright, had returned to coaching for the first time since his tour of duty with the navy. The game was completely sold out by August. Even professional scalpers had trouble securing tickets, which were as scarce as Republicans in the state capital. Then about a week before the game, tickets were mysteriously available for purchasing. Printer C. Miles Morrison, who had printed the genuine tickets, discovered there was something wrong with the type that appeared on the new supply of tickets. He called the police, who then questioned the people selling the tickets. They finally admitted that they had brought in a batch of counterfeit tickets from an out-of-state printer.

It was only the beginning of the problem. On game day, an untold number of fans holding counterfeits were denied admission to Carolina Stadium. Near game time, the angry crowd had swelled to thousands. Even Howard encountered trouble getting his players though the gates. He had to identify every player near the entrance. After he had finally gotten all his players through safely, Howard was stopped by a guard. He was taken aback for a moment.

"It doesn't matter if you let me in or not, but if you don't, there isn't going to be a game," Howard exclaimed.

As soon as the kickoff took place, the frenzied mob stormed the gates, succeeded in crashing through, and headed straight for the sidelines. They ringed the entire field, five and six deep. They covered both benches, and fans who were sitting in the lower stands couldn't see the field.

Until he died in 1964, leaving a void that no one would dare fill, Frank B. "Gator" Farr, a 1930 graduate of Clemson, returned to Clemson every year the week before the South Carolina game to preach the mock funeral of the Gamecock. It was no ordinary funeral but a colorful ritual with enough pomp and ceremony as would be befitting a king's funeral. Farr would arrive at Clemson, having made the journey from his home in Palatka, Florida, and perform his ceremony that same night dressed in split tails and top hat at a giant outdoor pep rally. An honor guard and pallbearers carried a coffin that had a stuffed chicken protruding at one end of the open box.

The coffin itself dated back to 1940 when Clemson played in its first bowl game against Boston College. The Eagle students were so confident that they would devour the Tigers in the Cotton Bowl, they brought a coffin to Dallas all the way from Boston. After Clemson upset Boston College 6–3, the Eagles fans gave the coffin to Clemson to take back.

The last Big Thursday game occurred on October 22, 1959. By that time, even the mild-mannered and jovial Howard was weary of the arrangement after having taken part in 30 of them, more than any other single coach.

"We always had to sit in the sun, and we got tired of going down there every year," Howard said. "We weren't getting half of the tickets, half of the program and concessions sales, and it knocked one game out of our schedule because we couldn't play the Saturday before or after the Thursday game."

Sources

Periodicals
Greenville News
The State
Seneca Journal
Anderson Independent
Charleston Post & Courier Journal
Charlotte Observer
Tiger News
Sports Illustrated
ESPN
Associated Press
Washington Post
USA Today
New York Times
Wikipedia
Orange & White
Clemson Insider

Books
Big Thursdays & Super Saturdays by Don Barton (Leisure Press 1981)

Death Valley Days by Bob Bradley (Longstreet Press 1991)

Classic Clashes of The South Carolina-Clemson Rivalry by Travis Haney & Larry Williams (History Press 2011)

Clemson Football Media Guide, published annually by the Clemson Communications Office, Clemson University, Clemson, South Carolina, 1981–2013.